Lighting the Sky

Book Five of the *Coming Back to Cornwall* series

Katharine E. Smith

HEDDON PUBLISHING

www.heddonpublishing.com
www.facebook.com/heddonpublishing
@PublishHeddon

Katharine E. Smith is a writer, editor and publisher.

An avid reader of contemporary writers such as Kate Atkinson, David Nicholls and Anne Tyler, Katharine's aim is to write books she would like to read herself. Katharine has written and published eight novels to date, with bestselling *A Second Chance Summer* marking the start of the Coming Back to Cornwall series.

She also runs Heddon Publishing; working with other independent authors all over the world.

Katharine lives in Shropshire, with her husband and their two children. She hopes she will be able to add '(and their dog)' to this very soon.

This is for Catherine Clarke – my fellow landlocked Cornwall lover, fantastic friend and cover designer.

It's possible nobody would have looked twice at these books if it wasn't for you!

Lighting the Sky

Deep down at the tail end of the country (or perhaps the head, if you're from this neck of the woods; Cornish folk are renowned for their pride, and may not take kindly to being cast as the rear end of anything) – far from London, miles from any motorway, sits a den of tranquillity which is well worth the journey.

Amethi, the brainchild of two childhood friends from the Midlands, is less than two miles away from the nearest popular 'destination' town (guaranteed to be drenched with holiday-makers from May till September, and beyond) and yet it could be anywhere, or even the middle of nowhere. Entry is granted through a screen of trees, which feel like they might block your way if they deem you unworthy.

Leaving the open fields and the sea behind, you find yourself on a sweeping drive, flanked on each side by wildflower meadows, guiding you to a neat parking area and a set of old stone buildings.

You wanted peace and quiet. You wanted to get away from it all. Here, you have it. It is, quite simply, heaven.

1

I clutch Julie's hand, glancing up to see if she's read as much as I have. We have just this morning received our copy of *Staycation* magazine, hot off the press. It's taken every ounce of willpower for me not to open it before now but I promised Julie we would read it together and, once I'd told her it had arrived, she was up here like a flash.

Sitting in our little office, trying not to shiver, we both take our time to read the whole thing, and to look at the pictures which Nick – the slightly odd, yet exceedingly good-looking photographer – had taken. Whatever his personality, you cannot fault his pictures. The first shows Julie and me walking side-by-side along one of the meadow-side paths. We are laughing, and the sunlight glints through the trees, casting a glow behind us and picking out some of the details of the meadow.

I can't help but sigh to look at this picture. It seems so long ago that the days were warm and the meadows vibrant and lively with busy insects. Now, the grass and wild flowers are gone; reduced to a neat, short stubble, and the fields lie dormant, hibernating through the winter. Underground, all kinds of magic is taking place, but only the moles and the worms are privy to this.

I cast my eyes over the other pictures in the two-page spread dedicated to Amethi. The communal area; a bedroom; one of the kitchens. I re-read the article, taking in all the details which Catriona has included. The yoga retreats, and writing courses. The dinners Julie cooks for the guests, and the organisation I provide for days out, restaurant bookings, etc. A beautiful description of Amethi, highlighting many of the features I love, and even a focus on our environmental credentials. She has really gone to town on writing this article, and I could not be more grateful, particularly after our horrible experience with negative online reviews earlier this year.

And we are on the cover, too! That same picture, of Julie and I walking alongside the meadow. It is the perfect image at this time of year, when the days are short and the mornings dark and it is near enough impossible to believe it could ever be hot enough to go outside without a coat.

The magazine comes out in December, and will be on the shelves for two months – slicing through Christmas and New Year, right into the heart of winter, when people start to dream of holidays and sunny days. And while lots of people want to go abroad, presumably people who buy *Staycation* magazine want to holiday in this country. A little shiver runs across me and I look up to see my grin mirrored on Julie's face. We stand and hug each other, dancing around as much as the limited space allows.

"Ow!" Julie clonks her head on the sloping ceiling.

"Are you OK?"

"Yeah! Who cares about a little bang to the head? I've got another."

"Erm… not sure how to tell you this but you've only got one."

"Damn. Let's get the champagne out, Alice! This is something which needs to be celebrated."

I look at my watch. "It's only seven minutes past eleven."

"Who cares? Sometimes, Alice, you have to grasp the nettle and just go for it."

I look from my watch to my computer screen, where my calendar is open.

"I don't think I can, Julie, I'm really sorry. I've got to pick up Sophie from town later."

"Oh, OK, I suppose it can wait."

"But we could go out for coffee and cake?" I suggest. "I know it's not the same but, you know, we're in our thirties now. You're a married lady. Well, you're married at least. And we're business owners."

"You sure do know how to suck the spontaneity out of a situation, Griffiths."

"Hey, coffee and cake can be spontaneous. I tell you what, we'll go to McGinty's, we've been saying for ages we should give it a try."

"Woo. Wild. McGinty's it is, I suppose."

"Come on! Get your coat," I say. "Last one to the car's a rotten egg."

I make a run for it, leaving Julie to lock up. I can just hear her muttering something about Enid Blyton.

"Can I have one latte and one decaf latte, please?" I have sent Julie to secure the best table in the café, which is perched high on the cliffside at the far end of McGinty's farm, with floor-to-ceiling windows on one side, that give the impression that we are teetering on the edge of the cliff.

A roaring fire crackles heartily on one side of the room, throwing out enough heat for the whole place, and buffing everyone's cheeks to a rosy red; a stark contrast to the moody weather outside. The wind is doing its best to rattle the window panes but they are made of hardy stuff. Every now and then, however, even at this height, a shower of sea water splashes against the glass.

"Who says coffee and cake can't be wild?" I set the tray down on the table, making sure I move the decaf coffee in my direction, and quickly stirring a sugar in, swirling the foamy D before Julie has a chance to notice. She would want to know why I am drinking decaf and I can't tell her. Not yet.

It is becoming increasingly difficult to keep this secret from her. And I don't feel comfortable doing it. But I can't tell her before I tell Sam; even though I am pretty sure she'd tell me before Luke if it was the other way around.

I think Sam would be gutted, though, if I told Julie first. I know how straight he is. But right now he is also majorly stressed. I just want it to be right, when I tell him that he and I are having a baby. I want to see his face break into a huge smile. I want him to sweep me up into an all-encompassing embrace, and for the news to make his day. Right now, I'm worried that it might be swept up in everything else that's going on; even worse, I am scared that it may not be welcome.

I sit down and take a sip of the coffee, then a bite of the cake; tiny crystallised ginger pieces providing a sharp contrast to the sweetness. Julie is having a scone with clotted cream and jam. She layers it up thickly, takes a huge bite, licking the cream from her top lip. "Mmm. There's definitely something to be said, having somebody else cook for you, even if it is just a cake."

"How does it compare to yours?" I ask.

"I wouldn't like to say! But this is delicious. And you're right, this is a perfectly great way to celebrate our amazing write-up. I can't believe it, Alice, can you? I just feel like everything's coming together. I think next year's going to be the best yet."

She lifts her coffee cup and I do the same with mine, clinking it against hers.

"To us," Julie says.

"To us," I echo, "and Amethi."

"And an amazing year next year," Julie smiles, her face shining with joy.

I smile back at her, my oldest friend, then look out of the window, out to sea. It is raining further out but closer to shore, although it is grey, the air is clear. I sink back in my seat, feeling the heat from the fire, hearing the chatter of conversation, and watching the gannets dive-bomb the waves, fearless and bold.

2

I wasn't making it up when I said I had to collect Sophie. Sam is at work on the other side of the county; something to do with a seal count, or survey, or something. Sophie, meanwhile, is refusing to go back to Kate and Isaac's, which is heart-breaking – for Kate as much as Sophie, if not more. The flat where the two of them lived together for so long has now become home to Isaac, and baby Jacob – Sophie's little brother. To those not in the know, it might appear that Sophie has not been able to adjust to the changes, to the late-night crying and the early starts, and the usurper in her midst. But the problem is not Jacob; it's the fact that Kate and Isaac are planning to leave Cornwall for Devon. Not a million miles away, of course, but still not home for Sophie, and away from Sam, as well. To top it all off, the whole enterprise had been kept secret so both Sophie and Sam are fuming that they had to find out about it all along with everybody else.

This is why Sam is so stressed at the moment, and why Sophie is living with us. Not in itself a problem but the reasons behind it are, and I know that adding another baby into the mix will only complicate matters. So here I am, literally carrying this secret around with me; knowing full well that one of the reasons Sam is so mad at Kate is that she kept him in the dark about something which is having such an impact on his life. Also aware that years back, I was angry at him when he didn't tell me about Sophie. Yet now I am keeping this from him.

And this little secret is going to get bigger; there is no way

7

I can keep it quiet for long. Already, I feel like my waistline is expanding, although I could just be imagining that. If my calculations are correct, I am a little over two months pregnant. The doctor has given me a due date of mid-June, based on when my last period was.

I have to tell Sam soon, I know, and I am desperate to. I just have to find the right moment.

I sit in the car just round the corner from the school and wait for Sophie. Little gangs of kids come past, laughing and joking with each other; one boy gets pushed into the side of the car and I feel an intense irritation rise within me but he looks round, shocked, and mouths "Sorry!" at me. I can't help smiling at him, and see Sophie not far behind, with Amber, and Josh, and a few other kids I don't recognise.

She sees me, and I watch her say her goodbyes to Amber – a hug, as though they won't see each other for weeks, when in all likelihood they will be messaging each other from the moment Sophie gets into the car, throughout the evening, and then all the way to school tomorrow, until they are able to speak in person again. And they will greet each other with another hug. I love it. Not the constant messaging, but the joy they take in each other. Until Amber moved nearby, Sophie didn't have any particular friend. Now, she and Amber are inseparable.

I am thinking back to when Julie and I were that age when I notice Sophie glance quickly in my direction; almost guiltily, and I catch a glimpse of her hand in Josh's. She pulls it away quickly. *Interesting*, I think, but I am not going to say anything.

She walks towards the car, and I see Amber wave to her dad, Simon, in his Land Rover a bit further along the street. Sophie's little gang of friends disperses, blending into the other groups of children in blazers, and Sophie herself opens the passenger door.

"Hi, Alice." I can see her looking at me, trying to gauge whether I saw her and Josh holding hands.

I busy myself fiddling with the radio. "Hi, Soph, how was your day?" I ask casually. I can almost feel her relief.

"Oh, you know, the usual," she says.

"Straight home?" I ask.

"Yes, please."

I check the mirrors and indicate, then check the mirrors again; you can't be too careful round here, with the hundreds of children, and multiple cars, not to mention the school buses. It's a nightmare, and I hadn't expected to be doing the 'school run' at this stage in my life, but I guess it's practice for the future.

As predicted, Sophie has her phone in her hand almost as soon as we have pulled out. In fact, she is already messaging Amber at the time that my car passes Simon's Land Rover, and I can see Amber also has her head down, no doubt bent over a screen; probably messaging Sophie. Simon and I give each other a wave, then he heads one way and I head the other, and soon we are up and out of town, winding our way along the roads to Amethi.

Despite my best intentions, I can't help myself.

"Soph…"

"Uhuh…"

"Was that Josh?"

She looks up sharply. "Was what Josh?"

"Well, no, let me rephrase that." I keep my eyes on the road. "Were you and Josh… holding hands?"

From the corner of my eye, I see her turn her head away.

9

She says nothing. I berate myself internally.

"Yes," she says, not turning back to me. "He's my… boyfriend."

It's like she is trying out the word, never having said it before. As far as I am aware, she has not had a boyfriend before. Possibly this is the first time she has said it aloud.

"OK," I say. "That's good, isn't it?"

"Yes," she turns to me, smiling like she used to, before the world came to rest on her shoulders. "I think so. But," her smile fades, "I don't think Dad will."

"Why not? You're thirteen. I think it's OK to have a boyfriend."

"Do you think so?" The hope in her voice could almost make me cry. I remember being that age; I remember it so well.

"Yes," I say, "and I am sure Sam would agree." I hope he would.

"It's just he always says I should put work, and friends, before boys."

"Well, he's right," I counter, thinking that sounds just like Sam, "but it doesn't mean you can't have a boyfriend. Just that you shouldn't let it become the most important thing. You've known Josh for a while, haven't you?"

"Yes."

"So you know him as a friend, which is good. And you don't want to lose his friendship if things, you know…" I let this sentence peter out, realising that Sophie probably doesn't want to contemplate splitting up from him.

"He's a really good friend," Sophie says, either not picking up on what I was saying or deliberately ignoring it. "And he knows what I'm going through, with Mum and Dad being apart, you know… not that I don't love Dad being with you, Alice."

"Sophie, you don't ever have to add that. I understand, it's not ideal for you that your parents aren't together. I'm not going to take that personally."

"Are you going to tell Dad? About Josh?"

"I think it would be better if you did."

She grows quiet again.

"OK," she says after a while. "But will you talk to him about it, if he's not happy?"

"Yes, I will, if you promise that you will keep talking to me, and your dad, about things. And if you don't leave it too long to tell him." I could really do without having another secret to keep from Sam.

We sit in silence for the rest of the journey, Sophie tapping away at her phone and me contemplating the complexities of life, and wondering at what point it might become more straightforward.

I really enjoy having Sophie around. And for the moment she is refusing to go back to Kate's – although she will spend time there at the weekends. Poor Kate is all over the place, with all this going on and a new baby to take care of. Although when she was pregnant she was adamant that she and Isaac would be sharing parental responsibilities, and she would be back to work quite quickly, she has confided in me that she has changed her mind.

"It's not that I don't trust Isaac," she said, when she and I were having a cup of tea last week, "but I don't think he's the kind of parent I imagined he would be. He's not like Sam," her cheeks flushed. "I hope you don't mind me saying that."

"Not at all." I really didn't.

"Sam was great; just kind of intuitive – getting stuck in, not asking if I want a hand with anything. It's like Jacob is

11

my responsibility and Isaac thinks he's doing me a favour. *Helping out.* It's his child, for god's sake! Sorry. It's just that attitude, like if the mum goes out in the evening, the dad is babysitting. Not just looking after his kids, as he should. I shouldn't slag Isaac off, I know. And he is working really hard on this Devon thing, so much of his energies are going into that."

She didn't sound overly enthusiastic about the 'Devon thing' but I know where the boundaries are in terms of what I can discuss with her. It is too big a thing for Sam and Sophie for me to get involved with. I can only sit back and observe, and support them when I am able to.

"God, Alice, Sophie hates me, doesn't she?"

"No, she doesn't. And neither does Sam. You know that. But it's all a bit... of a mess... and the way it was announced was a shock."

"I could have killed Isaac for doing that, I don't know what got into him. Well, I do; it was about four pints of ale. And he can't hold his drink, at all. It was almost farcical, in the labour ward. He was a mess; totally useless. In the end, I asked him to sit down on a chair in the corner of the room and I was willing him to go to sleep. And he did!" She laughed. "Lizzie managed to wake him up for the moment Jacob was born; I couldn't let him miss out on that, but I couldn't have his beery breath all over me, and him trying to tell me what to do. Thank god Lizzie was there."

Lizzie was meant to be the stand-in for Kate at Amethi, taking the yoga classes and courses until Kate was ready to come back to work. Now, Kate won't be coming back to work with us, and I think Lizzie is a long-term prospect. But, while she is an excellent yoga instructor, and a lovely person, I can't imagine having her by my side while I'm giving birth. She's 'a character', for want of a better expression. But Kate knows her better than I do. And the guests at Amethi love her. She's calm, patient and welcoming, and incredibly strong. Once she whips off her regulation poncho to reveal – often – a shiny leotard, reminiscent of the Green Goddess from the 1980s, you can see she is all muscle.

"I was quite shocked by Isaac," I admitted to Kate. "And I'm surprised he isn't pulling his weight more with Jacob."

"He's not so bad," Kate said, suddenly defensive, possibly realising that she shouldn't be bad-mouthing her partner.

"Good. You must just be really tired, and quite stressed."

"Understatement of the year," Kate had laughed. "If you ever have kids, Alice, make sure you look after yourself, OK? Although, you're with Sam. He'd look after you. You'd be fine."

I smiled, my stomach churning quietly. I almost told Kate. I can't bear keeping this secret all to myself. But, while I am pretty sure she wouldn't tell anybody, I would know that I had told her before Sam, and before Julie, and it would feel like a betrayal.

"Well, take your time, with everything. And look after yourself, too. And don't forget Sam and I are around if you need anything."

"You're doing enough already, looking after my daughter." Suddenly, tears were spilling from her eyes. "I miss her, Alice. I miss her so much. I just, I love Jacob, and Isaac, I really do, but sometimes I wish I could go back to just me and Sophie, in this little flat. Just me and her."

I put my hand on her arm. "I know you miss her. I know. And she misses you, don't think she doesn't. She just doesn't know where to put herself at the moment, but she'll work it out. We'll all help her work it out. And remember, when it was just you and her, you were lonely. You know you were."

I remember her well; Casey, as I'd thought she was called. The glamorous mum, who stayed in every night, drinking alone, once her daughter was in bed. Sometimes before. She was very lonely, and needy, and while Isaac may not be meeting her needs right now, it's obvious how happy he has made her. I'm sure it can all come right.

"You're tired, and stressed, and have probably got post-pregnancy hormones causing havoc for you. And you're missing Sophie. Jacob is a gorgeous little boy, and Isaac is a good man; he's probably a bit stressed himself; this is his first go at being a dad, isn't it?"

"Yes," Kate had sniffed, "it is. I know. I'm so hard on him."

"No!" I said. "That wasn't meant to make you feel bad. I'm trying to make you feel better! It is a weird time at the moment but it will get better, and we'll work it all out between us. I promise."

3

When Sophie and I arrive home, she disappears up to her room, ostensibly to do homework. I have to take her at her word, and I'm not about to take the role of parent with her. She doesn't want that any more than I do.

"I've got to go to the office," I say as she's heading upstairs, "and see Julie. Just come and find me if you need me."

"I will." Sophie turns to me. "Thank you, Alice."

"No problem."

"I mean about... Josh," she says, shyly.

"That really isn't a problem, either. I remember what it's like being your age!" I hate those words as soon as they've left my mouth. Sophie doesn't seem to mind, though.

"You're pretty cool, for an old lady!" she grins and runs up the last couple of steps, swinging round the top of the banister before I have a chance to retaliate.

"You'll pay!" I call and I grin as I leave the house.

Crossing the gravel, I see the lights are on in the only holiday house which is occupied this week. The day is already turning dark and the soft glow through the windows is inviting and cosy. I shiver and pull my cardigan around me; it's not yet full-on winter, but it's not far off, I can sense it. And it gives me a little thrill, to think of Christmas just around the corner, and New Year. I won't be able to drink this year, I think – which doesn't bother me. In fact, I like it. I love this reason for behaving differently, and taking better care of myself. I love knowing that within me is a tiny being; with me wherever I go. I am aware I have already started absentmindedly placing my hand on my stomach. It's protective, but also a way to communicate the overwhelming love I already feel. To let this baby know I love it and will do everything I can to keep it safe. It's hard to believe that I'd had no thought of getting pregnant just yet. I would not have said that this was an ideal time. The business is still very young, and I feel like I am, too – although, medically speaking, I am not young at all to become a mother. I am close enough to being 'geriatric' in terms of pregnancy. What a thought.

In practical terms, we have a small two-bed cottage, which actually belongs to the business, and, as things stand, it doesn't look like Sophie will be leaving us any time soon. Not that I want her to, but where will the baby sleep?

Then there is Julie. She is longing for a baby. I wish she was pregnant, too. But I cannot do anything about that. And now that I am pregnant myself, I wouldn't want it to be any other way. But I know how much this is going to hurt her.

I know all of this, and more – and yet, I wonder if there is any such thing as an ideal time to have a baby. When Mum and Dad had me, they were just starting out; had been married less than a year, and were still living with Dad's mum. She was very cool, so that wasn't a problem, but it certainly wasn't ideal.

Luckily, Mum and Dad are away at the moment. They are travelling across Canada by train, and having a wonderful time, judging by the messages they are sending. I say it's lucky they are away at the moment because I would find it very hard not to tell them, if they were here. They are due back in ten days, and I must make sure that I have told Sam, and probably Julie, before then.

The office is cold, and dark. I clatter up the steps and switch on the heater before I turn on my laptop. There is an email from Shona, subject line: **Have you seen it?**

I pick up the phone immediately.

"Alice?"

"Hi, Shona. I just saw your email. I am so sorry, I meant to call you earlier. I haven't even read your email but I guess you mean *Staycation*?"

"Yes! Are you happy? And Julie?"

"Happy doesn't even begin to cover it! It is wonderful. Thank you so much, Shona."

"Ach, it's nothing, it's all down to you and Julie, anyway. All your hard work."

"Well, thank you. It's like the perfect antidote to all the nastiness earlier this year."

"You can put all that behind you, Alice. This is on the shelves in the next week or two and I can almost guarantee you that your phone is going to be off the hook. Or your booking system will go down, whatever the modern alternative is!"

"I hope so."

"I'm sure of it. Now, are you ready for some more news?"

"I don't know. Am I?"

"Yes. Is Julie there with you?"

"No, she's making dinner for our guests."

"Oh, of course, I've lost track of time. My god, is it dark already?"

I peer out of the window. "Yep."

"I hate winter! Can you take the phone down to Julie? Interrupt her for a minute?"

"Sure." I am intrigued as I head back down the steps and into the kitchen, where Julie is humming to herself as she stirs a delicious-smelling risotto. She looks round at me and I gesture to the phone, mouthing, "Shona."

"OK," I say to Shona, "I'm in the kitchen with Julie."

"Can you put me on speakerphone?"

I put the phone on the spotless stainless steel counter top.

"Hi Shona," Julie calls. "Sorry, I can't leave my spot by the hob, I am making a risotto which, as every *Masterchef* viewer knows, is a labour of love."

"That's a fact," Shona laughs. "I've got some good news for you, girls."

"We've seen the article," Julie says, looking at me. I shake my head.

"That's just for starters," Shona says. "How do you feel about Amethi being shortlisted for Best Young Business in the Tourism & Travel Awards?"

"Erm... let me think about that... pretty good," says Julie.

"I thought you would!" Shona laughs again. "And how about the Women in Business category?"

"Shit! No way!" I want to grab Julie, but I know better than to mess with her risotto. She is smiling at the phone, absently still stirring away.

"What do you think, guys?" Shona asks.

"Seriously? Really? This is for real?" I ask.

"Yes! This is for real! You're on both shortlists."

"Fucking hell! Sorry," Julie says.

"No need to apologise," Shona says and I think back all those years to the sales training at World of Stationery – where we were told that you could 'hear a smile' down a phone line. I can definitely hear Shona's smile.

"So now's a good time to celebrate," Shona says. "They're both tough categories, but in all honesty, although it would be amazing to win, you've kind of made it, just getting onto the shortlists. You can add the badges to your website and all your marketing literature – and this is the best sort of free PR. The awards are on 28th February, so keep that date free. I'll book us a table."

"Oh my god, I can't believe this. Thank you so, so much, Shona. We wouldn't have any of this without you."

"It's my job," she says. "And when it goes well, like this, it makes it extremely worthwhile. Now, listen, don't let me ruin that risotto. I'll talk to you soon, and I'll send you all the info about the awards."

"Thank you, Shona," Julie says. "I think I love you."

We can hear Shona chuckling as she ends the call. Julie and I just look at each other.

"Did that just happen?" Julie asks.

"It did. I really think it did."

"And I'm right in the middle of this risotto," Julie groans.

"Well, that sounds messy. Look, I'm going to go and get some tea ready for me, Sam and Sophie. Why don't you come round after?"

"We could have the champagne!" Julie says.

I can't think of a good excuse not to. "Great idea."

I go back up to the office, check through the inbox. There is nothing which can't wait until morning. I switch off the heater and lights and head back down the stairs, out into the cold night air. It's only just after five but it is now properly dark and the darkness at Amethi seems to me to have a special quality all of its own.

It's a cloudy night so there are no stars to be seen, and the moon is hiding, too. The lack of light amplifies the sounds; I can hear the few leaves which remain on the trees rustling in the gentle breeze, and I can hear something small scurrying across the gravel. Probably a mouse. Hopefully not a rat.

The guests have closed their curtains now, so there is only a small line of light around the edges of their windows, but I can hear laughter from within, and the pop of a cork. It really is a pleasure to have a job that is all about helping make people happy.

I crunch across the gravel to what was once my home, which became Sam's and mine, and is now Sophie's, Sam's and mine. The lights are on in Sophie's room and her curtains are open. I can see her head, bent studiously over her desk by the window. Maybe she really is doing her homework.

I open the door. "I'm back!" I call.

"Hi, Alice!"

"Julie's coming round for dinner."

"Brill! Do you need a hand?"

"No, you crack on with your work. That's fine."

I switch on the kitchen lights, swap my boots for slippers to protect my feet from the cold of the red-tiled floor. As I check through the cupboards and fridge, making a plan for dinner, my mind is more focused on the fact I cannot keep my pregnancy a secret any longer.

4

I message Sam to check what time he might be back from his seal count, then I get to work making a quiche, and baking sweet potatoes. It's a longstanding joke that I can't cook, and I've certainly had my share of disasters in my time, so nowadays I like to keep things simple. I also have to avoid things like soft cheeses and raw eggs (I don't think that will be too difficult) now I'm pregnant.

As I whisk the eggs, my phone buzzes. It's Sam. He's about to set off and will be home in an hour or so. Julie will be another half-hour, I'm guessing, and I'm already ravenously hungry, so I open the crackers and get some mature cheddar out of the fridge. I have to stop myself finishing the lot. I don't know if it is the pregnancy, or that winter need to eat more. I am sure we should be hibernating through these colder months.

All is quiet in the house, which hopefully means that Sophie is working. I put the cheese away, allow myself one more cracker smeared with chilli chutney, then put the box back in the cupboard and chop onions, peppers and feta to go in the quiche. I am sure feta is on the approved list, or at least I think it is. I'd better do some more reading up on it all.

I sit in the warm kitchen while the quiche and potatoes cook, the only sounds the humming of the fridge and the steady hiss of the flame in the oven. I realise I am shaking but whether it is with nerves, hunger or excitement, I do not know.

I put the kettle on, make a cup of lemon and ginger tea,

21

and sip at it slowly. I haven't had morning sickness, but there are definitely some odd things going on; smells seem much stronger than they used to, and now, as I contemplate the quiche, I find that I can't bear the thought of eating the peppers. This is not good.

When Julie arrives, before Sam, bearing a bottle of champagne, I decide that one glass can't hurt. She hugs me, full of the excitement of the day, and ready to celebrate. We toast each other, and our success, and I take a sip, but it turns my stomach. Again, is it nerves, guilt, or the pregnancy? I don't know. But I do know it's time to come clean.

"Are you OK?" asks Julie.

"Yes, I'm…" I go to the kitchen door, listen out upstairs, but all is quiet and calm. Who said teenagers are hard work? I close the door, come back in, and sit next to Julie. "I don't know how to say this."

"Say what?" Julie's face falls, and I feel like I can see the whole range of possibilities flicking across her mind: illness; death; a problem with the business. I don't think she's considered the one thing that it actually is.

"Julie, I'm pregnant." I make my eyes meet hers.

She is silent for a moment. Then, "You're pregnant?" There is surprise, and shock, and sadness, and then a smile, but I am not convinced. "That's amazing. Congratulations!"

"Julie…"

"No, really." Suddenly she is business-like. I know her too well, to believe she is really OK. I recognise her pulling on a persona. "I mean, you are pleased, aren't you?"

"Yes, I am, but… it wasn't planned." Not the right thing to say to somebody who's been struggling to conceive. "What I mean is, I know how much you and Luke…"

"Oh, don't worry about us." She brushes my words aside unconvincingly. "We'll be fine. We'll get there."

"You will… oh, I hope you will, Julie." I am floundering, knowing there is nothing I can possibly say to make this any better. I can't tell her she'll get pregnant. I don't know that any better than she does. And I also fear it will make me seem smug. Like suddenly I know it all. How I wish she had got pregnant first. That we could be pregnant together; share all this. But it doesn't work like that. And I want to cry for Julie, but I know her, and I know she does not want sympathy. Right now, she wants to carry on like everything's fine.

"I bet Sam's delighted," she says.

"I haven't told him yet."

"What? Alice!"

"It's all this other stuff going on, with Sophie – which is why I hadn't told you till now. I really thought I should tell Sam first. It's messy."

"It's only as messy as you let it be, Alice," Julie says, and drains her glass, grasping the neck of the champagne bottle. "Right. You need to tell him. And I need to go, so that you can tell him. We'll celebrate another time."

Her face is almost blank, though I can see she is really trying to be happy for me. But she is also really trying not to get upset.

"Julie…"

"It's fine. I'm fine," she smiles, stands up, and kisses me on the head. "I will be fine. And I am happy for you, please believe me."

"Thank you," I say lamely and stand up, but her hand gently presses me back into my seat.

"It's fine," she says again. "Look, I'm sorry to run out on you when you've cooked for me, but hopefully you guys

23

can manage it all between you. And you're eating for two now, anyway."

I say nothing. What can I say? My friend opens the kitchen door, turning to send a smile back in my direction, but as she pulls on her boots and leaves the house, I feel like I can hear her heart breaking.

"Is that Julie?" Sophie calls from upstairs.

"She's had to go, love. Sorry." I can tell Sophie is disappointed. She pretty much hero-worships Julie. "Your dad'll be back soon, though, and then we can eat. And maybe you can tell him about Josh?" I venture, thinking that now one secret's been cracked, we might as well break the rest, too.

We sit quietly, each of us lost in our own thoughts. It's not an unpleasant silence; in fact, I love the way that we can all be quiet together. Nobody feeling the need to fill the gaps in conversation. The table is a screen-free place in our house and Sophie is not allowed her phone at all after half-past eight. She wasn't too happy about this at first, but I do think she perhaps has come to like having time away from it.

When we've finished the main course, I start to clear the table, casting a meaningful look at Sophie.

"Dad," she says. "You know Josh?"

Way to go, Sophie. There's no beating about the bush here.

"Yeah, well, I know who he is."

"He's kind of my, my… boyfriend."

"Oh yeah?"

I try to read Sam's reaction, but can't see his face clearly.

"Yeah. Is that OK?"

"Is he nice to you?"

"Yes."

"Are you still working hard at school?"

24

"Yes."

"And are you still spending lots of time with your mates, like Amber?"

"Yes, of course!"

"Great. As long as you're happy." He leans over and kisses her cheek. She beams.

Well, that was easy. Two down, one to go.

I start to scrape the leftovers from the plates into the small green compost bin, but feel queasy all of a sudden.

"Excuse me," I say and I dash out of the kitchen and upstairs into the bathroom. I pull the seat up and lean over, my eyes watering as I retch, but nothing comes out.

I hear Sam come upstairs. "Are you OK?" He knocks gently on the door.

"Yes, I'm..." I flush the toilet, although there is nothing there to get rid of, and I splash water on my face. I see in the mirror that I look pale and tired. Opening the door, I say, "I've got something to tell you, too."

Sam looks worried. I take a deep breath. Think of how straightforward Sophie was just now.

"I'm pregnant," I whisper.

"You're not?" asks Sam, incredulous, a smile spreading across his face. "Are you? Are you really?"

I feel tears running down my cheeks and an overwhelming relief washes over me. Of course he would react like this. I should have known, really.

"I am," I sob, smiling through the tears. "I really am."

In a whispered conversation, we decide not to tell Sophie yet.

"Can we talk about it all later?" Sam asks, and his face is a picture of excitement. A child in a sweet shop.

"Yes, of course," I laugh.

25

"I can't believe it!" he says, and he turns to hug me, smudging a kiss across my cheek and making me laugh. "This is amazing. But we probably ought to get back to Sophie."

"I had some other good news today," I say, as I follow him down the stairs. "Well, Julie and I both did, actually."

The thought of Julie makes me feel sad again. I am a complete mess, emotionally. But I tell Sam and Sophie about the article in *Staycation*, and then the tourism awards.

"That is amazing," Sam says, hugging me tightly, and I know it's not about the awards, it's about the baby.

Sophie pretends to be disgusted. "I'll get back to my homework."

Sam and I laugh, but he doesn't let go of me, and as Sophie leaves the room, I sink my head onto his chest, listen to his heartbeat, thinking that now there are three of us here in this embrace.

By the time we go to bed, the rain has stopped. The sky has cleared, so we keep our curtains open, allowing the moonlight into our room.

Sam has his arm around me. "I don't even know how pregnant you are," he says.

"I'm one hundred percent pregnant," I say.

"Very funny. You know what I mean."

"Well, I think I'm a bit over two months."

"Wow! And you've only just found out?"

"No," I admit. "I've known for a few weeks. And I'm really sorry," I say, before he has a chance to react, "for not telling you before. But I found out at almost exactly the same time Isaac made his big announcement, and there's been so much going on with Sophie... It wasn't that I didn't want to tell you, believe me."

I sit up and look at him. He looks thoughtful. "You've known for weeks?"

"Yes, and I'm sorry. I just wanted it to be perfect, when I told you. I didn't want it mixed up with all this other stuff that's going on."

"But there is no such thing as perfect, Alice. You know that. I wish you'd told me before. You can tell me anything, any time. And this is my baby, too."

"I know, and I really am sorry. And I have to tell you, Julie knows. But I only told her today," I quickly add, "and only because she really wanted us to have a few drinks, and I've just had enough of secrets."

Sam considers this. "How was she? About you being pregnant?"

"I think she was absolutely gutted. She pretended she wasn't, but I know her too well."

"I hope she's OK."

"I do, too. And I hope Soph's alright with it all. Suddenly she's going to have two new siblings." I start to feel doubt creeping in. "It is going to be alright, isn't it, Sam?"

"Alice," he pulls me back down next to him, "it is not going to be 'alright'. It is going to be brilliant. And part of the reason I wish you'd told me before now is so I could share all this with you. I bet you've been worrying away ever since you found out. Julie might be upset, but she will be OK. So will Luke. So will Sophie. People adapt, all the time." He sighs, kisses me. "And I can't tell you how happy I am. How lucky I feel." He kisses me again. "I love you, so much. And I love this baby, too."

He sits up, slides down the bed, lifts my t-shirt, and kisses my belly, sending goose pimples across my skin. He moves back up and kisses me again.

"Is this OK?" he whispers.

"Yes," I say; all worries, all stresses, forgotten, as I kiss him back, and slide my hands under his t-shirt.

"Your hands are freezing!" he exclaims in a whisper.

"I know," I laugh, and move on top of him, sitting up and pulling the duvet over my shoulders. "I love you." I lean down to kiss him again, feeling the warmth of his body, and the strength of his arms around me; his hands on me. I feel safe, and ready for anything, as we move closer together, in the soft blue of the night.

5

Julie is not alright. I know it, and she knows it, and she knows that I know it. But there's a block somewhere between us now, preventing us from being honest with each other; keeping communication on a far more superficial level than normal. It hurts, and I know it will be hurting Julie, too. I ache when I think of how she must be feeling. Her maternal tendencies took me by surprise and I think were a shock to her, too, but once she had started going down that route, there was no turning back and, for somebody who had always maintained they might not want to have children, it was unexpected.

Sam and I had been thinking more of marriage than of a baby; and I am slightly embarrassed to say that there is a part of me which is quite traditional in the way I view life: marriage first, then babies. But I know life should surely go the way that is right for the person living it, not just fall in line with other people's expectations.

Today is an exciting day, though, and I cast aside all thoughts of marriage – and try to push back my worries about Julie. Today, Mum and Dad are back from Canada, and I am going with Sam to tell them that they are going to be grandparents.

As it's Sunday, Sam and I have the day to ourselves. Sam is keen to have a lie-in, and I try, I really do.

"Come on, then," Sam mock-sighs, putting his book down and looking at me.

"What?" I ask innocently.

"Let's go to your mum and dad's. I know you're not going to stop fidgeting until we do."

"Oh, are you sure? We don't have to go right now. It is Sunday morning, after all."

"If you think you're fooling me, Alice, you must think I don't know you at all."

I grin. "I suppose, perhaps, we could go down to town, and pop in and see them. I mean, if you really want to."

"Yes, that's right, let's go because *I* really want to." Sam gulps down the rest of his mug of tea and swings his legs round, so that he is sitting on the edge of the bed. I admire his strong back as he leans forward to retrieve his jeans from the floor. I kneel on the mattress and lean over, kissing his bare skin, all the way up the length of his spine, wanting to feel every detail of it.

"You're not really helping the cause, Alice," Sam turns to kiss me. "How am I meant to get out of bed if you're doing that?"

"Sorry." I scurry back chastely, and stand demurely.

"Hey! You're already dressed!" Sam says accusingly.

It's true; I had a shower and got dressed while the kettle was boiling. Then I brought two cups of tea upstairs and snuggled back under the duvet while Sam was waking up.

"Oh yeah," I say, as if just noticing this. "I'm too excited, I'm sorry."

Sam just smiles. "Well, I think it's pretty cool that you're so keen to get to your parents'. I hope that Sophie's the same with me when she's older; and this little one, too, of course." He eyes my belly.

"I hope so, too."

It's another quiet week at Amethi, in terms of guests – two of the properties are taken, both by older couples, and there is no sign of life from either as we leave the house and walk as quietly as possible across the gravel and round to the car park.

As Shona had predicted, however, the phone has been – if not quite off the hook – ringing very regularly with enquiries. *Staycation* came out this week, and it seems people really like the idea of Amethi. Shona says we should expect the first two weeks to be busy, then the initial flurry might die down a little, but we could have a steady run of bookings for the two months the magazine is on the shelves.

"Then it's nearly time for the awards, girls, so you're not going to have time to sit still."

I saw Julie's eyes skim across my tummy as Shona said these words but I chose not to acknowledge it. Shona and Paul, of course, have no idea that I am pregnant, and I am still not sure how it's going to affect the business, but for now I am going on as normal and the timing of the article is good for Julie and me, giving us a focus on our business instead of our personal lives.

It's good to have this day off and, although it's cold, the sun is shining. I can't wait for the sight as the sea comes into view, and I toy with the idea of Sam and I having a walk after we see Mum and Dad; maybe going for lunch somewhere. Or just sitting on the harbour wall – though the thick stone is going to be extremely cold – and watching the comings and goings of the boats.

Now that we have another person in our household to think of, in Sophie, we are a little less free to do as we please, but she is with Amber this weekend and not due home till this evening. Sam and I should make the most of this day of freedom.

31

We park up near the top of Mum and Dad's street and, as ever, I feel a slight wistfulness as we begin the descent down the narrow road, lined either side with old townhouses. I'm always torn between here and Amethi. I absolutely love the solitude of the fields, the open sky, and the lack of people, but it was this town I fell in love with: its twisting, cobbled streets and alleyways, steep steps and fishermen's cottages; the harbour and the beaches, leading either side of town onto the coastal path.

And the history of the place; I feel like it's steeped in its past, and no matter how many tourists pass through, how many four-by-fours get stuck in one of the myriad of side streets, or how many houses get swallowed up into the tourism industry, nobody is going to take away the heritage of this place. Its fishing industry still struggles on and, although I don't support it in that I don't eat fish, I respect it. A way of life which is dying out or, possibly more correctly, being killed off. Meanwhile, the cottages where the fishermen of old would have lived are being 'refurbished to a high standard', seeing a steady tide of holiday-makers moving in and out on a weekly basis. I don't resent the tourists as some people do – I rely on them to make a living – but I do get how frustrating it is for people who have grown up here, to never have a chance of living where perhaps their ancestors did, in the heart of their town.

And now here I am, at my parents'; two more 'incomers', who have bought one of the best houses around (in my opinion). I squeeze Sam's hand as we stand side-by-side at the front door.

"They do know we're coming, don't they?" Sam asks.

"Er… no. I mean, I didn't call ahead."

"It looks like their curtains are closed," Sam says,

stepping back and peering up, just as I ring the doorbell.

"Bugger. Oh well, too late."

A bleary-eyed, dressing-gowned Dad opens the door. "Hello, you two!" He manages to look pleased. "What are you doing up so bright and early? I thought it was your traditional lie-in day."

"Hi Dad!" I step up and hug him.

"Hi, sweetheart," he returns my hug, reaches his hand out to Sam. "How goes it, young man?"

"Hi, Phil. Sorry for disturbing you." Sam has the good grace to look embarrassed, but I'm already in through the front door.

It's so familiar, this house. The first place Julie and I lived when we came down here; up in the attic rooms, while David lived downstairs. Now, it also has that familiar Mum-and-Dad smell, so it's an odd mixture of associations which assault my senses when I step across the threshold.

"Where's Mum?"

"In bed!" Dad laughs.

"At this time?" I pretend to tut, and consult my watch. "It's… nearly nine o'clock."

"Yes, and it's Sunday, and we're jetlagged, and knackered from travelling!" Dad protests.

"Come on, Alice," Sam says. "Why don't we go for a walk, and come back in a little while? We could go and get breakfast on the beach."

"OK," I say reluctantly, although my tummy is rumbling, and breakfast on the beach sounds great. But then I hear my mum's voice.

"Alice?"

I look up to see her, also in her dressing gown, at the top of the stairs – next to the stairwell window, bathed in the morning sunlight.

"Mum!" I embarrassingly find I want to cry. Mum looks worried and starts to come downstairs.

"Are you OK?"

"Yes," I laugh, brushing a tear away from my face, "I'm fine. I'm…" I can't help myself. "I'm pregnant."

I hear a gasp from both my parents.

"Oh, Alice! And Sam!" Mum exclaims.

"I wasn't expecting that," Dad says.

In the blink of an eye, there are hugs all round, and the odd tear here and there.

"Come through, come through," Mum says, ushering us into the lounge. "Come and sit down. Tell us all about it."

"I'll put the kettle on," says Dad, a huge smile lighting up his face.

"OK," I follow Mum in, "and you have to tell us about your holiday, too."

"Oh, it was wonderful," she says, "but that can wait. We'll have a slide show another day," she teases, putting her arm around Sam's shoulder and giving him a squeeze.

"How many months, Alice?" she asks.

"Nearly three, I think, and we've got our first scan this week!" I exclaim, so happy and relieved to be able to speak to my mum about this.

"Wow, that is going to be incredible. I can't believe you're three months already! Have you only just found out?"

"No…" I look at Sam. "I have known for a few weeks, but we've had so much going on, with Soph and all."

"Oh, yes. How is Sophie? Have you told her your news?"

"No, not yet. I think we should, though, Sam, do you?"

"Yes, I guess so." Sam looks thoughtful.

"And you need to tell your mum, too."

I have never met Sam's mum. She's in Spain and has

been for a long time now, having left Sam in Cornwall when he was sixteen. I think he's seen her only a handful of times since then.

"Yes, I guess."

Mum keeps quiet, but I know what she's thinking – Sam must tell his mum; she will want to know. Only, Sam's mum isn't like mine. She has met Sophie only once in all her life, and sometimes remembers her birthday, but often forgets, or doesn't bother. Sam says he hasn't had as much as a card from her for his own birthday since she went to Spain. Not that it's about birthdays and Christmas, but it does suggest she's not the most thoughtful of parents or grandparents. Nevertheless, she should probably know that Sam is going to be a dad again. And he can tell her that we've got engaged, too.

Dad comes into the room, bearing a tray of coffee, tea, and a toast rack. "Hang on," he says, putting it down on the table and leaving to return with a second tray, laden with butter and jam, and a bowl of cherries. "Here we go," he says, and he sits next to me.

"I can't believe it," he puts his arm round me. "My little girl. Pregnant."

"Dad! I am not a little girl." From the corner of my eye, I can just see Sam's grin.

"No, I know, but…" Dad sniffles.

"Oh, Phil," Mum says fondly. "Tell us the due date, Alice," she suggests.

"Mid-June," I say.

"Oh, that's lovely. A summer baby!"

"Like Alice," Dad says.

"Yes, but earlier in the summer," I say, smiling at Sam.

"And are you feeling well? Your mum had morning sickness."

"Yes, I'm fine," I laugh. "Although I seem to be going off some things. In fact, I don't think I fancy a cup of tea. Or coffee. Or anything milky." I do feel a little bit off all of a sudden. And the word 'milky'... urgh. I can't bear to think of it.

"How about some of those cherries?" Mum asks.

"Erm, no, I'm OK, thanks. I did eat earlier. I'm sure I'll feel hungry again soon."

I sit and sip a glass of sparkling water, feeling slightly envious as my parents and Sam tuck into coffee and toast with butter and jam; but I just don't think I can take it at the moment.

"We've got some news, too," Mum says. Dad looks confused. "You know..." she looks meaningfully at him. "My job."

"Oh, yeah!" Dad smiles.

"I'm quitting working at the hospice," Mum says.

"Are you?" I knew Mum wasn't finding it very easy working there but I'm surprised she's leaving. "Have you got something new?"

"No, not yet, but your dad and I were talking while we were away, and I realised how much I was dreading going back there. And that's not like me."

"No," Dad takes up the thread of conversation. "And after your mum's illness the other year, I don't want her getting stressed."

"I'm fine!" Mum takes back the reins, "But I don't have to work, financially, and I feel like I rushed into that position – and I also feel really quite, well, unwelcome there. It's not a nice way to feel, going into work every day. The hospice is lovely; in fact, I think I might volunteer there. I just don't want to work in that office anymore."

"OK," I take this in. "But you're not hugely unhappy?"

"Not now, no. And I wasn't desperately unhappy before. But your dad and I are in a fortunate position, and it seemed a bit daft to be doing something that I really wasn't enjoying. And there's so much resistance to change... I get it; people have worked there, and done things a certain way for so long, they don't want some upstart coming in, telling them to do things differently. But it is frustrating."

"What are you going to do though, Mum?" I know my mum, and I know she will get bored without something to challenge her.

"I don't know yet. But I have the luxury of a bit of time to think it all through."

"I think we should start a business together," says Dad. "Something food-related."

"I don't," Mum says firmly. "I mean, if you want to do that, Phil, you should go for it, but it wouldn't work, us spending all our time together. I love you dearly, you know that, but we might just drive each other mad."

I laugh at this, and so does Sam.

"Could you work with me?" I ask him.

"I don't know. I agree with Sue, it's good to keep some things separate. Anyway, you and Julie have it all sown up. I don't think I could compete with her."

Mum picks something up in my expression at the mention of my friend. "How is Julie?" she asks.

"She's OK, thanks," I say, knowing that my reply doesn't sound overly confident or enthusiastic. Mum doesn't say anything more, but a look passes between us. We can talk about it later.

Sam and I leave amid further congratulations and hugs. My queasiness has passed and I step lightly out of the house, onto the street and into the fresh winter air.

"Fancy a walk?" Sam asks.

"I was about to suggest exactly that!" I smile and place my hand in his, putting my other hand on his arm and holding on for a moment.

"Happy?" he asks, smiling and kissing the top of my head.

"Yes, very. And did you see how excited Mum and Dad are?"

"Just a bit!" he grins. "You're very lucky, having them."

"I know."

We walk in silence for a while, footsteps echoing off the walls of the houses. I cast my mind back fifteen years or so. Julie and I, fresh from the Midlands, heading down to town on our first evening out. It was a hot night, in the early summer, and the air seemed full of excitement; life filled with possibilities. We'd had a few drinks that night, Julie and I, and explored the town, chatting and giggling as we took it all in, unable to believe our luck.

Now, I feel older, and hopefully a little wiser, but I do sometimes miss those heady days, and right now I keenly miss that closeness with Julie. I hope that we can get it back. I know we've had our fallings-out in the past, but there is something about this situation that goes so very deep. It's not a disagreement, or a petty squabble. This baby is coming and it's going to take over my life; I realise that, more and more. There will still be Amethi, there will still be friendships, but having seen how Kate is with Jacob, I have realised how immediate a baby is. How his or her needs will have to come before mine, or anybody else's – to a great degree. I must be squeezing Sam's hand too tightly, as he gently eases my fingers loose.

"Are you OK?"

"I'm fine, sorry. I was just thinking about what it's going

to mean to have a baby. And what a responsibility it's going to be."

"You are going to be brilliant," Sam says, lifting my hand and kissing it. "And it's not just down to you, it's going to be the two of us, always."

I smile. "Kate said you were great when Sophie was a baby."

"Did she?" He looks pleased.

"Yes, and it didn't surprise me. You are great."

"I know." He suppresses a smile.

We round the corner onto the harbour road, past the Lifeboat station. The tide is in and it's calm today. I can see the resident seal bobbing up and down in the deep green water. As we pass a café, I have a sudden craving.

"A cheese toastie," I say. "With barbecue sauce."

"Is that the baby or you asking?"

"I think it's both," I say.

"I don't mind, either way. Wait here. Do you want a drink as well?"

"Lemonade, please."

"No problem."

I spy a bench being vacated by a pair of older women and I make a beeline for it, resting my feet on the harbour railings and watching the seal plunging under the surface and popping up closer to me. Its head swivels around and I might be imagining things but it seems to be looking at me. I look straight back; hold its gaze. The gentle waves rock it up and down but it continues to stare at me and then, all of a sudden, it turns and disappears into the depths once more.

A couple of turnstones hop close to the bench, eyeing me surreptitiously; not quite relaxed, ready to flee at any time if they need to.

I feel a gentle hand on my shoulder. "Here you go," Sam says, handing me a carton and a bottle of lemonade.

"Thanks!" The carton is warm and I realise how cold I've been getting. "Can we walk round to the pier?"

"Of course. Probably best; we can shelter from the gulls there."

"What have you got?"

"Same as you. Except I've got a coke instead of the lemonade. Oh, and a pasty instead of the sandwich. And a bag of crisps."

"We're like twins."

On the pier, we find a spot on the wall where we can lean back while we eat, making it harder for any gulls to launch a surprise attack on us. Sam hands me some sachets of barbecue sauce and I dip the hot sandwich in, making short work of it.

"I could eat that again."

"Not unless you regurgitate it," Sam says. "Sorry."

"Yep, thanks for that."

"Do you want another one?" he asks earnestly.

"No, I'd better not. They reckon that 'eating for two' stuff is all rubbish, you know. You only need a few extra calories a day, and that's at a later stage of pregnancy than I'm at."

"Yeah, but if you want another sandwich, you can have one!"

"I know. Thanks, Sam. To be honest, I'm more tired than anything. I could just sit here and go to sleep."

"Well, do it," Sam says, gathering our litter and stowing it away. "Here."

He puts his arm around me and pulls me in so that I can rest against him. With the thick stone wall behind us and the sun on our faces, it feels warm here. I close my eyes, listening to the creaking of the boat masts, and the soft, lulling waves against the harbour walls.

"What was that?" I ask suddenly, and Sam sits up.

"Are you OK?"

"Yes! It's just, I think I felt it. I think I just felt the baby!"

It was either that or indigestion, but it felt different to anything I've experienced before. Like a little stream of bubbles in my tummy. I sit, quietly, willing it to happen again, but it doesn't. I'm sure of it, though. *Thank you*, I think, as though my developing baby can hear my thoughts. Maybe it can. Who knows?

And, while I don't go to sleep, I nestle in against Sam again and we sit there until our backsides are numb and we have to get up, or risk never being able to move again.

The town is so much quieter at this time of year, and more relaxed. We walk along to the surfer beach, pop into the bar to see Andrew, who Sam has known since school.

"Beer, mate?"

Sam looks at me.

"Of course! Have a beer. Can I have an orange juice?"

Andrew nods.

"Can I tell him?" Sam asks. He looks so eager, it's impossible to say no.

"It means we're going to have to tell Sophie, tonight. And you need to tell your mum, too. Let's get it done; tell Sophie when she's back from Amber's, then give your mum a ring."

"OK," Sam says, and he goes up the bar, speaking quietly to Andrew.

"No way!" Andrew exclaims. "You're not going to believe this, mate, but Becky is, too! About three months, they reckon."

41

"Same as Alice," Sam says and it makes me smile to hear them talking about us like this, like experts. Of course, Sam is more of an expert than me, having gone through it all with Kate already.

"We might be in the same ante natal class," I say, and they both look at me blankly.

"Oh, yeah," Sam says, "I'd forgotten all about those. Probably blanked them out. We were so young when Kate was pregnant, it felt like the others were looking down their noses at us. In fact, I think we skipped the last two."

"Becky'll be pleased to have somebody in the same boat as her," Andrew smiles, leaning over the bar to kiss me. "Congratulations."

"And to you," I say. "Tell Becky to give me a shout some time."

"Will do."

After the bar, we walk the length of the beach, then back to town, and up to the car. I feel shattered.

"Let's get home and you can have a rest this afternoon," Sam says. "I'll get tea on and when Soph gets back we can tell her, together. I hope she's OK about it," he says doubtfully.

"Me too." I have a small fear that she's going to feel pushed out, with her mum and dad both having new babies. We will just have to make sure she doesn't.

6

As it turns out, Sophie is OK with the news. At least, I am pretty sure she is. She doesn't seem overly bothered, either way, which may be because she doesn't find babies interesting, or it could be that she is too cool these days to display emotion. Although she does look crestfallen for a moment.

"Oh, what about the wedding?"

"The wedding?" I ask.

"Yes, *your* wedding!" she exclaims, as though Sam and I are stupid. "You can't get married now you're pregnant, can you?"

"I could... we could," I correct myself, "but I don't know. We hadn't set a date yet."

"But I was really looking forward to it," Sophie looks genuinely put out.

"Were you?" Sam asks gently.

"Yeah, I was. I really was."

"Because you'd get a new dress?"

"Dad!" She looks seriously outraged, and I don't blame her.

"I didn't realise you were so into the idea," I say, taking the heat off Sam.

"Yeah, well, Luke and Julie had such a great day, I wanted you two to have the same."

"That is really lovely of you, Soph," I say. "And I definitely still want to marry your dad. I guess we just haven't had a chance to think about that side of things yet."

"Well, you should. It's romantic."

Ah, I think, *she's in love*. It's the romance which appeals to her.

"It will be romantic," I agree, "whenever it happens. And you'll be the first to know when we decide on a date. Whether or not that will be before the baby comes, I don't know."

"Yes, sorry Soph," Sam says, "I was only teasing about the dress. It's so sweet that you were looking forward to it so much. And I definitely still want to marry Alice, so don't worry – it will happen."

He looks at me and smiles, and I feel my stomach do a little flip. This time, possibly accompanied by the wriggle of our tiny baby. I put my hand to my tummy.

"Did it kick?" Sophie asks, and I realise she might actually be excited about this baby after all.

"I don't know if it's called kicking yet – I think it may be too small to kick! But it's something, I am sure of it."

"Urgh, Mum's tummy was all weird when she was pregnant. You could see Jacob moving about under her skin!"

"Well, that's going to happen to me, if all goes smoothly with the pregnancy. There's a lot less space for the baby to move as it gets bigger."

"It's freaky," Sophie says.

"I'll look forward to that."

"Do you know what's really great, Soph?" Sam puts his hand on his daughter's. "You're an expert already on looking after babies. Kate says you're brilliant with Jacob. You'll be able to give us a few pointers, cos I'm a bit rusty."

"And I've never done it before!"

I see a tiny flash of the younger Sophie as she considers this, looking pleased to be in such a position.

"You'll both be great," she says, almost shyly.

"Oh, Sophie. I love you," I say, leaning across to hug her. And I think I have never told her that before. She holds onto my arm, tightly. "I love you, too, Alice."

When we let go of each other it's just in time for me to see Sam swiping at the tears which have formed in his eyes.

Once Sophie is in on the secret, we are free to tell anyone we care to, but decide to hang on until the scan, just to make sure everything's OK. I've tried to get Sam to call his mum but as yet he hasn't. I think it's a bit rubbish of him; she needs to know. But I know better than to push it. It's his mum. I can tell he's struggling with this. The last time he contacted her was to say he'd graduated. He left her a message, and he emailed her, but she didn't respond. He'll tell her soon, I'm sure.

On the way to the hospital, I am nervous like I've never been in my whole life. I try to keep it in, and at the same time try to ignore my full-to-bursting bladder. Apparently, it's easier to perform the scan if my bladder is full, but it's getting really uncomfortable.

"You alright over there?" Sam glances my way.

"Yep," I say, tight-lipped.

"I hope they don't keep us waiting ages."

"Thanks, Sam, that's just what I needed to hear."

"Don't worry! And if you have to go to the toilet, you have to go. I'm sure you wouldn't be the first one."

"What, in the scan room?"

"No, you wally! Just use the Ladies, like a normal person."

"Oh." I fiddle with the radio station, find Bob Marley's *Three Little Birds*. It makes me smile. I am determined to do this right.

They want me with a full bladder, they are going to get me with a full bladder.

We don't have to wait long at the hospital.

"Alice Griffiths?" An older woman, with tight grey curls and a very serious look, calls me through. I stand and Sam stands beside me.

"Just through here," she says, all brisk efficiency. Sam squeezes my hand and away we go.

I note that she barely acknowledges Sam, who sits on the side-lines while I remove my shoes and shift myself onto the bed. A younger woman, who was already in the room, smiles reassuringly at me.

"Hi, I'm Angela. I'm going to put some gel on your tummy, it's going to be quite cold, sorry. I just need to tuck this into your waistband first," she waves a wad of blue paper at me, "so we don't get the gel all over your clothes."

"OK, thanks," I say, happy to lie back and let them do what they need to do. The first woman, who has not introduced herself, but I assume is the sonographer, moves to the other side of the bed, where there's a screen and some kind of machine attached to it. She picks a handset up, looking at the screen while the cold gel is applied to my skin. I am too nervous to speak now and a quick peek at Sam tells me he's much the same. I feel sorry for him, over in the shadows. But maybe this is one of the few places and times when a woman is put first.

"OK, Alice." Somehow the use of my name makes this woman feel a bit friendlier. "Let's see what we've got, shall we?" She moves the handset onto my tummy.

"We don't want to know the sex!" I exclaim.

"I meant, let's see this baby. Of course we couldn't tell its *gender* at this point. Unless you've got your dates very wrong," she chuckles drily. Angela casts a very quick, sympathetic, look my way, but I feel my cheeks flush.

"She won't have got them wrong," I hear Sam speak up. "I expect she's just nervous, seeing as she's never done this before."

There is no response from the sonographer, who appears not to have heard Sam, and is intent on moving the handset firmly across my tummy, pushing it harder in places, her eyes not leaving the images on the monitor for more than a split second. I send a smile Sam's way then return to watching the screen. It is a mass of weird shapes, and I can't work out what anything is but then, "There we go." Her voice has softened slightly. "There's your baby."

Involuntarily, I take a sharp inhale, as I see our baby for the first time. It is blurry, it is tiny, and it looks like no baby I've ever seen before, but there on the screen is the little person who I now feel like I've been waiting for all my life.

"Its head," the woman continues now in her more gentle tone, moving the handset with one hand and pointing to the screen with the other. "Its spine… and can you see that? That is your baby's heart beating."

I gasp again and I feel Sam take my hand. I can't look at him, I can't tear my eyes away from the screen, but I feel him shudder a little and I am sure he is crying, too.

"Now, everything looks as it should." Is that a smile on her face? Surely not. "I just need to try to work out your due date, by doing a few measurements." There is silence for a few moments while Sam and I look at our baby in awe. "OK. That's looking good. This looks like a twelve-week pregnancy so you obviously were spot on with your dates." She doesn't look at Sam. "I'm going to give your due date as… let's see… June 24th."

June 24th. My new favourite date.

"Would you like printouts to take away?"

"Definitely!" I say, turning to smile widely at Sam.

"OK, just hold on, let me see if I can get a nice clear picture. Oh look, I think it's waving at you."

I turn back, see a tiny arm movement. This woman may not be as cold and hard as she first seemed. She manages to get a fantastic image, which she sends to be printed as Angela helps me clean the gel off my tummy.

"OK. All looks excellent, Alice. I'll send a copy of the report to your doctors' practice and they can share it with your midwife, but if you have your folder I can add a copy to that, too."

"I do," I say, suddenly aware that I am desperate for the loo. I sit up slowly. "Could I quickly go to the toilet?"

"Of course!" Angela laughs, helping me off the bed, although I am not yet that heavily pregnant that I couldn't manoeuvre myself. "Out of this door, and it's the next on the right."

"Thank you!" I exclaim and I am out of there, not even stopping to put my shoes on.

I sit for moment, enjoying the relief of being able to empty my bladder at last, but also considering what I have just witnessed. That little shape on the screen; that is Sam's and my child. It is hard to believe. Me and Sam. Sam and me. And my heart is bursting with love for that tiny little being, which is still here with me, not on that screen back in the sonography room but right here, and it will be with me every step I take for the next six months.

Tears stream down my face and I take a moment to compose myself, blow my nose and dry my eyes, then I head back to the scan room with as much dignity as I can muster. Sam is holding my shoes at the door. There is no sign of the older woman but I offer my thanks to Angela.

"Have you got the picture?" I ask Sam.

"Yep, two copies," he says, brandishing two white folded cards, decorated with a picture of a stork carrying a baby in a cloth. I think somebody needs a refresher course in sex education. I take a card from Sam and open it to reveal a copy of the image we'd seen on screen. Marvelling at the size of the head, I try to pick out the different details, and remember seeing that tiny beating heart.

"It's so cheesy to say this, but it feels like a miracle!"

"I know," Sam smiles at me, kisses my forehead, then hands me my shoes. "Now get your shoes on! Before they think you're an inpatient and whisk you away."

When we leave the hospital it's raining and Sam tucks the pictures into his coat then we run hand-in-hand back to the car. It's a bit of a trek across Cornwall, and the windscreen wipers are going hell for leather as we drive, passing fields of subdued cows, and woodlands stripped bare of their greenery. Even the wind turbines are still; beaten into submission by the downpour.

It is December but it hasn't yet turned cold – meaning it doesn't feel exactly festive right now. But waiting back at Amethi is a load of organising which I need to do, and as we get closer to home my mind tucks away all thoughts of the scan, and turns instead to my ever-growing, never-ending to do list.

Before Christmas arrives, we have a special yoga retreat, celebrating the winter solstice. I am really excited about it and Lizzie has gone to town on writing the themed lessons, while Julie and I have been putting together a menu culminating in a winter feast, on the eve of the solstice. The starter is spiced pumpkin soup, topped with roasted pumpkin seeds and accompanied by home-baked rye bread; main course is vegan butternut squash pizza, accompanied by roasted vegetable salad and, for those who dare, warm brussels sprouts salad. For non-vegans there is rum-spiced egg nog and for vegans, or those who don't like egg nog, a rum and ginger cocktail.

Our regular hosts for the writing courses – Vanessa and Rosie – have agreed to join us for the feast, and provide some poetry readings. There will be candles, an open fire, and a fire outdoors, and Lizzie is going to educate us in some pagan traditions, including the welcoming of the sun on the solstice morning. The course has been booked up for months, and I can't wait. I love traditional Christmas celebrations but it's going to be great to do something completely different. The solstice itself is on the Friday and once the yoga guests have gone, all our properties are booked out from the Saturday, by people looking to spend Christmas away from home – whether it's because their kids won't be with them this year, or because they want more space to get all the family together, without being on top of each other.

We've ordered a huge tree to go in the yard, but we won't be putting it up until after the yoga retreat. Doing it so close to Christmas is going to feel extra exciting, I think, and Julie and I have invited all the usual suspects up to Amethi for a mini Christmas party, and to help us decorate the tree. Mum and Dad; David, Martin and Tyler; Bea and Bob; Jonathan; Stef and April, plus Annabel and Reuben; Paul and Shona. Luke is going to be off work over Christmas, and driving back from London that day, and Sam will be off for a few days, too. There is an awful lot to look forward to.

I just wish that things were better for Julie. It feels incredibly unfair that I am experiencing so much luck; so much happiness. She's OK, or so she says, but I know she's aching and I know that me being pregnant can only be making her feel worse. It is frustrating that there is absolutely nothing I can do to make her situation better. I just have to hope that things work out for her and Luke, and soon. But I feel like whatever I might say to her will sound shallow and futile. I don't want anything to drive us apart, and I really wish I had my friend alongside me now, in this exciting, scary time of life, but I cannot expect her to support me in my pregnancy; it would be rubbing salt in the wound.

We take the coast road, then pass around the back of the town just as the rain is stopping and the sun begins to break through. I will never get bored of this view, across the lichened rooftops which tumble down towards the sea. Seagulls ascend over them, gliding lazily on warm currents of air, while far out at sea a tanker passes slowly by. Over the Island I see a rainbow, curving up and out of the waves. Bob Marley's voice creeps into my mind. Everything's going to be alright.

7

"How did it go?" Julie emerges from the kitchen just as I get to the doorway of the office. I was going to go straight up; not make a big deal of it.

"It was fine, thanks," I say, kicking myself for feeling awkward with my best friend. It's like I can feel her pain. Maybe I'm making too much of it. But I've seen her abject disappointment when her period has come, month after month; and her excitement the time she thought she was pregnant.

"Come on then, where's the picture?" She smiles at me.

"I think it's in my bag, hang on."

"Alice…" she says warningly, putting her hand on my arm so I look up from my bag. "Alice, stop it! You don't have to play it down for me, you know. I'm happy for you. I am delighted for you. You should know that."

Tears spring, unannounced, to my eyes. "Julie…"

"Alice!" she says sharply. "You have nothing to feel bad about. And nothing to hide. You're my best friend, and you're having a baby, and I want to be part of it all."

She reaches out and pulls me to her and I feel weak, and stupid, allowing her to comfort me when it should be the other way round.

"Damn hormones," I say.

"Yep," she agrees, and pushes me back gently so we are looking at each other eye-to-eye. "Can't bloody win with them. But I mean it, Alice. We are best friends, and we are business partners, and more than that, you are my family. Which means I'm here for you. And I want to share in your happiness now. This is an exciting time. And before you say anything else, let's just get it all out in the open. We both know it anyway. I want a baby – I really badly want a baby. And it hasn't happened yet, but that's not to say it won't. But it is happening for you, right now. You and Sam. And I'm genuinely, honestly, really happy for you. You will be the best mum."

"Bloody hell, Julie." I want to say that she will be the best mum but I know I can't say that. It is a stupid thing to say when she is having trouble conceiving. "How can you be so brilliant?"

"You shouldn't be surprised," she smiles. "You've known me long enough. But I mean it, Alice, let's be upfront and honest about it all. I've felt like we've been slightly distant lately and I don't want that. Life happens differently for all of us, and if we can't accept that and see each other through the hard times, as well as be happy for each other in the good times, then what's the point? Now, speech done. Let's see this picture."

Of course, I knew exactly where it was all along. As if it would be just 'somewhere' amongst the detritus of my bag. I pull it out and hand it to her. She opens the card and looks for a while. I watch her face as she examines the picture.

"OK. I don't get it."

I laugh. "Look," I move round next to her, and point out the various things which the sonographer had shown us.

"Ohhhh," Julie says. "I did guess that must be the head but… wow… they're a really odd shape at this stage, aren't they? I mean that in a nice way," she smiles sweetly.

"Yes, they are! But I now have a due date. June 24th."

"Now that is exciting. And it's midsummer! We'll have to tell Lizzie."

"If she doesn't already know," I say facetiously. "Has she been in touch? She was meant to be calling today; the Johnsons wanted some sessions next week."

"Yes, she rang earlier. Told me that there would be snow at the solstice."

"Where does she get her news from?"

"I think it might be Facebook but she's sure it's a higher power. She said the other day that she just tunes into it."

"Like a radio?"

"Yes, exactly."

"I do love her. I think she helps make Amethi even more unique."

"That is one way of putting it."

What a relief to have had that talk with Julie. I feel like a weight has lifted, and definitely as though whatever barrier had built itself up between us has been knocked down. I marvel at my friend's immense strength, and generosity. I don't think I could love her more.

When she goes back into the kitchen, I head upstairs to the office, and I can't help myself. I begin to spread the news.

"Oh my God!" David shrieks. "Martin! Alice is preggers!!" I hear Martin's excited voice in the background, shouting congratulations. "Tell me all, Alice," David says, "although you can leave out the very beginning bit."

I fill him in, as requested, and feel my excitement rise as he joins in my amazement at the idea of the baby which is growing inside me, and the weird way I'm feeling about certain food and smells.

"We've got some news, too," David tells me.

"Oh yeah?"

"Yes… we might be having number two."

"Another baby?" I ask, imagining David and me as new parents together. Cosy parenting groups, afternoons drinking coffee while our babies sleep side-by-side in their Moses baskets. Conveniently forgetting a marauding Tyler would be on the scene.

"Not a baby, not quite. Another toddler. About the same age Tyler was when he came to us. But a little girl this time."

I find I am in tears again. I'm becoming a nightmare. "David, that is lovely."

"Well, it isn't quite definite yet; they contacted us to say this was a possibility, and to find out what we think. She will be quite close in age to Ty; about eighteen months between them. And obviously we have to think about how it might affect him, after all he's been through already."

I actually don't know what Tyler has been through already; Martin and David have kept this information to themselves. "Of course."

"But I love the idea, and so does Martin. So watch this space."

I call Bea next, who is equally overjoyed. "Oh, Alice," I think I hear her sniffle. "That is wonderful news. I can't believe it, I still think of that shy eighteen-year-old that came to work for me so many years ago. Look at you now! It's making me feel old."

"You are definitely not old," I say.

"Ha, you say that now. Please come round one evening, with Sam. Let Bob and me take you out for a meal to celebrate. Hey, and Sam's got a ready-made designated driver now!"

I laugh. "Yes, I had thought of that before. Christmas is going to be different this year. And New Year's Eve! But I really don't mind." I put my hand on my tummy.

"We're really looking forward to your party, too. And Bob and I have just booked our January break. We're going to Borneo! Stef's holding the fort while we're away, but you know how quiet January is. Although I do love being here while it's quiet."

Me too. The town in January, and for much of February, feels like it is in hibernation. There's a quiet, comfortable air, while the residents, and streets and beaches, can take a breath, relieved for a while of holiday-makers. Because of the New Year celebrations, it is almost as busy in late December as it is in the middle of summer. But once the partying is over and the street cleaners have done their work, there are a few weeks' grace in which to take stock, before it all begins again.

"That's lovely, Bea. Sounds amazing, in fact."

"You should get away, too. Make the most of it while it's just you and Sam."

"That would be nice," I say thoughtfully, "but I guess we need to save our money now. Plus there's Sophie to consider, of course."

"Of course. Is she with you permanently now?"

"She's certainly with us full-time, but she and Sam are going to Devon with Kate and Isaac and Jacob next weekend, to see this place. I might go up later on Saturday, if I'm not too tired."

"That sounds positive. See how you feel, though. Maybe you should make the most of any chance you have to put your feet up."

"You're probably right – but I'd like to see this place, out of nosiness, and also support Sam and Soph – and even Kate. It's a tricky situation."

"It is that," Bea laughs. "But at least life's interesting! I'd better go. Give my love to Sam, and get back to me with a date for going out. I know it may not be till next year now, but if we don't put a date in the calendar it will never happen."

"I'll do that, Bea. Thank you."

I take a break from the phone calls to check the general Amethi emails. There is one from the Tourism & Travel Awards. I open it up.

We are delighted to confirm your place in the following categories:

Best Young Business
Women in Business

The competition is high in both categories, of course, but it would not be worth competing against any lesser adversaries.

We can offer you a table for up to twelve guests at the gala dinner on February 28th and ask that you respond by January 21st with your final numbers, and the name of each guest, along with any dietary or access requirements.

My heart begins to beat faster as I read the email again. I pick up the phone and get Julie on the intercom.

"We've got our invite to the awards dinner!"

"Really? That is exciting! Can we bring guests?"

"Yes – we've got a table for twelve if we want it."

"Wow, that's loads. Who should we invite?"

"I was thinking… Sam and Luke, of course. Then – I don't know. How about Cindy, and maybe Lizzie and

Kate? They're all part of the team."

"That would be good – although does that mean they should invite partners? And what about your mum and dad? They do a lot for us, especially Phil."

"That makes twelve, if Isaac comes, and if Cindy and Lizzie bring partners."

"That was easy. Although... does Lizzie have a partner?"

"I'm not sure. And I don't know if Rod would be up for an awards ceremony."

"We should definitely ask, though."

"We're not going to win, are we?"

"No, of course not. But it's all good publicity, as Shona would say. Shit, shouldn't we invite Shona?"

"Yes, we should, really. OK, let's think it through before we do anything. We can add it to our list to go through tomorrow morning."

"Excellent. Now, are you busy or are you too excited after your scan to do any real work?"

"No," I say defensively, determined that being pregnant won't make a difference to how I work.

"It's OK if you are!" laughs Julie. "It's just, I'm done here. There are no orders for tonight, as you kindly arranged dinner reservations for our guests. I've just been taking the chance to sort things out in the kitchen. Why don't we bunk off, go for a walk? I could do with a bit of sea air."

"That sounds perfect," I scan the inbox to confirm there's nothing urgent.

"But we're not allowed to talk work, OK?"

"Of course. No work."

"And you can talk babies if you like."

"I'm sure we have other things to talk about than work and babies, my friend."

The wind is strong down on the beach, whipping sand into our faces and whisking our breath away. Julie and I laugh, shocked by the strength of it, clutching each other's arms.

"We've so many memories of this place!" Julie has to almost shout to make herself heard.

"I know," I say, pulling her close to me then freeing one arm to pull some hair from my mouth.

"Remember that night, when we'd just come back here? And we bumped into Luke again?"

"How could I forget?" I had also seen Sam, from a distance, but he had mysteriously vanished and I'd wondered if I'd imagined him. Now, I know he had been going to pick Sophie up from a school trip. Luke had been evasive about Sam, but quite obviously was immediately smitten by Julie. "He was so excited to see you. He's never been much of one for a poker face, has he?"

"No," Julie smiles. "I think he might not be so keen on me at the moment, though. I'm being horrible to him."

"Are you?" This is news to me. "Why?"

"I don't know!" she says. "Well, I do. I think it's to do with this baby, or not-baby. I know it's not his fault – and we are trying, believe me – but he doesn't seem to care about it like I do. When I thought I was pregnant back in the summer, and then I wasn't, I don't think he got it. He wants to be a dad, but I don't think he wants it as badly as I want to be a mum."

"Oh, Julie," I say. "Maybe it is different for men, I don't know. I suppose they don't have the physical side of it, but remember you hadn't even told him you thought you were pregnant. He hadn't had the chance to feel excited."

"No, I told you, didn't I? And when he found out, I don't think he was very pleased."

"Well, I told you I was pregnant before I told Sam."

"We're not very good, are we?" Julie laughs.

"I beg to differ. We are both excellent."

She squeezes my arm and we walk on, footprints trudging into the damp sand. It is hard to catch our breath, never mind have a conversation. And in the grey, nearly dark, December day, the beach seems deserted – just a man and his dog, which is running maniacally into the sea and back, barking at the waves.

We walk the length of the beach, to the slippery rocks which mark the end of the sand and the start of the steep ascent to the coastal footpath. We look at the rickety wooden steps and handrail then at each other, both thinking the same thing.

"Nah!" we say in unison, and laugh, then turn and retrace our path. I'd like to take my socks and boots off, feel the sand between my toes and the rough shale sloughing away the dry skin on my feet, but I know the drive home will be cold, damp and uncomfortable if I do.

"Fancy a drink?" I ask, gesturing to the café which sits above the beach, lit from inside and glowing like a beacon in the increasingly dark day.

"Sure," says Julie.

We get inside, shaking off as much of the damp as we can, and are led to a table by the window – the kind of table which is at a premium in the summer, when the view is vast and the sky is blue, and the beach an array of colours, with windbreaks, beach tents and kites separating the rows of skimpy-clothed holiday-makers. Today, the view is limited, and the sky a threatening gunmetal grey. Soon, it will be swallowed into the night and I think of our upcoming yoga retreat; the winter solstice and the turn of the seasons, when the nights begin to draw out again, like a wave retreating from the shore.

Of course, it's a long, slow drawing out and it will be months before we see those longer, lighter evenings again. It's hard to believe at this time of year that it can ever be that way; so hot that the Amethi office is almost suffocating, and the merest movement causes me to break out in sweat. By the time it's like that again I will be, or nearly be, a mum, if all goes as it should. I hold this thought close to me, thrilled by it.

"Hot chocolate?" Julie asks as the waitress appears at our table.

"Yes, please."

"With all the trimmings?"

"Just the cream for me, please." I smile at the waitress and she makes a note of this.

"Are you really worried about Luke?" I ask Julie when the waitress has retreated.

"No. I don't know," Julie sighs. "I feel like we were having so much fun, and now I'm sucking all that fun out of our relationship. I'm not meant to be like this," she says in anguish.

"There is no 'meant'," I say, putting my hand on hers. "Life changes all the time, and you're having a hard time of it now. You and Luke are there to support each other as much as to just have fun, and you both know that."

"You're right, I know, but I am not making it easy for him. I don't know what's wrong with me."

I want to say 'nothing' but I know it will sound trite so I opt instead to literally say nothing. Let Julie speak instead.

"He wants to talk to me about it, but I just can't. I don't know why. I'm better at talking to you about things, and he knows that. It's not that he resents our friendship, but he said the other week that he wishes I'd treat him more like I treat you."

"Oh, Julie," I say, and I feel for Luke. I know my friend, and I think I know why she is finding it easier to speak to me than to him, about the problems conceiving. I may be pregnant but I am not tied up in their situation.

"You know this already, Julie, but you need to be doing this together, not apart. You need to open up to Luke about it all. You were amazing earlier, saying all that to me, and I can't tell you how much I appreciate it."

"So why can't I be the same way towards Luke?"

"Well..."

"I don't know," she sighs and slumps, just as the waitress brings our drinks over.

The mugs are huge, emitting a lava flow of whipped cream and, in Julie's case, marshmallows. I smile and thank the waitress.

"I think I know," I return to the conversation.

"Of course you do," Julie gives me a small smile.

"I am not as close to all this as Luke is; that's why you can speak to me about it. You two both have a vested interest and I do, of course. I can't tell you how much I want this for you, but I'm still an outside party." I pause for a moment, trying to assess Julie's expression; whether she thinks I am speaking out of turn. "Neither of you know if there is an actual physical, or medical, reason that this hasn't worked for you yet. And I don't want to sound like I think I know it all, just because I am pregnant. I don't for one minute think I know everything. But I do think you probably need to consider, at some point, going to see a doctor. I am sure it takes some couples ages, when there is no problem at all, and hopefully that is all that's happening with you. But if it's damaging your relationship, you should think about it."

I suspect that to say as much to Luke will make it more

real to Julie, and she's worried where the next step will take them. But I hold my tongue again.

"You're right, of course," Julie smiles as she slowly swirls the cream and marshmallows into the hot chocolate. I push a spoonful of sweet cream into my mouth. It's delicious. I seem to have found something which doesn't turn my stomach.

The windows of the café are steaming up but all is darkness out there now; the mist has moved in as well, and Julie and I are the only customers left.

We sit quietly, contemplatively, and I feel suddenly exhausted.

"Thanks, Alice," Julie says.

"For what?"

"For making sense. For telling me what I already knew, but I needed somebody else to say it to me."

I just smile and sip my drink.

8

I am now thirteen weeks pregnant. Thirteen weeks! This is the end of the first trimester and by all accounts the second trimester will be the best in terms of energy levels, and any morning sickness – which thankfully hasn't really happened for me – should be gone, but I'll soon be visibly pregnant and I must admit, I'm looking forward to it.

The weeks are flying by, and I can't believe that I am already a third of a way through the pregnancy. And there is so much that needs to be done before the baby comes; not least making a plan for work. I have always imagined that, should I ever be lucky enough to become a mum, the baby would fit around Amethi and my work here. Now, the reality of the situation is sinking in, and I have to concede that when people (Mum) tell me I am going to be exhausted, and that a baby won't wait if it's hungry or tired, or needs its nappy changing, they might just be right.

"Don't underestimate it, Alice. It's true that you do not have to give up everything. But a baby will not just sleep and feed – and certainly not at times which are convenient for you. You were a terrible sleeper, and you cried non-stop through every evening for the first few weeks of your life. But every baby's different. Maybe yours will sleep through the night – though if you're planning on breastfeeding, I suspect it might not."

I sit quietly, mulling over what is being said. We're in the dining room at Mum and Dad's and it's another dark day out there, so that even though it's early afternoon, the lamps are on, and the fire is roaring away in the front room, but it was too hot for me. On the garden wall sits Gerald; Mum's 'pet seagull'. She swears she doesn't feed him but he's always there, watching and waiting. In the summer, Mum and Dad eat outside a lot so Gerald gets the crumbs, but I'm not convinced that's all.

"If any of the locals catch you feeding him, you'll be lynched!" I've told her. "Bloody out-of-towners, coming and causing havoc with our gulls."

"I don't feed him!" she insisted, continuing sheepishly, "He just likes me."

Now, he sits atop the wall, looking slightly forlorn, wing feathers ruffling in the winter wind. I almost feel sorry for him but remind myself he is a gull and well able to look after himself. If indeed he is a he.

"More than anything, Alice, you need to enjoy being a mum. And it might not come easily. It is a huge shock to the system, a massive change. You will hopefully love your baby more than you'd ever thought possible, from the minute he or she is placed in your arms, but your life will change in ways you can't even imagine now. No amount of reading will prepare you for it. I was lucky to have your grandma to help me, and you'll have me and your dad, of course. Especially now I'm out of work," she adds ruefully.

"You make it sound like you've been sacked!"

"I know, I know, I chose to leave. I just need a plan. I don't like having nothing to do."

"Are you going to volunteer at the hospice?"

"Yes, I think I will, but it won't be enough to fill that gap."

"I'll keep an eye open for anything suitable."

"Thank you, Alice. But back to you, and your work."

"I can't imagine not being there every day. I really love it, Mum."

"I know you do. And you should. You and Julie should be so proud of yourselves. How is Julie?" Her mind flits quickly to my friend; a second daughter to her, really. "Is she OK with your situation? It can't be easy, if she's wanting a baby of her own."

"No," I frown. "It can't. But she is being amazing, and supportive to me. I feel pretty awful about it."

"You shouldn't. And at least you're aware of it. And who knows, it might all work out for her and Luke soon, too. Although how you're going to run the business with two babies about, I have no idea."

"Maybe we'll start a creche as well."

"You might have to!"

I look at my watch. "I'd better get going, Mum. I need to check back in with the guests, make sure they're OK, then it's off up to Devon."

"Are you sure you don't just want to take the opportunity to rest?"

"As lovely as that sounds, I really think I need to go up, support Sam and Sophie."

"You're already halfway there; being a mum, I mean. Sophie's giving you some practice!"

"I feel awful for Kate, though. She is really torn."

"I bet. You never know, maybe Sophie will start to see things differently when she's actually able to see the place, and imagine living there."

"I don't know, Mum. She's pretty adamant she doesn't want to leave Cornwall. And she's not Isaac's greatest fan at the moment."

"It's a tough time for her. So much to adjust to. And she's still so young."

We both go quiet; both transported to our early teenage years. They don't seem long ago to me, and I suspect it's the same for Mum. Maybe we never feel truly old – it's others' perception of us, rather than how we feel inside.

"It's so much to think about. If she wants to live with us, she must. But where we're going to put this baby, I've got no idea!" I laugh slightly mirthlessly. I have to take a deep breath when it comes to these things and trust that we will find a way to make it work. Right now, though, I have literally no idea what that might be.

"Go on," Mum pats my leg. "Get going, and give me a call when you get there. I don't like to think of you driving all that way when you're pregnant."

"Mum!" I say, outraged. "I'm pregnant, not ill. And it's only about two hours' drive. But I'm getting the train anyway – Julie needs the car as Luke's away this weekend."

"OK, OK," Mum laughs. "I know. You're perfectly capable of driving to Devon. But I'm pleased you're getting the train. Is Sam picking you up when you arrive?"

"Yes, don't worry. I'm being looked after."

Mum laughs again. "I get the message. Stop being smothering."

"Not smothering," I stand and kiss her. "I appreciate it. But I am just fine and I can look after myself."

Up at Amethi, I find Julie in the office. I can tell straight off that she's not herself.

"What's up?"

"Oh, nothing. Just had an argument with Luke. Again."

"Oh no. On the phone?"

"Yes. I was a total bitch. I don't know what's wrong with me. Probably hormones," she says. "It feels like PMS."

A small glimmer of hope passes through me, that it may be hormones of a different type, but I am not stupid enough to suggest this.

"Can you call him back?" Luke is staying in London this weekend, trying to fix some problems on the project he's working on.

"I tried, but he was just getting on the tube. He's going to some work meeting or something, and it's running late, so I won't be able to speak to him till later."

"Text him?"

"I will. But I think he might be fed up of my apologies. I'm sick of them myself!"

"Oh, Julie."

"Don't worry," she says. "You need to grab your things and get to the station."

"Are you sure you don't want me to stay?" Inwardly, selfishly, I'd quite like her to say she would. The thought of a quiet evening at home, rather than potentially landing in the middle of an argument between Sophie and Sam, Kate and Isaac, is appealing.

"No, no, you go. Everything's quiet here, anyway. I'll be happy as Larry staying at yours, and Sam might need your support."

We walk together to my little two-bed house. At first, there was just me here and it seemed roomy; then Sam came along, and it seemed perfect. Sophie made three, which was not a crowd, as the old saying might suggest, but I do wonder how we're going to manage four. I think of the Julia Donaldson book, *A Squash and a Squeeze*, only in that case she kicks out the cow and the goat and the pig, and the chicken, and realises that actually she had plenty of room for herself all along. This is not an option for me.

Breathe, I tell myself. *We'll get to this next year.*

I lock the door, hand the key to Julie. "The bed's got fresh sheets on it, and there's a bottle of red in the kitchen, so help yourself. There are logs for the fire, too."

"Thanks, mate. I think I'll have a bath, get into my PJs, and settle down on the sofa. I might pick up a pizza on the way back from dropping you off."

"You should definitely do that. You do more than enough cooking."

The light is fading as we drive the short distance to town and Julie deposits me in the train station car park. It's just light enough to make out the beach down below, and a family with two small children carving out some shapes in the sand, while two small dogs chase each other in circles.

"Thanks for the lift," I lean over and kiss Julie.

"No worries. Have a great time."

"I'll try."

The train is already at the platform and I climb aboard, sinking gratefully into a window seat. I will have to change at St Erth, but it's a good twenty minutes away. I look out of the window, back towards the town, and see the Christmas lights glittering along the streets. A warmth floods through me at the thought that this time next year, I will have my baby. All being well.

I always want to add 'all being well'. I know things can go wrong. But I am positive and I cannot wait for him or her, and their first Christmas. And what a place to be born! Will my child be Cornish? Their dad is, and they will be born here. Surely that qualifies them for being a true child of Kernow.

There are very few other passengers when the train pulls out, moving slowly as it goes through the tunnel and picking up speed when it emerges, tracing the coast. I look out at an ever-darkening sky, picking out the Christmas lights across the estuary, and the dark shapes of the winter wading birds in the shallows.

At St Erth, I change trains, and text Sam to let him know I should be on time.

Can't wait to see you! I miss you xx he texts back.

I only just saw you yesterday! xxx

I think you mean you miss me too?? xxx

Oh yes, sorry – bloody predictive text. I miss you too xxx

It's dark outside as the train makes its way past small villages and towns, all decorated for Christmas, most with shining stars atop church towers. It's a pleasure to be able to sit back and see the county from this vantage point, and I hug my coat to me, across my belly, thinking of the baby within as my secret. Nobody on this train knows I am pregnant. *But I know you're there*, I think, and as if in answer I feel a little movement inside me, like a tiny frog kicking its legs or a miniature whale flicking its tale. I smile, put my earphones in, and listen to a playlist I've been working on for our Christmas party. I really need to work on something for the winter solstice too, although Lizzie says she's got it covered. It's not that I don't trust her, but the control freak in me says I need to have a backup plan, just in case. But what do we listen to for a pagan-like celebration? I need to do some research. I really don't think Slade is going to cut it.

The journey passes quickly and at Totnes I disembark to find a smiling Sam waiting on the platform.

"Hello!" he kisses me, and he seems cheerful.

"Hi," I kiss him back and think that I have missed him,

even if it was only for a night. I enjoy the familiarity of him; his aftershave, and the softly prickling stubble of his face. Now he's with me, it feels at once as though we've never been apart and as though I haven't seen him for ages.

"So how's it going?" I ask as he takes my bag from me, then takes my hand, and we walk out towards the car.

"It's alright, actually."

"What's it like, the place?"

"It's great. You'll love it."

"And how's Sophie?"

"She is surprisingly great, too. I think now it's not quite as alien a concept, and Isaac's making a real effort to show her everything and make sure she knows exactly what's what."

"That sounds positive."

"Yeah, I don't know if they're trying to sell it to her a bit too much, though. Or if I just don't like the idea of her living up here."

I squeeze his hand. "Just because she likes it doesn't mean she's going to want to live here."

"But Kate's her mum, and they've always been together – apart from these last few months."

"And you're her dad, and she loves living with you."

"But I buggered off to North Wales, didn't I? When she was ten. Kate put in all the hard work. She always has."

This is true. Kate has always been a fantastic mum. And even though I am not yet a mum, I am starting to get an idea of how impossible it would be to imagine living away from your own child.

"Let's just see how it goes, shall we? Nobody needs to make any decisions yet, do they?"

"I guess not," Sam says, "but Isaac reckons he's going to be up here a lot after New Year, getting the place set up."

"What about Kate and Jacob?"

"It's not really ready for them to move in yet, plus Kate's still got her flat. Isaac says he's got to finish the studio first so he can start running classes as soon as possible, to get some income coming in and start building their reputation."

This sounds quite different to what Kate had said about her and Isaac sharing the parenting of Jacob, but then I think back to our conversation when she'd expressed some doubts about this anyway. It is none of my business; apart from the effect it will have on Sophie, and really, that is more Sam's business than mine.

We get in the car and I'm glad of the warmth when Sam turns the engine on. "Cold, innit?" he asks.

"Yes. It is actually starting to feel like Christmas."

"You're not allowed to say that till after your yoga retreat."

"OK," I smile, "it's starting to feel like the pagan festival of Yule."

"That's better."

Sam drives us out of Totnes and into the darkness of the countryside.

"Look at that!" An owl is illuminated in the full beams of the headlights, swooping above the road in front of us.

"That was amazing." I crane my neck for a further sight of the bird but all is darkness either side of the car. I turn to look behind us and see only the inky night sky. We are definitely going uphill and there seem to be far fewer trees up here but it's difficult to tell, really.

"Is it really remote, this place?"

"Quite – although maybe not that much more than Amethi. And the nearest neighbour's a micro-brewery."

"For when the yogis have had enough healthy living?"

"Exactly! I can imagine them sneaking over there of an evening."

"Hopefully Isaac will stay off it, though."

"Ha! Let's hope so. Ah, here we are. I managed to drive past this three times yesterday!"

Sam takes a sharp turn onto a narrow, bumpy drive and I see a couple of buildings up ahead. One of them has its lights on.

"That's the house, I guess?"

"Yeah, and it's lovely. Needs some work, but it is really nice. A lot bigger than our place."

"Hey, size isn't everything."

"So they say." Sam smiles and pulls in next to Isaac's car.

Sophie emerges from the darkness, holding Jacob securely in her arms.

"Alice!" Sophie beams.

"Hello, you two!" I say, kissing her and then kissing the soft baby-warmth of Jacob's head.

"Come and see! This place is amazing," Sophie says.

I turn back briefly to look at Sam. He shrugs and smiles and we follow Sophie inside.

Kate and Isaac are in the kitchen, which opens onto the dining area and lounge.

"Hi, Alice!" Kate hugs me and Isaac kisses me on the cheek. "Thank you so much for coming."

"It's a pleasure. This place looks great, even in the dark!"

"It is," Kate agrees, "I'd almost forgotten quite how great it is."

"I know what you mean. Sometimes you're so immersed in what you're trying to do, you forget to look at it from an outsider's viewpoint."

I think back fondly to those early days at Amethi, really not that long ago. It was so exciting, but also really scary.

"Wait till you see the view in the morning," Isaac says, almost shyly but there is definitely a touch of pride in his voice. "Here, take this," he hands me a glass of red wine, "and take a seat."

"Thank you, but actually, I shouldn't be drinking."

"Damn! Sorry. Kate did tell me. Congratulations!" His face flushes.

"Don't worry!" I laugh. "To be honest, a glass of red would be perfect – and I am sure that one glass would be fine, but I'm staying off it. Just trying to be sensible! I'm sure Sam will take it off my hands, though."

"It's from the local vineyard," Isaac says. "I don't drink, as you know – well, apart from… well, the less said about that, the better."

"I've seen far worse than that," I say cheerily, "don't worry about it!"

"I guess I'll have to do the honours," Sam says, Sophie hanging onto his arm. "Cheers!"

Kate hands me a glass of cloudy apple juice, pouring another for herself, and one for Sophie. Isaac agrees to a small glass of wine – "Just to support local business, you know" – and we all move through to the sitting area, where a fire is crackling merrily in the hearth. The fireplace walls are thick stone and the beamed ceiling is low. The furniture is old but comfy.

"It feels like a proper old farmhouse," I say.

"It is." I don't think I've ever known Isaac so vocal before, and again that note of pride has edged into his voice – but it's not an unpleasant pride; in fact, it's quite endearing. "This was a dairy farm once; the cows had so much space to roam the hillside, and the old farmer pioneered a lot of organic techniques. His kids didn't want to carry on the farming, though, and when the old man

74

died, they sold off the building and the land and – a bit like Amethi when you moved there, Alice – this place has been partially developed. Not the house, as you can see, but in the morning you'll be able to get an idea of what we've got here."

"This is really exciting!" I say, and I glance at Sophie to check she doesn't mind my saying that, but she is happily settled into the crook of Sam's arm, encased in a large, soft armchair. Jacob is now in his mum's arms, gurgling on Kate's shoulder.

"It is," Kate agrees. "But we've a lot to think about. And so much to do."

I want to know how much has been discussed already. Did they get to speak last night; Sam, Sophie, Isaac and Kate, about the future? I know if I was Sophie, at her age, there is no way I would have wanted to leave my home town and the friends I'd made. She and Amber are pretty much inseparable, and then there is Josh. Although it seems unlikely that will last forever I can tell how important he is to Sophie now. And I don't think telling her it's 'just' a teenage romance would go down too well.

"It's endless," I agree, "and even when you're up and running, the list won't be completed – it will just be a different list!"

"You're definitely taking on a lot," says Sam and I feel like Isaac bristles.

"No more than Alice and Julie did," he says, and I want to point out that we didn't have any children to think of when we started Amethi but luckily we are saved from any further discussion by the bubbling-over of a pot of rice.

"Come on, let's eat," Kate says, expertly manoeuvring herself up and out of the seat, gently placing Jacob into his baby carrier, and taking the rice off the boil. It looks like one fluid movement. How does she manage to always look so blooming graceful?

We follow her to the dining table. The room is comfortably warm, from the fire and the insulation of those thick walls, I guess; there doesn't appear to be any central heating. We take our seats at the round table; me next to Kate, with Sophie on my left and Isaac on her right, and Sam in between them both. Isaac brings over a huge pan of rice and another of vegetable chilli. There are homemade tortilla chips, and salsa and sour cream, and a huge tub of cheese. I realise I am extremely hungry. It appears that everybody feels the same as there is definitely more eating than talking going on. I am longing to ask Sam how it's been; what's been said. Yes, I want to know if Sophie still intends to live with us. I'm trying to get a sense of any atmosphere, but conversation seems generally to be laidback and pleasant; Isaac asks Sam about his work, Kate tells us about a baby group she belongs to, and some of the other mums she's met. Apparently, there is one full-time dad there.

"I feel sorry for him – it's like none of us quite dare to talk to him. Not because we think he's weird, but we all know his wife, who's back at work at the council now that Billy is six months old, and the husband – Pete – is lovely, but it feels like being too friendly might look like we're trying to chat him up."

"Poor bloke," Sam laughs.

"I know. I just can't imagine asking him round for coffee, like I would one of the mums. Which I know is really wrong, but it would just seem weird."

"Are baby groups a nightmare?" I ask.

"No, they're not – I never really went to any with Sophie." Kate looks at her daughter lovingly. Sophie is too busy spooning salsa onto a tortilla chip and trying to cram it into her mouth to notice. "I tried, a few times; the health visitor said I should give it a go, but I felt like I was too young, I had nothing in common with the other mums." I think back to what Sam said about the ante natal groups. "Now I feel like I'm the expert – although actually I've forgotten most of what I used to know about having a baby. It's like learning it all again. But people are nice; generally. Like everything, you get the snobs, and the show-offs, but I've met some really nice people."

"You'll meet nice people up here, too," Isaac says.

"I know," she puts her hand on his. "I do know that." Kate smiles at Isaac, and again I check on Sophie. Again, she seems more concerned with food than conversation.

After dinner, which is finished off with apple crumble and custard ("Vegan," says Isaac) we return to our seats near the fire and by and by I find myself nodding off.

"Are you OK?" Sam nudges me.

"Yeah," I yawn. "Just really tired."

"Go on up," Kate says. "Don't feel like you have to stay down here to be polite. But it's a lot cooler in the bedrooms. Here, I'll get you a hot water bottle."

"You don't have to do that," I say, but I'm grateful and even more so when I do get upstairs. Sam shows me our room, which is large and cold, and could definitely do with more than a lick of paint – but the bed is comfortable and the sheets pristine. I climb in, pulling the hot water bottle to me. I think I feel the baby kick in protest and I move the heat away from my tummy, up to my chest.

Sam kisses me. "Mind if I stay up a bit?"

"Of course not. It's only..." I check my watch... "nine-forty! Oh my god, I'm so old and boring."

"No, you're pregnant and tired." He sits on the bed.

"Thanks for coming up here, Alice. I know you could have had a day resting tomorrow, and maybe you should have."

"Don't be daft," I protest. "This is important. How's it going?" I add quietly, as if Kate and Isaac are listening outside the door.

"Oh, OK," he says, "but I don't think Sophie has the slightest intention of living up here. The only draw for her is Kate, of course, and I have no idea how Kate will feel if Sophie decides to stay with us. Or where we'll all sleep," he adds.

"We'll deal with that if and when we need to," I say. "Right now, I think we need to make sure Kate and Sophie are alright."

"You are amazing," Sam kisses me on the forehead. "And I am now going to let you have some sleep. Shall I switch the light off? There isn't one near the bed."

"OK, but hang on." I fish my phone out of my bag. "I'll just keep this nearby, in case we need a torch during the night."

"Great idea." Sam waits, then turns off the light and creaks back down the rickety staircase. I have half a mind to check messages, but I really am so tired, I just put the phone on the floor and fall straight asleep.

Later, I am dimly aware of Sam coming into bed beside me. "Your hands are cold," I say.

"Sorry," he whispers, and he sounds like he's had a few more glasses of that wine.

"Are you OK?" I mumble.

"Yeah, fine," he flings his arm across me, and is soon asleep. But now I'm awake. And I can hear the wind whistling through a gap somewhere in the room; the windowsill, maybe. I'm cold, I realise, and gently extricate myself from Sam's sleeping embrace; switch my phone on to torch mode, and look at the time. 1.53am.

I dig around in my bag for a cardigan and some extra socks, pulling them on before climbing back under the duvet, but I still feel cold.

Outside, it sounds windier than ever and rain is now tapping on the window. I huddle closer to Sam and think what life must have been like for the generations of farmers who have lived here over the years. Probably a bit like this, I think, then wonder if any of the children were born in this room. It used to be the norm for births to take place at home. I know that people are becoming increasingly keen on home births again now, but I can't imagine it, somehow. I like the idea of being in hospital: close to medical support if it's needed but also not having to think about the mess. I know I wouldn't be expected to clear up after myself if I gave birth at home – at least I hope not – but there's something about the thought of being in hospital, in a place designed for giving birth, which feels right to me.

In the darkness of the night, thoughts of what giving birth might be like fill my mind. During the day, I barely think about this kind of stuff. Now, while Sam slumbers next to me and the rest of the household are presumably fast asleep as well, I can't stop thinking about it. I'm not worried, I don't think – it has to happen, and the end result will make it more than worthwhile, I am sure. But sometimes things go wrong, and these are the kinds of thoughts which now creep into my mind while the rain and the wind seem to pick up strength, rattling the windowpane. There is a sudden sliding sound above my head, which makes me jump, then the unmistakeable crash of a tile hitting the ground outside. It's enough to shake me out of those unhelpful thoughts, and I think instead of Amethi and how lucky we were to get it after Paul Winters had worked his magic. He'd fixed it all up; reroofed where necessary; put in new windows and doors, and heating. Really gone to town on the place. Then decided he didn't want it. All the work he'd done may have driven the price up, but it saved Julie and me a lot more work. Isaac and Kate really have got their work cut out here.

I turn away from Sam, then back again. One of my legs feels twitchy. I think I need some warm milk.

As I tiptoe to the doorway, I hear Jacob crying in the room next door. I really hope I haven't woken him up. I hear Kate's soft voice and I creep downstairs, picking my way carefully through the darkness. By the time I reach the bottom step, the crying has stopped.

In the lounge, the fire has reduced to a few glowing embers. The curtains are open but reveal only darkness. The rain lashes at the windows but downstairs seems more airtight than the bedroom and the room still feels warm. I find milk in the fridge, and a small pan, which I half-fill then put on a low heat.

There is a huge pile of logs by the fireplace and I place a couple onto the smouldering remnants of their contemporaries. While the milk heats up, I keep checking on the fire and see the logs catch nicely. I check the milk with my little finger then pour it into a wide white-and-blue striped mug, turning the gas hob off and bringing the mug over to the settee where I'd sat earlier.

My phone is upstairs and there is no TV here. For entertainment I have the fire, and the sound of the weather battering at the windows. Together, the two are strangely soothing.

I think of Kate's yoga sessions, where she would

encourage us to be 'in the moment'. Lizzie's, where she talks of doing everything mindfully.

The centre of my mind is surrounded by all sorts of thoughts jostling to get in: the upcoming yoga retreat and winter solstice; the Christmas party; keeping well during pregnancy; wanting Julie to be pregnant, too, and hoping she and Luke are OK; the tourism awards; Mum being jobless, and having left a job she loved to live closer to me; Sophie, and what we will do if she wants to live with us — and if she doesn't. The list goes on, but I don't want to let any of those thoughts in now.

Instead, I pull a throw around my shoulders, swivelling round so that my legs stretch out in front of me on the cushions. I sip my milk. Watch the fire grow in strength. Listen to the wind, and gaze out at the blackness of the Devon night. Then I turn my eyes back towards the fire. It is growing. It is mesmerising. When I've finished my milk, I place the mug on the floor beside me. I should go back to bed, but I don't want to move. I pull the throw over me and I curl up on my side, letting the warmth and the sounds of the weather lull me back to sleep.

9

"Alice?" An unfamiliar voice is whispering. "Are you OK?"

I open my eyes unwillingly. I was asleep. I was dreaming about something but already the dream is escaping me. But here is Isaac, and there is Jacob, in his arms.

"Are you OK?" Isaac asks again, and I can't help wondering why he woke me.

"I'm fine," I say.

"You were kind of shouting," Isaac says.

"Was I?" That's weird. I thought I was having a nice dream. Maybe it was so nice I had to shout about it.

"Yep."

"What was I saying?" I feel suddenly wide awake, and I sit up and smile at Jacob, who is only just really beginning to smile himself. He grins at me now, his pink gums making my heart melt.

"I don't really know, sorry. And I'm sorry to wake you, but you seemed kind of upset. Here, can you hold the little guy?" Isaac passes Jacob to me before I have a chance to answer, then goes over to the fireplace, building up a small pile of kindling and using the poker to try and jostle some life back into the fire.

"Sorry, I couldn't sleep…" I say, holding Jacob so that he is lying in my arms, looking up at me. His eyes are a deep, dark blue and his head is covered in a very fine dark hair. I realise I haven't really held him before. Haven't held that many babies at all, in fact.

I smile at Jacob, he smiles at me. I close my eyes then

spring them open, wide. He gurgles.

"No worries," Isaac says, his back to me as he fiddles about with the fire. "Looks like it's going to be a nice day."

I look towards the window. It must be later than I'd imagined, as it's light out there. The rain seems to have stopped and I can see small clouds moving rapidly across what is otherwise a bright blue sky. Altocumulus, I think – if I've remembered correctly.

I move Jacob so he's resting upright against me. Check his face is above my shoulder level, and he holds his head up for a moment then rests his cheek against me. It feels like an honour for him to be so comfortable with me. Jogging him gently up and down, I walk to the window. Isaac's back is still turned.

"Wow!" I breathe, and I feel Isaac turn.

"Oh yeah, I forgot you hadn't seen it yet."

In front of me is a glistening green hillside, rolling down steadily towards a woodland. Beyond that are fields filled with tiny dots of sheep, shadows of clouds scudding across them all. Further still, the sea. A dark, brilliant navy blue today. Awash with white tops, still unsettled after last night's weather.

"Why did nobody mention this?" I exclaim.

"I don't know. It's pretty special though, isn't it?"

"I'll say! I can see why you're so set on this place," I smile at Isaac.

"Want to see the rest of it?"

"Yes! For sure!"

"Let me get him wrapped up," Isaac takes Jacob from me, zips him snugly into his full snow suit. "It's going to be cold out there. You'd better bring your coat," he adds.

The rest of the house is quiet; presumably all the other occupants are asleep. I follow Isaac, who is carrying Jacob, and hasn't bothered to get a coat for himself, outside. We are hit immediately by the wind, which takes hold of me and makes me laugh.

"That happens a lot up here," Isaac grins. "Come on, I'll show you the studio."

We walk to the long building, which is made from the same brick as the farmhouse, but which could not be more different inside. It is sleek, and whitewashed, and the whole of one side of it is glass. Along the opposite wall, like a dance studio, is a long mirror, although there is no barre to hold onto.

"Here, stand here," Isaac says, and he positions me so that I am looking along the mirror and see immediately why it is there. I see sky, and greenery, and sea, along the whole length of the wall.

"That… is… stunning," I say.

"I know!" he grins. "Here, do you mind holding the little fella again?"

I gladly take Jacob, already feeling the familiarity of his weight, and how I think he likes to be held. He grasps some of my hair and Isaac turns to face the picture window. Without saying another word, he puts his hands into the yoga prayer position and proceeds to do two sun salutations. Wearing no coat and just a thin t-shirt and jogging bottoms, it seems every sinew of his body is visible as he performs the practised movements, perfectly.

I have never seen him like this; so at ease with himself.

I spy some large beanbags at the end of the room and I move over, put Jacob on one and sit on another, next to him. Isaac pulls up a third beanbag and sits on the other side of Jacob, gazing at his son.

"I need to thank you, really, Alice."

"What?" I am startled by this, wondering what he's

going to say.

"Yes. You've inspired me. You and Julie. You've done so well with Amethi. And I've wanted to do something on my own for a long time. I just wasn't sure what. Then I came back to see Mum one weekend and saw this place was up for sale by auction."

"Is your mum up here, then?"

"Yeah, this is where I was born, where I grew up. Well, down the hill. Over... that way," he points.

"It's beautiful. I can see why you'd want to come back."

"I do love Cornwall, you know. But this is home for me."

It's not for Kate, though, or Sophie, I think, but Isaac is right there with me.

"I know it's selfish. Especially when it comes to Sophie. But I brought Kate here and she fell in love with the place, too. It's all very well us working for other people – and believe me, Kate has really loved working with you and Julie – but I want more for us all." Isaac's eyes haven't left Jacob. "For this little fella, and for Kate, and for Sophie – but I know that's more complicated. I'm a bit stuck there." Isaac looks up at last and his eyes look glassy. "I've never been a dad before, and I've obviously never been a teenage girl. I don't know if she hates me."

"She doesn't," I say, pretty sure this is true. "And I get it, I totally get it. It's difficult for Sophie, though, she's got all her friends."

"And Sam, and you."

"Well, yes, certainly Sam."

"She loves you too, Alice. You're her idol."

"I don't know about that. I suspect Julie's more the idol sort."

"Don't be so sure! Kate says it. Sophie's always talking about you."

85

I blush now. "Really?"

"Yes. And I think Kate knows Sophie's going to want to stay in Cornwall." Isaac tickles Jacob's tummy lightly, and Jacob smiles, waves his legs in the air.

"It's difficult," I acknowledge, "for all of you. Really difficult. I guess Sophie's old enough to know her own mind, to an extent. And I know what I was like at that age. I am happy to do whatever works for everyone. But I think what is really important is that, whatever happens, we do make sure it works for *everyone*. All of us. I guess it's just a shame you couldn't find somewhere closer to home for Kate and Sophie."

"Yes, well, the market's already a bit saturated there," Isaac grins. He stands suddenly, as a cloud moves to reveal the sun and the room is bathed in light.

Isaac goes to the centre of the room and leans forward so that he is resting on his knees and elbows, then the next thing I know he has unfolded himself upwards so his body forms a vertical line, feet pointing straight to the sky. His t-shirt falls down over his face, revealing a ridiculously toned body, each tiny movement and adjustment visible right below his skin, lit up by the sunshine.

I watch, mesmerised, until he refolds himself, returns to an upright position, and grins at me. "We can make this work, can't we, Alice?"

His boyish smile, his little boy next to me, grasping my finger, and the untouched sunlight streaming through the glass, fill me with warmth.

"Yes," I say. "We can. And we will."

10

I return to Cornwall refreshed and positive, if a little tired. In fact, I fell asleep in the car on the way back and I wake with a start as we pull into the Amethi car park, Sophie delighting in telling me that I was snoring.

"Thanks for that," I say, turning uncomfortably to look at her.

"It was really loud, wasn't it, Dad?" she's grinning.

"I barely noticed a thing," Sam smiles. Puts his hand on my knee. "You're exhausted. You should have stayed here."

"No, I'm really glad I came up to Devon." I release my seatbelt, open the door and get out of the car. All my joints feel stiff. "I thought this second trimester was meant to be the one where I'd be full of life and energy, not aching and snoring."

"I guess it's different for everyone," Sam says. "Here, Sophie and I have got the bags. You go through and we'll be there in a moment."

I trudge across the gravel, my joints thankfully easing with every step. Sunday has its own feeling, I always think, setting it apart from the six other days of the week, and that is certainly true at Amethi. It's the one day that Julie and I aren't at our guests' beck and call – and it's often the first full day of people's holidays, so they are just starting to relax. Possibly sleeping off the over-indulgence of the first night, or off out, exploring.

Today, all is quiet, and the clouds hang low across the landscape, providing cover and comfort, and muffling the sounds of the afternoon. While a gang of jackdaws squawk from the now-bare line of trees, there is little else to be heard. *All is calm, all is grey.* I quite enjoy this wintry murkiness in the run-up to Christmas and I don't think I am alone in relishing the excuse to just hunker down inside, get the fire going, grab a good book and a hot drink, and curl up in a comfy chair, occasionally glancing through the window to confirm that staying in and doing very little was definitely the right decision.

I reach the front door and push it gently. The little red car was in the parking area so I know Julie is about, and I know she won't have locked the door if she's in. I never used to, but since the incident with Tony earlier this year I have been a little more aware that I share this place with strangers.

"Hello?" I call.

There is no answer. I can hear Sam and Sophie not far behind me. Something urges me on, to find Julie before they get here. I go through to the lounge and there she is, earphones in, eyes closed, humming to herself. I fill with relief. I am worried about her at the moment but I don't know what I feared I'd find just now. I realise I am shaking slightly. Maybe pregnancy is making me go a little mad.

"Oi!" I prod her with my toe and her eyes open immediately.

"Hello!" she smiles, pushing herself up. "How was Devon?"

Sam and Sophie are in now. "Hi Julie!" Sophie calls.

"Hello, you two! How was Devon?" She asks the question again, addressing the group this time.

"It… was… amazing!" Sophie exclaims.

Julie looks at me, raises her eyebrows. I offer a tiny shrug in return.

"Wow, that's great, Soph," Julie sits up straight, stretches her long legs. "So what, you're thinking you might want to move there?"

I can't look at Sam. He and I haven't talked about this yet, so I don't know exactly what was discussed with Kate, and Isaac, before I got to Devon.

"No!" Sophie says, as if it's obvious. "I'm going to stay with Dad and Alice, but I'm going to have a really cool place to go at weekends and holidays."

"Oh, right," Julie sends a fleeting, apologetic glance my way and then Sam's. I can't look at him. I knew this was probably how it would turn out, of course, but I would have liked to have chatted more with Sam – found out exactly what has been agreed. It does, after all, also affect me.

"God, is that the time? I'd better get going," Julie says. "Your bed is so comfortable, you two, I slept till about ten this morning."

"Where's Uncle Luke?" asks Sophie.

"Oh, he's been in London this weekend."

"Will he be back yet?" I ask.

"Dunno, I haven't spoken to him today," Julie tries to sound nonchalant, but I know better. And this is not like her. Normally, she and Luke speak a minimum of five times a day, when they've seen each other in the morning, and they know they're going home to each other in the evening. I say nothing. What can I say? Especially with Sam and Sophie there.

"Any problems while I've been gone?" I ask, to change the subject.

"No, nothing. Good as gold, this lot. It's Sleepy Winter Syndrome. And it's so quiet here, I bet everyone got a good lie-in this weekend."

"That's what I like to hear."

"Right, I'll grab my bag, and I'll be off." Julie retrieves the bag, and her jacket, pulls on her boots and kisses Sam and Sophie in turn. "Glad you had a good time."

"I'll walk you to the car," I suggest.

"You don't have to."

"I want to."

Outside, I put my arm through Julie's. "Is everything OK?"

"With Luke?"

"Yes, it's not like you to have not spoken."

"He's not answering my calls," she admits.

"What? That's not like Luke."

"I went a bit mental at him on the phone last night."

"Oh."

"He was going out, with some of the people from that meeting, including *Sinead*," she says with derision.

"OK, well that's OK, isn't it?"

"Yes, of course. Although I don't like her. She's always texting him."

"I wouldn't worry about that. It's probably work stuff."

"It's not."

"How do you know?"

"I've looked," she admits, shamefaced.

"Oh," I say again. "Shit."

"I know. I never thought I'd be like this. I'm turning into one of those women. I'm needy, I'm suspicious, I can't seem to find a nice word to say to him. And once I'd started reading their texts, I couldn't stop."

"So what do they say?"

"Oh, nothing – well, something and nothing. I guess they could be interpreted as flirty – or just friendly. And I choose to interpret them as flirty."

"But Luke wouldn't…"

"No, he wouldn't. I know."

We are at the little red car now and Julie leans against it. I lean next to her. It feels cold through my clothes.

I look at the pillowy grey clouds moving so slowly, filling every inch of the sky. I feel like they could envelop us, this whole place; swallow us up and move on, and it would be as if we'd never been here.

"And she's probably just being friendly, really," Julie says. "But I feel so crap at the moment, and I'm worried Luke's going to find somebody better than me. Who doesn't give him shit all the time, and makes him laugh, and can… can get pregnant."

I turn to see my friend's face crumple and I put my arms around her, pulling her to me. I don't think in all the years I have known Julie that I have seen her like this. She is such a strong person, so positive. She's a driving force, in so many things. And I know she's not always happy, because nobody can be − and that the strong, determined outlook on life does not always come easily − but I've never really known her doubt herself like this.

I hold her and let her cry. Words at a time like this would be pointless. I wait until the sobs subside and I pull her closer. I wish so much that I could make this better for Julie. And I am aware that tucked away in my belly is a tiny being which is literally between us right now, and which I fervently hope won't drive us apart.

"You were gone a while. I thought you'd fallen down a well!" Sam says when I finally get back.

When Julie stopped crying, we had talked a little and I'd made her call Luke. He had answered this call.

"Sorry I couldn't answer earlier," I could hear him

saying, and something about another meeting.

"That's OK," Julie said, "I'm sorry for being such a bitch. Are you coming home?"

She listened for a while then said, "OK. Love you, too," and ended the call. She looked a little brighter.

"What did he say?"

"He was with the client they'd met with last night; he said if he didn't see him today he'd have had to stay till tomorrow, and he wanted to get back to me today."

"There, you see."

"You sound like a mum!" Julie said. "You'll make a great mum, Alice." She took one of my hands, holding it gently with both of hers.

I hugged my friend again. "I wish I could make this better for you, Julie."

"I know. I know you would, if you could. I need to stop making it worse for myself, though, and Luke."

"No more reading text messages," I said sternly.

"No. God, what an idiot I'm being."

"Stop being so hard on yourself, too. You need to book your holiday in January, just you and Luke; get away for a bit." *You never know what might happen*, I thought but I was not stupid enough to say it. I do wonder if she wasn't so stressed about it all whether that might help but that is pure conjecture, based on my ridiculously limited knowledge of the whole thing. And I know that the last thing somebody struggling to get pregnant would want is advice from somebody who already is pregnant.

"I did fall down a well, didn't you hear me shouting?" I pull my shoes off, tuck myself in next to Sam on the settee. He's already got the fire going and the small room feels warm and cosy. "Where's Sophie?"

"She's doing her homework," Sam says.

"But there's hours yet! What happened to cramming it into as little time as possible at the end of the day?"

"I don't know. I feel like she's changed somehow this weekend. Weird. It probably won't last."

"Maybe she's relieved to know a bit more about how things are going to be."

"Yes," Sam turns to me. "About that. Is it OK? Really, I mean, if she lives with us?"

"Yes," I reply firmly. "Of course. And I was thinking, while the baby is little it's going to be in our room anyway, isn't it? So we've got a bit more time to think about what we'll do."

"I am stuck when it comes to that," Sam admits.

"There'll be a way. We'll make sure of it," I kiss him. "But what about Kate? Did you three get to speak together about it all?"

"Yes, and it was Kate I was up talking to last night. I hope you don't mind?"

"Of course not." I think of Julie's feelings towards Sinead – although I suspect if it wasn't Sinead, it would be something, or someone, else. Julie's just finding a target for her unhappiness. I realise I don't feel any unease about Sam and Kate, and I like the fact they have a close relationship these days. It says something great about them both. "Is Kate alright with it all?"

"I don't know," Sam says, "but she realises it's her choice to move to Devon; hers and Isaac's. And, as she says, Sophie's a teenager now. She's growing up, and in a few years she'll be leaving home... probably. I did feel sorry for Kate, but she knows that Sophie's only ever going to be a couple of hours away."

"I can't imagine living apart from my child."

"No, but I did it, didn't I, when I was in Wales?"

"Oh, I know, and it wasn't a criticism. I just feel sorry for Kate, that's all."

"She's also worried that Sophie's going to think Jacob's taken her place."

"It didn't seem like it, did it? Sophie is brilliant with him!"

"Yes, and long may it continue… I hope she's the same with this one," Sam puts his hand on my belly and I hold it there.

"Can you feel anything?"

He is quiet and still for a while, but I can't feel anything either.

"No," Sam admits.

"I wish you could experience being pregnant," I say.

"Me too."

"Really?"

"No way! But I'm glad you're enjoying it."

I lean into him. "You know you've still got to tell your mum?"

"Yes," he sighs.

"Why don't you do it today?" I know I'm pushing it but really, why wait? She needs to know, and then the deed is done, and he doesn't need to talk to his mum again for another year, or however long it's been since they were last in touch.

"It's going to be a long call," he says. "But you're right. No time like the present. Here, you make yourself comfortable and I'll go through to the kitchen, empty the dishwasher while I'm talking to her – might as well make use of the time."

I am so grateful that my relationship with my parents is strong. I prop myself up with some cushions and pick up the TV remote. I haven't watched Sunday afternoon TV in a long time. It soon becomes apparent why, as I flick through the channels, settling eventually on *Four in a Bed*. I can at least pretend it's research for work.

"Hi, Mum," I hear Sam's voice sounding unnaturally strained just before he closes the kitchen door.

11

As Julie commented on Sunday, the guests this week are as good as gold, and they ask for very little. Julie is kept busy cooking for them, but I have time to run through the details for the upcoming yoga retreat, which is only just over a week away now, and I feel satisfied that everything is in place. I'm looking forward to it from a personal perspective; I am quite intrigued about an alternative winter celebration.

I also have to go to Penzance to do a bit of shopping, as my trousers are too tight to ignore now and my tops are beginning to feel a bit snug as well. I take Mum with me.

"Oh look, Alice," she makes me stop and look at packs of babygros, and tiny bootees, which I have to admit are really sweet. "Can I get you some?"

"I'm meant to be getting larger clothes, Mum, I don't think I'll squeeze into those."

"You know what I mean," she swipes playfully at my arm. "My first grandchild! I can't wait."

"Go on," I say. And we end up with a huge bag of things, including impossibly small popper-fastening vests; little baby sleeping bags, which fasten over the baby's shoulders; scratch mitts and bootees. They are all so little, and so soft. I pick up a cotton blanket, decorated with pictures of giraffes.

"Do you want it?"

"Mum! Stop encouraging me!" I laugh.

"Go on, get it. You can put these things away in a drawer somewhere, for the time being."

"OK," I sigh, as if she's making me do something awful. Then I smile. "Thank you, Mum."

We move on, pick some maternity clothes for me. I love the waistbands on the trousers, which may not look particularly attractive but feel like they're going to be really snug during the winter. The tops are a stretchy material and don't look that big but the woman in the shop assures us they will grow with me.

At lunch, we sit surrounded by shopping bags.

"You haven't got yourself anything!" I say.

"I'm not bothered, this is much more exciting."

I tuck into a cheese and mushroom toastie and drink a smoothie; although it is cold outside, the shops and the café are almost too warm, especially the changing rooms, and I feel the need to cool down.

"How are you getting on, with work and everything?" Mum asks.

"Oh, fine," I say, surprised. "There's no reason I shouldn't be," I add, almost defensively.

"I know that!" Mum laughs. "I was just trying to find a way to bring the conversation round to an idea I had."

"Oh yeah?"

"Yes, well, please say no if you don't want to do this, I won't be offended, but I wondered if you wanted to train me up at Amethi? So I could cover for you when you need it, especially in those first few weeks after the baby's born – and beforehand, too, if you start to find it a bit much. It will save you having to find agency staff."

I roll the idea around my mind, like a marble. How we'll manage at Amethi when I have this baby – especially considering it is going to be the start of the summer – has been on my mind. We will have to get somebody in, which is going to cost, and that person will probably have to shadow me for a while. It's such a unique role, and both Julie and I need to know that person can do things just right, and will act with the best interests of Amethi at heart.

"Would you really want to do that, though? What if your dream job comes up in the meantime?"

"I don't think I have one!" Mum smiles. "Not anymore. I know you probably don't want to think of me like this, but I'm getting a bit long in the tooth, you know. I'm not looking for a new career, but I do want to keep busy. And I think I'd enjoy working at Amethi."

"Really? You're not just doing it to help me out?"

"Really."

"Thank you, Mum. Can I think about it? And I'll have to talk to Julie about it."

"Of course. There's no rush, from my point of view. I just wanted to give you that option, and if you decide against it I won't be offended. Not very offended, anyway."

We finish our lunch and head back to Mum's car. She drops me off at Amethi. "This place is just beautiful, even in the winter. Seriously, if you would like me to work up here, I'd be more than happy to. It wouldn't just be doing you a favour."

"Thank you, Mum. And for that bootful of stuff, as well!"

"Go and put some of those comfy trousers on! And put the baby things away before Sam sees them and thinks we're becoming obsessed!"

"Good idea, I'll do that."

I wave Mum off then traipse round to the house, laden down with shopping bags. Just as Julie comes around the corner.

"Successful trip?" she smiles.

"You could say that!"

"Here, let me take some of those."

"Thanks," I say, and I reach into my bag for the key.

"Can I see what you've got? Oh…" Julie is already looking in one of the bags and of course it has to be the one with all the baby stuff. It's too late to stop her. I unlock the door, not sure whether to react at all.

"This stuff is so cute!" she says.

"Come on, I'll show you what I've got," I say, feeling like life from now on is going to be full of these little moments, and it's going to become very awkward if we're not careful. The only way to face it is head-on. "I'll put the kettle on."

"No, don't worry, I'd better get back to the kitchen soon. Let's see what you've got, though."

So I carefully unpack the blanket, and the vests and the scratch mitts and bootees. She handles them all carefully. "These are lovely."

"I know. Mum got a bit over-excited!"

"I can imagine. Your baby is going to be very lucky, having Sue and Phil as its grandparents."

"And Sam's mum," I grin, taking the items back from Julie and packing them away. I'm glad for this opportunity to change the subject. "Did I tell you he finally called her?"

"No, how did it go?"

"He was on for ages. He had to tell her we'd got engaged, too."

"Was she excited?"

"Not particularly, according to Sam. He said she was more concerned with telling him about this new man of hers."

"Hmm. Great! Luke says she's not exactly prize mother material. Makes my mum look like a saint."

"Your mum's lovely," I say.

"I know. She's just not a 'Mum' mum, like yours."

I decide now is not the time to mention Mum's offer. I'm

99

not sure what I think about it, anyway. "I don't know how I'll react if I ever meet Sam's mum. She sounds like a nightmare."

"Good job she's in Spain!"

"Yep, thank god."

"Shit," Julie looks at her watch, "I'd better get back! You're going to have the best-dressed baby in town." She smiles and hugs me before she leaves the house and rushes back across the gravel, towards the kitchen.

I feel my heart breaking for my friend.

12

Having the yoga retreat to plan for is a blessing to us all. It pushes me to finish my Christmas shopping, most of which I do online. It's quite a list these days, but I find most people easy to buy for. As usual, it is Sam I struggle with.

For Sophie, I buy some Bluetooth earphones and a top I know she's been after. I don't know why, but Sam and I have not yet got into buying presents for her from both of us. I still feel like an extra, I suppose – although I am marrying her dad (at some point, if we ever get round to it), I don't expect Sophie to see us as a package – he is her dad, I am her… well, I don't know what. When I think of Isaac suggesting I'm her idol, I confess it makes my head and heart swell a little, but I have taken that with a pinch of salt. He's obviously not very sure of his place in Sophie's world, and it would be easy for him to compare his relationship with her to mine.

David and Martin get a new tree for their garden, and I enjoy choosing some books for Tyler; *Revolting Rhymes* and *Dirty Beasts*, by Roald Dahl. "Don't you think those are a bit old for him?" Dad asked. "No, I loved them when I was a kid!" I protested. "Yes, but you were a bit older. They're pretty gruesome." When the books arrived, I started to read them and realised he might be right. Oh well, I can imagine David and Martin enjoying them. They can read them to Tyler when he's older – or maybe doctor them a little for now. I'm amazed how well I recall these stories; the details come flooding back and I remember how I felt reading them time and time again, as a kid.

I get Bea and Bob some whisky, and Jonathan a new jumper. For Mum and Dad, I buy vouchers for a spa, and then I take a while thinking about Julie and Luke. I would normally get them something to share, these days, but I feel like I need to get something special for Julie this year. I think back to her hen do, and the night away that we had. We promised each other that we'd do it every year but, inevitably, life has got in the way and we've managed it once. I book us a night in the same hotel we went to then, and I hope that it will do us both good. Then I have to think of something for Luke. Inspiration strikes. I book him and Sam a night away, the same date as my night away with Julie. They will stay for a night in a yurt in the woods, and be taken on a guided walk to learn about foraging for mushrooms, and the host will then prepare a mushroom-themed meal for them. Five courses, apparently. It might be a bit random but they'll have a laugh, and it will give them a chance to spend a bit of time together, before this baby comes. The booking is not until April, when I hope that the temperature will be picking up and they won't be too cold. Whatever the weather, Julie and I will be fine, although I am going to be pretty big by then.

This leaves presents for Cindy, our excellent housekeeper – I know she and Rod love a particular seafood restaurant so buy them vouchers for a meal there. Paul and Shona, Julie and I buy for together, which helps maintain that slight necessary distance between Paul and me. After all, we very nearly had a relationship and I don't really feel comfortable buying him something just from me – more from Sam's and Shona's viewpoints than mine and Paul's. It doesn't feel right, somehow.

On top of the presents, there are Christmas cards for friends and family, and an electronic mail-out to all of

Amethi's guests from the last two years. This is in tiers, so that people who have stayed with us more than once get something a little more personalised and also receive a voucher for 10% off future stays. The design is the same; a clever image of Amethi in the snow, although since we have been here we have had little more than an icing sugar-style dusting. It looks beautiful. I secretly hope, as I do every year, that it snows this winter. Even though it could cause havoc for the business. It could mean people cancelling or delaying their holidays. I still can't help imagining how much more magical it will feel here if it snows.

Once the messages are set up and ready to go, I call Julie up to check them over.

"They look great! Look at our little place, all cold in the snow!"

"It looks really realistic, doesn't it?"

"Yes, and like winter, rather than specifically Christmas... I like your choice of wording, too."

The e-cards, along with the snowy image, bear this message:

With thanks for your custom and best wishes for a warm, restful winter and a healthy, happy New Year. We hope to see you again soon.
From all at Amethi xx

I have avoided Christmas, I have avoided holiday season, and festivities – and hopefully made it sincere, with no remnant of cheesiness. I am always aware of the sadness that accompanies these times of supposedly intense joy. It's often a lovely experience to share with family and friends, but not if you're recently bereaved, or somebody you're close to is ill, or you're alone, newly single, depressed, living in poverty or an unhappy relationship… the list goes on. All the while, the TV displays unlikely scenes of perfection, unachievable for most – and people spout messages of good will to all, and peace on earth, while all around the world there are terrible things happening. They aren't going to stop for Christmas, and a printed message on a greeting card will not make any difference. Words are never going to have more effect than actions.

But merry Christmas, one and all!

As a contrast to the overwhelmingness of Christmas, I'm really looking forward to the yoga retreat. I know I sound like a hippy, but I want to find out how things might be done differently; in touch with the world, and with nature. I think Lizzie is getting to me.

She comes to see Julie and me on the Saturday before the course is due to start. Emerging from her car in a fantastically fluffy poncho and matching hat, her trademark glimmering green leggings poke out from below the hem, reminding me as they so often do of frogs' legs.

Amethi is silent; the resident jackdaws have moved on, cackling, over the frozen fields. We expect them to return at dusk. Julie and I have been in the communal area, checking the heating is working, and that our yoga guests aren't going to freeze, or overheat.

We have shifted the furniture – "I'm not going to tell you not to, Alice; you're pregnant, not ill, but if you think you shouldn't be doing stuff like this, please say" – and made sure the table has enough seats for all the attendees, plus me, Julie and Lizzie. By the time Lizzie gets to us, we are ready for a break.

"Hi, Lizzie!" I am on my way back from the recycling

bins as she pulls up so I wait for her. She embraces me warmly and although she is quite a bit shorter than me, I feel like she could lift me in the air if she so wished. Much like Isaac, it seems like Lizzie is composed entirely of tight, sinewy muscle.

"It's so peaceful here!" she exclaims, stopping for a moment and turning slowly in wonderment, much like a child. I smile benignly at her and wait. She turns her attention to me. "This one's growing nicely," she beams at my stomach and I wonder if it is my expanding waistline or the baby she's referring to. She places her hand lightly on my abdomen – "Do you mind?" she asks without waiting for approval – and smiles. "Yes, she's very happy. Very happy," she murmurs, smiling more to herself than me, or so it seems.

She? I pay this no mind. It's fifty-fifty on the gender of the baby. David is sure it's going to be a boy. But he's not as tuned in with the world as Lizzie thinks she is – and might actually be, for all I know.

"Have you been drinking the tea?" she asks now, and I'd been hoping she wouldn't.

"Erm, no… I just don't fancy it, somehow. There are lots of things which are turning my stomach at the moment," I add, not wishing to offend her.

"Ah, but you need to look past that initial queasiness, it's good stuff, full of folic acid. And iron." Sounds delicious. "Great for you and Baby."

"Maybe I'll try it tonight," I say unconvincingly.

"You do that. Now, where's Julie?"

"She should be in the communal area, where I left her."

"Lead on!" Lizzie says cheerfully. I do as I'm told.

"Hello, my lovely," Lizzie greets Julie with another of her tight hugs and Julie looks over the top of Lizzie's head at me, her eyes wide in mock-panic. I grin. "How are you?" She stands back and casts her eye over Julie, who watches her curiously. Lizzie says nothing more and instead turns towards the dining table. "Shall we sit?"

"Yes, let's. Do you want a drink?" I ask.

"No, I'm fine, thank you. I'm too excited about showing you these plans..."

She draws out a sheaf of papers and it's obvious how much work she has put into the week ahead. Lizzie may come across as slightly dippy, but she is an extremely hard worker and she really knows her stuff when it comes to yoga. She's also providing invaluable help when it comes to putting together the solstice celebration.

"One early morning active session, one mid-morning meditation, then I thought lunch and a rest, followed by an early evening session and meditation an hour before dinner. It would mean a later dinner than normal. Will that be OK, Julie?"

"That will be fine. As long as I know what time to cook for, I can fit your schedule. It's nice to have somebody else taking control, to be honest."

"Do you want to stay up here this week, Lizzie?" I ask, as she has done before and it will save her driving along the icy early-morning and late-night roads.

"I think I will, if you're sure that's OK, darling."

"Of course." I hate being called 'darling'. Have I always been this uppity about stuff or is just an effect of being pregnant? I suspect I have always been this way. "I'll make sure Cindy knows, and we'll have a room ready for you."

"I can't wait for this," she turns to us both. "I really do think it is going to be an unforgettable week."

13

Sam and I enjoy a quiet day together on Sunday, while Sophie is at Kate's.

"Have you heard any more from your mum?" I ask him, tucked cosily into the crook of his arm and luxuriating in the late lie-in we're allowing ourselves. The curtains are open but that same low grey sky remains, and there is not much to be seen, aside from the occasional flock of gulls moving across the square of sky afforded by the small window. They fly slowly, almost lazily, lethargic in the winter weather and limited light.

"No, nothing – but I only spoke to her last week. We've got another fifty-one weeks to go before I expect to hear from her again."

"What about a Christmas present? Should we get her something?"

"No, I'll send something for Janie, I think, but present-buying for Mum deteriorated into us buying each other gift vouchers. Impersonal, and pointless. I decided we might as well keep the money, save the hassle, and buy ourselves something we actually want instead."

"I'm sorry your mum's like that," I say tentatively; although Sam is not enamoured with her, she is his mum and I don't like to offer criticism or even suggest that there might be anything to be critical of.

"Well, I'm used to it. And it's made me a better dad," he says, adding doubtfully, "I think."

"You are a great dad. You must know that." I turn, leaning on my elbow, and kiss him. It seems a while since

I've kissed him like this, and I let my lips linger on his, excited by his familiarity. Scenes flash through my mind, of the time on the beach when I'd gone swimming drunk and he'd told me off – which was also the night of our first kiss. The kiss itself, as he sat on a wall and slipped his arms around me, inside my jacket. His lips on mine, and the feeling of excitement and safety wrapped up together, much as I am feeling now.

"Hello," he smiles, his voice gruff and low.

"Hi." I kiss him again, and he shuffles down the bed, pulls me to him.

"We don't do this so much these days," he acknowledges.

"No, I guess having Sophie over the landing makes it a bit tricky."

"*Do* you mind?" He pulls back, looks concerned. I've told him so many times that it is more than fine to have Sophie here, but I know he still worries about it.

"No. I don't. Of course I don't. It just makes times like this more special."

The time for talking is over. I imagine viewing us from above, zooming out; the two of us, together – no other soul in sight for miles around, safe in each other's arms, cushioned by the soft winter's day. A bird's eye view of the bed, then the house, then all of Amethi, and the fields surrounding it. I feel dizzy and overwhelmed and I let myself go.

On Monday morning, Sam is up bright and early to get to Launceston, where there is going to be a meeting of all the wildlife charities working in Cornwall.

"When I get back, will the place be over-run with hippies?"

"Yes, a dozen Lizzies strutting about in ponchos. Snacking on seeds. It'll be like a flock of exotic birds. You'll love it."

"I can hardly wait," Sam grins, kisses me, and is gone.

I allow myself the luxury of a hot drink in bed before I get up and face the world. I tentatively suggest tea to myself but my stomach protests. I opt instead for boiled water with lemon. Not the same, somehow; there is not a whole lot to enjoy in such a drink, but at least it won't make me sick. I really hope my body returns to normal after I've given birth. I miss coffee and tea from my day but there's no point in forcing them down.

I pile Sam's and my pillows together, propping myself up against them and pulling my knees up, warming my hands around my unexciting drink. Today's weather is a marked contrast to yesterday's; the bedroom window displays a clear winter-blue sky, currently being crossed by a double-vapour-trail plane, the straight white lines already disintegrating and curling into new shapes. I'm unable to relax, keen to get going with the week, knowing we are doing something new and exciting. I hope Lizzie was right, that it will be an unforgettable week, for the right reasons.

A shower and hair-dry later, I am exiting the house, locking the door, walking over to the office. I stop for a moment. Revel in the stillness. It is winter, but the sunshine holds some warmth and I turn my face to the sky with pleasure. The jackdaws hop about and caw in the trees then something makes them rise, as one, directly upwards, where they flap around each other and caw some more before returning to the bare branches, grumbling.

A lone robin is watching me from the top of an outdoor chair that is leaning against a table. Its shiny black eyes are focused on me. I must refill the garden feeders. Maybe that's why the robin's here, to pass that message on.

I hear a high-pitched cry from high above and I see now what had unsettled the jackdaws; a buzzard is gliding in slow circles above the trees, gradually drifting in my direction. Shielding my eyes from the sun, I watch its progress. One or two of the jackdaws make a half-hearted attempt to fly at it; *yeah, that'll show 'im*, but the buzzard is too high up, and seemingly too content to be bothered.

Come on, I tell myself. *It's time to get moving*. I unlock the door to the office, climb the stairs, and switch on the heater before I turn on my computer.

"OK, let's see what we've got," I mutter to myself, placing a hand briefly on my tummy. There is a fluttering within and I am sure these feelings are getting stronger. The next scan is due in February, a couple of weeks before the tourism awards ceremony. Already, I can't wait. Although I have also heard the baby's heartbeat now, whooshing and whistling along so fast, and it seemed to me that was maybe even more exciting than seeing the images from the scan. The very sound of life itself. Sam wasn't with me for that appointment as he had to be at work and it was just a routine check-up. I described it for him later, wondering if it is less exciting for him as he's been through this all once before.

As I open the email inbox now, a series of pings tells me I have quite a lot of mail, and the number 36 pops up on my screen. I scan them first, for anything urgent.

Ursula Murray. The name rings a bell. It's one of our yoga course participants, who was here for a retreat earlier in the year.

Subject – last minute cancellation

Oh no. This is disappointing. I remember Ursula being a good person to have about; gregarious and laidback. Somebody who helped the group to gel.

Dear Alice and Julie,

I am very sorry to say that I won't be able to make the yoga course this week, due to an accident, which I am embarrassed to say was all my fault.

I decided to get some boxes of Christmas decorations down from the attic – up a ladder, in an empty house. As you have probably already guessed, I've fallen and injured my ankle. There is no way I can drive to Cornwall, never mind participate in a week's worth of yoga.

I know you will not be able to refund me for my place, and I wondered if instead I might send somebody in my place? I have a friend who I think would enjoy it and I'd rather she came than the money be wasted. She'll just have to buy me a nice Christmas present! But I wanted to run this past you first before I ask her. Please can you give me a ring when you get this message? I didn't want to call you on a Sunday night.

I am so sorry to miss out; as my family will tell you, I have been really looking forward to this week and seeing you two again. I know Kate must be on maternity leave by now. Please pass my regards to her, I hope that she and the baby are also keeping well.

With best wishes,
Ursula

That's a real shame. I find her number and pick up the phone.

"Hello?"

"Hi... Ursula?"

"Speaking. Is that Alice?"

"Yes, it is, I've just read your email. I am so sorry."

"Oh, don't, I know. What a silly sausage I am. My son is really cross with me, but I'm even more cross with myself. What a thing to do, and what a time to do it!"

I can't help thinking she doesn't sound particularly cross with herself.

"But I did have some good news last night, as well. My son who lives in New Zealand is coming back for Christmas!"

"Oh, that's lovely."

"Yes, but I am still absolutely devastated to miss out on coming to lovely Amethi again. Would it be OK to transfer my place to my friend, assuming she can come?"

"That should be fine," I say. "Can you just let me know if she's coming – and send me her details, plus estimated arrival time?"

"Of course. She's only in Somerset, like me, so it's not too far."

"Great, just let me know. I'm sorry to rush but I have to get things ready. I am really sorry you can't make it."

"Thank you, my lovely, I am too, but I'm lucky to have my family around me at Christmas. My friend is on her own, so it will be nice for her to have this week if she can make it."

"I think that's lovely of you. She's lucky to have a good friend!"

"Thank you, Alice. I'll ring her now, and send you her details if she's coming. I hope you have a wonderful week."

"Thanks, Ursula. I hope you have a wonderful Christmas."

I smile as I hang up, touched as I always am when our customers are so thoughtful and warm. While there is plenty of opportunity for criticism and complaint in this business, I've definitely found the majority of people want to be pleased.

I make a note for Julie, and to remind myself, that Ursula isn't coming, then I read each unopened email in turn, deleting, replying to and filing as necessary. The initial flurry of enquiries about bookings after the *Staycation* article has died down, but I would say there are more than normal for the time of year. I open our booking system, enjoy clicking through until September next year and seeing that there are very few free weeks. Of course, by September, the baby will be here. I keep telling myself things like that because somehow it still doesn't feel real.

Julie arrives at about ten, in time for the food delivery, and I help her carry it through to the kitchen. The guests are not due until after lunch so there's time to go back through all the meal choices and dietary requirements.

We stop for a short lunch; a bowl of spicy butternut squash soup and some crusty bread, and then do a final walk-round of all the properties, listing the names of the guests and making sure each is allocated a room appropriate to their needs.

As we exit the final building, I hear the instantly recognisable sound of car tyres crunching over the gravel of the parking area. Julie and I go together to greet the first of our guests and, over the next two or three hours, ten more turn up. This leaves one empty space, after Ursula's cancellation, and despite having checked my emails numerous times, I have received nothing further from her.

There is no time to dwell on it, though – we have a nearly full complement of guests and Lizzie is ready and waiting in the communal area. At five, the course participants are expected to gather there and I will give a brief welcome, after which Lizzie will talk to them about what they can expect in the coming week. I stop in at the kitchen before going through, for a quick chat with Julie.

"Are things any better with Luke?"

"Kind of," she says reluctantly. "He's in London now again, of course, and I'm still driving myself mad thinking about him and Sinead."

"There isn't any 'him and Sinead'," I say sternly.

"I know, or at least I think I do. But I spoke to him last night and I could hear her in the background. She's the customer and he's working to her command so he said he was working late because he's trying to get this site finished before the weekend, so he can get back here for the party."

"And you have no reason not to believe him!"

"Oh, I know, Alice. When I'm here, during the day, I know – it's when I'm home and I have nothing to occupy my thoughts, my mind starts going to lots of dark places."

"How dark?"

"Not *dark*-dark, nothing like that," Julie says. "I'm not massively depressed or anything."

"This is going to sound like terrible pop psychology," I say, "but do you think you're distracting yourself from the real issue?"

"What? Wanting to have a baby?" Julie looks at me and sighs. "Yes, possibly. But it's the way Luke talks about Sinead, all the amazing work she does for this charity."

"Well, it is entirely possible he really does just admire her professionally. You have no reason not to take him at his

114

word. Luke would never jeopardise things with you."

"I hope not."

"I know not."

Back outside, I take a moment in the fresh air. It is still and cold, the sky as clear as it was this morning, but now a deep, dark blue, and dappled with stars. The light from the kitchen window illuminates my breath. I feel so bad for Julie, but I am also feeling sorry for Luke. I do not for one moment think he would be remotely interested in another woman. I have to get on, though, so I take a deep breath and walk in, smiling, to greet our guests.

The meeting goes well and everybody seems incredibly enthusiastic about the week. When Lizzie suggests starting early in the morning, one of the older men asks if it's possible to have a session sooner.

"I'd love to say yes," I say apologetically, "but Julie's in the kitchen, putting the finishing touches to your delicious dinner, and I suspect that after you've all tucked in, the last thing you're going to want to do is headstands and forward bends. I promise you will have plenty of yoga this week, and I am really looking forward to rounding it off with our solstice party."

Just before dinner, I pop outside for a moment. I hear a car coming up the drive so I go around to give Sam a sneaky kiss. I notice there are two cars, one unknown to me. A woman gets out. I don't recognise her.

"Are you Alice?" she asks.

"Yes," I say, thinking there is something familiar about her, which I can't place. Sam's car draws alongside hers. Sam gets out. "Are you Ursula's friend?" I ask the woman.

"No," she smiles. "I'm Sam's…"

"Mum!" he exclaims, and even in the poor light I can see all the colour drain from his face.

14

I look from Sam to his mum, and back again.

"You look like each other," I say stupidly.

"Well, yes," says Sam's mum. "He's my son."

She walks towards me and I glance to Sam, to see his reaction. I wonder dumbly what she is going to do, but she reaches out her arms and pulls me to her.

"Alice," she says, almost wistfully. "It is so good to meet you at last."

At last? I wonder, knowing Sam barely speaks to his mum. How long can she have been waiting to meet me?

I return her embrace hesitantly, meeting Sam's gaze behind his mum's back. I am desperate to know what to think; how he wants me to act in this unplanned for and completely unexpected situation. He just looks shocked.

"OK then," I pull back slightly, not allowing myself to lose sight of the fact I have to be back for dinner with the yoga crowd. "Sam, are you OK?"

"Yep."

"Great." It looks like I'm going to have to get things going here. "Right, well, it's lovely to meet you, too…"

"Karen," she supplies, and I realise Sam's never mentioned his mum's first name.

"Karen," I repeat. "I'm afraid I am about to dash back to work, though; I was actually just popping round to see Sam as I heard his car. Have you had a good day, Sam?"

"Yep."

He is the definition of slack-jawed.

"Sam!" His mum – Karen – now goes to him, pulls him

into her arms. He is a good half-foot taller than her and allows her to hug him but does not reciprocate. "I've missed you."

Sam says nothing.

Now I am stuck. What do I do? I have to get back for dinner; it's the first night, and I'm the host.

"Karen," I say, breaking her spell. She turns to me, her hands still on Sam, who takes the opportunity to step lightly away. "I have to go to work," I remind her, and Sam. "Would you like to come and see where Sam and I live? Have a cup of tea? Have you eaten?"

I worry slightly that Sam will hate me for this hospitable attitude. Should I even be inviting her in? Is she like a vampire? Is she actually a vampire? I know so little about this woman, and Sam's lack of feeling – or possibly excess of feeling – towards her is clear.

"I wouldn't want to put you to any trouble," she says, "but I'd love to see where you live."

"I'm really sorry," and I mean this as much to Sam as to Karen, "but I am going to have to leave you two to it. The guests are expecting me to be there for dinner."

"You have guests? You should have said. Silly me, just turning up unannounced. I can always come back…"

"No, no, not guests like that." Should I have accepted her offer to come back another time? "These are paying guests. Staying in our holiday lets."

"Oh, is that what this place is?" I realise just how clueless she must be about her son's life. "And they want you to go for dinner?" She sounds puzzled.

"We're running a yoga course, and we lay on the dinners. My friend, Julie, is the chef. It's the first night. I really do have to go," I say apologetically.

Sam seems to snap to attention. "Of course. Go, Alice."

"Yes, you must go, Alice, but I hope I'll get to meet you properly later."

"Well, it could be quite late," I say.

"That's fine. I'm a night owl anyway."

I kiss Sam, trying to pack as much meaning as I possibly can into the look I give him. He offers a small smile. I hate to do this, but I am going to have to leave him to it.

"Oh, Sam, it's so good to see you again," I hear behind me as I walk purposefully back round the corner. I can't believe she has just turned up like this, but I can't really think about it now. I have to put my work head on. I will get back to this later.

"Sam's mum's just turned up," I hiss to Julie as I help her carry in the hot dishes. It's a curry tonight; sweet potato, chickpea and aubergine, with brown rice, tarka dhal, and the biggest naan breads you've ever seen. Julie went on an Indian cookery course and she came back proficient in making these amazing breads. Tonight's are garlic and coriander. They smell mouth-watering.

"How are you all?" Julie treats the seated guests to her wide smile. "Hungry, I hope?"

"Julie is the best chef in the county," Lizzie smiles, "and she's not afraid to take meat out of the equation."

I smile around the table. "I'm sorry I'm a couple of minutes late. We had an, erm, unexpected visitor turn up, but now, please, tuck in. We don't stand on ceremony here, that's for sure."

The evening passes so pleasantly and, unlike the writing courses, this is not a booze-fuelled night. Everyone here is hoping to go away feeling wonderful. Starting the course with a hangover is not on the cards.

I keep my mind on my work – if you can call eating

delicious food and chatting with interesting people work – and try not to think too much about Sam and his mum. Will they be talking? Arguing? Will she still be there when I get back home? I can't help wondering why she has just turned up, with no warning. Sam doesn't talk about her much, at all, but I know she's been unreliable, and shown very little interest in her son. I think one of the saddest things is that he's all but lost touch with Janie, his sister, who was eight when her mum took her off to Spain, so must be in her mid-twenties now. Then again, imagine not having your mum in your life – knowing she is alive but just not all that bothered about seeing you.

I do wonder sometimes about Sophie's decision to stay here, and not go with her mum. Sam is a wonderful dad, but Kate is the person Sophie has lived with most of her life. Maybe because I am soon to become a mum myself, I can't help feeling that there is a unique bond with the person who carried you, and gave birth to you.

As well as being booze-free, this first night is also an early one. The course participants seem keen to head off to their own separate spaces, and I am grateful for this. I help Julie clear up and make the breakfast things ready for people to help themselves in the morning, then walk her to her car, filling her in on Karen's sudden appearance. We round the corner to the parking area.

"Her car's still here," I say.

"Shit. Good luck."

"Thank you," I kiss my friend on the cheek. "Is Luke still away?"

"Yes, I'll make the most of the peace and quiet." Julie's words don't quite ring true to me. She looks a little sad.

"Are you OK?"

"Yeah. Just tired!" She smiles, and again I think she's not fooling me.

"Why don't you come for the yoga in the morning?"

"I might just do that. Yeah… great idea, in fact. I think I could do with it."

"Me too," I say, circling my head slightly so that my neck clicks.

"How are you?" Julie asks suddenly. "Are you OK? Enjoying being pregnant? You can talk to me about it, you know."

"Oh, I know. Thank you," I smile and it's my turn to be unconvincing. "I think I'm just getting on with it, you know?" No, no, she doesn't know, I kick myself. "I mean, it's so busy. Maybe in the New Year I'll be able to be more focused." I am babbling. What am I talking about? I take a deep breath. "To be honest, I'm shattered. All this talk about the second trimester being when I'm meant to feel full of energy. I feel anything but."

"Ah, mate," Julie puts a sympathetic arm around my shoulder. "You need a rest. It's these dark afternoons that do it, too. We should be hibernating, not putting ourselves through all this work nonsense!"

"It's coming… the break, I mean. Just two weeks to go."

"Yeah, topped off with New Year's Eve. The most mental night of the year."

"I do love it, though."

"Me too."

"Just got to push on through till then. Have you and Luke booked a holiday?"

"No, we're going to do it at the weekend. What about you two?"

"We're looking." I don't know what I'll feel like in a couple of weeks' time. Although I have to admit, the thought of a week in the sun, just swimming in a pool and lazing on a lounger, is becoming increasingly attractive.

"It's the last chance, just the two of you," Julie squeezes me. "Make the most of it."

"I will." I hug her, and send her off home. I have a mother-in-law (well almost) to attend to.

All is quiet in the house when I push open the door. Is this a good thing? I don't really see how it can be. I hear a noise in the kitchen so I go in there. Sam is washing up.

"Hello?" I say cautiously.

He turns. He looks tired. "Hi," he smiles.

"Your mum still here?" I whisper.

"Yep."

"In the lounge?" Why am I still whispering?

"Yep."

"OK. I think that has to be enough yeps," I say quietly, walking to him and taking his hands. "What's going on?"

"Oh, I don't know. I don't know what the hell she's doing here."

"She hasn't said?"

"Nope."

"Enough!" I laugh and gently shake his hands.

"Sorry."

"I'll ask her."

"What?"

"I'll ask her why she's here. It's a reasonable question. I'll say I'm tired and hormonal if she takes offence."

"You can't…"

"I can." I am not sure what has come over me, but I feel fiercely protective of Sam, and I'm not having this; his mum walking in unannounced and turning him miserable and monosyllabic.

Before I know it, I am in the lounge, where Karen looks very comfortable, legs tucked under her on the settee, reading glasses on and a book in her hand.

"Oh, Alice, how was dinner?" she looks up. The glasses make her look older.

"It was great, thanks. But I'm really tired, and so is Sam. We both have to be up for work early in the morning. So I was wondering, if it doesn't sound too rude, if you could tell us what your plans are?"

Damn. I'd been quite excited about coming in and being all hard-nosed. Might have known I wouldn't be able to pull it off.

"I'm sorry, Alice, I wasn't thinking." Karen untucks her legs. Puts down the book. *My* book, I notice. "Of course, you need to get to bed. I'll get going."

"Where... where are you staying?"

"In a B&B in town, it belongs to a school friend."

I want to ask who, but I also don't want to prolong the conversation.

"I thought I might come back tomorrow, see Sophie as well. I didn't realise she'd be at her friend's."

No, well you wouldn't, seeing as you just rocked up here without checking first. "I'm going to be working tomorrow night, too – all week, in fact. I don't know what Sam's plans are."

"She can come tomorrow." Sam is standing in the doorway now.

"Thank you, Sam," Karen ignores his coldness. "I can't wait to see her. What is she now... twelve?"

"Nearly fourteen," Sam states.

"Oh, well, time does fly, doesn't it? Well, I won't stay any longer tonight. Alice, it was lovely to meet you. I hope we can spend a bit more time together later in the week, if you're not too busy."

Was that a barbed comment? I feel my hackles rise.

"Alice is working. She runs this business, and this week she's got a yoga course going on. She can't just drop it all to suit you."

"No, no, of course not. Yoga, though? I like a bit of yoga. I go three times a week in Spain."

Neither Sam nor I respond to this. I'm biting back my natural inclination to offer her the spare space on the course. I assume that Ursula would have been in touch by now if her friend was coming.

"Right, OK," I say after a moment or two's awkward silence. "Let me walk you to your car."

"I won't hear of it. You need to put your feet up! Sam?" Karen turns to her son.

"OK," he almost huffs, and for a moment I want to laugh – partly from the sheer stress of this situation and partly because I have a glimpse of what he was like as a teenager. It reminds me of Sophie when she's not happy about something. He pulls on his trainers and opens the door.

"Bye, Alice," Karen says as she follows her son.

"Bye," I say limply into the darkness, moving to stand in the open doorway.

It's cold and still outside, and the sound of two sets of footsteps on gravel is clear. I hear murmuring, then a car door being shut rather hard. As the engine starts up, I shiver, pulling my cardigan closer around myself. A sudden breeze ruffles the furniture covers and caresses my skin. I tuck a strand of hair behind my ear and wait for Sam. It's a while before I hear his footsteps and I wonder what he's doing.

An owl hoots in the treeline and then I hear Sam, coming back to me. I wait for him, leaning on the doorframe in the light of the hallway.

"Hi," he smiles when he sees me. "Aren't you meant to be putting your feet up?"

"I wanted to make sure you were OK," I say, hooking my arms around his waist and pulling him into the hallway, pushing the door closed with my foot. "Are you?"

"OK?" He laughs without any humour. "I guess."

"And she didn't say why she's here?"

"No. Well, she said she wanted to see us. But it's never as simple as that, with her."

"Do you think she's alright?" I take Sam by the hand and draw him down onto a settee with me, so that his head is on my shoulder. I think of Luke's mum, her illness and death. What if Karen's ill? Maybe she wants to see her son and granddaughter before she dies. Maybe my imagination's running away with me.

"Yeah, she's OK. She makes sure of that."

"You really don't get on, do you?"

Sam sits up, leans forward, rubbing his eyes. "It's not really about getting on. I just… when I was growing up, she was always off with some bloke or other. Always total losers, too, like my dad. She just couldn't be arsed, I don't think, with being a mum; at least that's how it felt to me. Then along came Janie, and that was like a novelty – a little girl to dress up – but the novelty soon wore off. I was about Sophie's age and I had this little sister to look after, while Mum went out, or had mates round, or some bloke."

"I'm sorry."

"It's OK."

"My god, it's not OK at all." I am fuming now. I want to go out there, run after her car and drag her back to explain herself.

"I'm used to it," Sam says. "And it made me determined

to be different."

It fits, I think – how Sam stayed with Kate when they discovered she was pregnant. Became Sophie's dad.

What's that Philip Larkin poem? Something about your parents fucking you up. It's not true, of course. Well, maybe for some people, but I don't think it's true for me. And Sam's waste-of-space parents have inadvertently created the best, most brilliant man I could ever hope to meet. Against the odds, if Larkin is to be believed.

"I cannot think of a better man to have a baby with," I say, lifting his head gently and kissing him on the lips. "I am just so sorry you had such a crappy time growing up."

Sam smiles, slightly sadly. "I'm not having a crappy time now."

"Good. And you won't, if I have anything to do with it."

Thankfully, we don't see much of Karen during the next few days. She comes up on Tuesday night and sees Sophie, but I miss her entirely. When I come back from dinner – another blessedly early night – she is already gone.

"How was it?" I ask Sam, kissing him. Sophie is sitting reading, so I don't want to make too much of it.

"How was Grandma Karen?" Sam asks his daughter.

"OK," Sophie keeps her eyes on the book, not giving much away.

"How old were you last time you saw her?" he prompts.

"Dunno... Seven? Eight?"

"You were eight," he confirms. "So, what, nearly six years ago? And yet she thinks she can just flounce back into our lives..."

I put a calming hand on Sam's arm. "Was it nice to see her again, Sophie?"

"I guess. It's not like she's been an important person in

my life. I mean, I know she's Dad's mum and all that, but I never hear from her. I see your mum and dad more than her, Alice. Like, a lot more."

"Well, she does live in Spain…" I have no idea why I'm defending her.

"Yeah, but she could Skype, or email, or even write. She never does." I know Sam is right.

"Did she say when she's going back to Spain?"

"No…" he says. "And I think she was a bit disappointed that our house is so small. I think she was hoping for a place to stay while she's back."

"We can't help her there," I said, adding before thinking, "it's tight enough with the three of us."

At this, Sophie looks up. I try to qualify what I've just said. I don't want her thinking she's unwelcome.

"I mean, there's not enough space for anybody else."

This is still the wrong thing.

"But you're having a baby," Sophie says, and I genuinely think it is the first time it's occurred to her that we have a bit of a space issue here.

"Oh yeah, but not for ages," I say airily, hoping Sophie won't realise how ridiculous that sounds.

She returns to her book. Phew. Crisis averted. For now.

"I might go and have a bath," I say.

"I'll run it for you," Sam offers, following me upstairs.

"It really hits me every now and then that we really are going to be pushed for space," he says, coming into our room after he's started the taps.

I am pulling my top over my head. I hope it hides my expression. I finish the manoeuvre, come out smiling. "It will be fine. We'll think of something. We'll make it work. Other people do, with much less than we have. And the baby will be in with us for the first few months so we've got at least a year before anything becomes an issue."

We both take a look at our room. Love it though I do, it's not the biggest space.

"I guess," Sam says doubtfully.

"Don't worry!" I say, longing to see a real smile on his face. "We will be fine, whatever. And think, both Sophie and this little one —" I touch my belly lightly "— are going to have us looking out for them. Space issues or not, that has to count for a lot. Even if we all had to share the same bedroom."

Sam shudders. "I don't fancy that much."

"Nor me!" I laugh. "But other people live like that. And my grandma, when she was little, had to share a bed with two of her sisters! That was pretty normal then."

"But it isn't now," Sam says slightly grimly and I have to agree. But more than anything, I want a happy evening, and I want to relieve him of some of the weight on his shoulders, landed there squarely by the arrival of his mum.

I sink gratefully through the bubbles, the lights switched off and a sizeable camomile-scented candle flickering away on the windowsill. The water accepts me, closing around me, lapping gently at the slightly rounder bump of my tummy. It is like an island, I consider, as I admire the way the light licks across my shiny skin. And inside is this tiny being who I cannot wait to meet.

The bath is not as hot as I would normally like but even so, the change of temperature seems to wake the baby and for the first time I feel something really resembling a kick.

"Happy in there?" I ask out loud, my voice sounding loud and strange amidst the acoustics of the bathroom.

"What was that?" Sam calls. I left him lounging on the bed, idly scrolling through screens on his iPad.

"Nothing," I say. "Thank you, this bath is lovely."

"Good!"

I lie back, hearing the fizzing of bubbles in my hair and ears. I consider the yoga course. It is going well, I think, although given the nature of the course and the people on it, I wonder how it could go anything other than well. The general atmosphere is overwhelmingly positive and just... so... relaxed. I love it.

Julie came for the morning session, and it seemed to do her a lot of good as well. We chatted over lunch.

"What do you think Luke's getting you for Christmas?"

"I hope it's a baby." The words were out of her mouth before she'd had time to think about it. Her hand flew up, as if to cram them back in, but it was too late.

"Oh, Julie." What could I say?

"I'm all about positive thinking now, Alice. I'm going to enjoy the rest of this year. Eat, drink and be merry – then next year we'll try again. And maybe it will be our year."

"I really hope so." I squeezed her hand.

I sigh now, sinking right under the water, letting the bubbles close over my face, eyes clenched shut. *Stop. Don't even breathe.* Hold the breath as we did in yoga. Then up and out, and inhale.

"I'm off to bed, Alice," Sophie calls.

"OK. Hang on, though. I'll get out of the bath. You'll need to use the bathroom."

"I don't want to make you get out!"

"I know, but you need to use the toilet and brush your teeth." I hope I don't sound like I think I'm talking to a child. I grasp the handles on the sides of the bath and pull myself up, water whooshing one way then the other, slapping the sides of the bath and splashing onto the floor. Wrapping a towel around my body, I tread wet footprints across the landing. "It's free now!"

Sophie emerges from her room, already in her pyjamas.

"Those are new." I don't recognise the lace-edged vest top or silky material.

"They're from Grandma Karen."

"They're too old for her," Sam mutters.

"Dad doesn't like them!"

"Well, OK, it's, erm, nice she got you a present."

"For god's sake, she thought she was twelve yesterday. Now she's buying her silky pyjamas."

"They look very comfy," I say supportively and Sophie flashes a grateful smile my way. "And anyway, it's not like anyone other than us will see them!"

"They'd better not," Sam says quietly.

"Night, Sophie. Sleep well," I say loudly and she goes into the bathroom.

"Sam," I say, closing our bedroom door. "I know you don't want your mum about, and I do realise those pyjamas are a little bit grown-up for Soph, but it's not like your mum's bought her a negligée. And it really isn't as though anyone else is going to see them. We can tell her to only wear them at home – not take them on sleepovers or whatever."

"I guess."

"It's nice to feel a little bit grown-up, you know, when you're that age."

"I suppose you're right."

"If anybody else had bought them for her, I don't think you'd have such a problem."

"The point is," he says through gritted teeth, "nobody else *would* buy them for her. Mum is, and always has been, completely unaware of what is appropriate."

I can feel the anger seething within him. I lie next to him, still wrapped in my towel. Shift onto my side and look at him. "Just try and keep calm, if you can. She'll be gone again soon."

By Thursday, the yoga folk are a delight. They are glowing; particularly those who have accomplished new positions. Lizzie is a hit with them all.

"You're great at this," I say over lunch.

"I love it," she says simply.

"I can tell, and your enthusiasm is infectious. I've had more than one person tell me they'll be coming back, and that they're going to recommend us to their friends and yoga classes back home! So thank you very much."

"Yeah, cheers Lizzie," says Julie, who has been getting as much out of it as the guests have, I'd say. I just wish I'd had the energy to join in, too. Julie raises her glass of water and Lizzie and I join ours to it.

"I can't wait for the solstice celebration!" I say. "I've never done anything like this before."

"You will love it." Lizzie smiles but her brow furrows for a moment. "Should a cloud pass before the sun, don't let it spoil the view."

Julie and I look at each other. I look away quickly so that I don't laugh.

"I've got to say, Lizzie, although we miss Kate, I am so glad you're working with us. Are you up for doing more of the same next year?"

"Yes, of course. More of the same, and new, too. A summer solstice?"

"Hmm. That could be trickier. It cuts right into the high season." I don't want to add it's also pretty much bang on my due date.

"You should pitch that to Kate and Isaac!" Julie

130

suggests. "They've got that hillside field, haven't they, Alice? You could have a midsummer yoga festival."

Lizzie's eyes light up. I wonder if this might be stepping on Isaac's toes a little but they can work that out between themselves. I could see it happening, though; tents glistening on the Devon hillside in the early morning dew, interspersed with gracefully posed figures silhouetted against the rising sun.

There is one last yoga session before a couple of hours' rest. Neither Julie nor I are able to join in the last session, now working against the clock to prepare for the feast. I rush around while Julie cooks; making sure we have everything we need in terms of glasses, plates, cutlery, drinks, etc. I receive delivery of a load of holly wreaths, which will take centre stage on the table. Tomorrow, once the yoga guests have gone, we will attach them to the doors of each property at Amethi.

"Could have brought your tree as well," the delivery man half-grumbles.

"Ah, but we're keeping it simple today," I say. "Saturday's Christmas Tree Day."

"If you say so."

I grin to myself and roll my eyes once he's safely on his way back to his delivery truck. As he pulls away, I wave to him, but expect, and receive, no return gesture. So much for the Christmas, or solstice, spirit.

A low mist hangs over the fields and the air is full of a fine, soft drizzle. I hope it clears for the morning; a solstice celebration with the sun obscured could be disappointing. Although, of course, I should heed Lizzie's words. I am sure they have some meaning, to her if nobody else.

A flock of wild pigeons rises above the bordering

farmland. There must be 200 of them, grey against the grey sky. I look at the pile of wreaths and think how none of this means anything to those birds. Have they any sense of the solstice? I suppose there's more chance they are aware of it than of Christmas, but I guess to them all that matters is the shift in the year, as the hours of daylight become gradually longer.

Is it ridiculous, this season of jollity and over-indulgence? Probably. And even the solstice, tied to nature as it is, seems like something only the luckiest among us might be able to enjoy. Not many people can afford to come to a yoga retreat – most people lacking time if not money. And while nature is free, and there for all of us, it's harder to feel connected from the centre of a city, or elevated away from the world in a high-rise flat. My mind flits to other parts of the world. War-torn countries. People fleeing aggressive regimes. Right now, I tell myself, as I stand in this spot, preparing for a week of fun with the people I love, there are other people in the world risking their safety and their families', trying to find a better life for themselves, with little more than hope to keep them going. They cannot take time out to revel in anything.

We are a lucky few, and it's not that I think we don't deserve to enjoy these things – rather that others do, too.

15

The end of the course is marked by the celebration dinner, with readings from Vanessa and Rosie and afterwards the lighting of a fire by Lizzie.

Sam never comes to the dinners, although he is always invited. "No, no, it's your work," he will insist. Tonight, though, he comes across, with Sophie, as both of them helped Lizzie build the fire earlier. The three of them worked together remarkably well, choosing the best position for the fire so that it is safely within the gravelled area where we normally put tables and chairs in the summer – and visible from within the communal area.

"There needs to be enough space for us all to gather round," Lizzie insisted. "That includes Julie, and you two, I hope?"

Sam looked doubtful. "It's a school day."

"Dad! It's the last day of term, and how often do I get to come to a winter solstice celebration?"

"Once a year?" he grinned. "Go on, then. I have to admit, I'm intrigued. We need to make sure there's no chance of the flames or any floating embers getting onto the building."

"We'll keep it small, Sam, don't worry," Lizzie said. "And I have assurance that no harm will come to the place."

"Assurance? From whom?"

She just smiled and looked serene.

Now, bellies full of delicious food, and bearing cups of egg nog or the rum cocktail, we all traipse outside.

"What a perfect night!" Vanessa exclaims.

I look past the fire, up to the sky, my eyes adjusting quickly to the dark. Where it had been cloud and mizzle, all is now peaceful, calm and clear. Stars are beginning to reveal themselves, pricking holes in the sky, one by one.

"It's the solstice," Lizzie says knowingly, although I can't believe that every solstice eve is like this. "It's a shame there's no full moon but since 1793 there have only been ten full moons on the winter solstice."

"Really? I had no idea."

"This is fascinating," Vanessa says. "Can I pick your brain about it, Lizzie? I feel a poem coming on!"

I think Vanessa is drunk. I look to see Rosie grinning at me. I laugh, then feel a hand on my shoulder. Turning, Sam kisses me on my cheek. Sophie is behind him.

"Look what I found, Alice!" She whirls a sparkler in the air, to admiring comments from some of the guests.

"I'm not sure it's that kind of bonfire," I say, wondering if the spirits – or at least Lizzie – will be annoyed at this flippancy.

"Course it is!" Lizzie calls. How did she hear that? Vanessa is bending her ear. "This is a celebration. If Sophie chooses to celebrate with sparklers, so be it!"

"Egg nog?" I ask Sam. He wrinkles his nose. "Or rum and ginger?"

"That's more like it."

I go back inside, get a cocktail for Sam and a mug with warm ginger wine for Sophie.

"Thanks," Sam says. "So what happens now?"

"I don't know, actually. It's nearly half-nine and we all need to be up early in the morning, to celebrate the return of the light."

"Sounds exciting!"

"Do you know, I can't wait. Normally by now, everything feels a bit too sickly-sweet. I mean, you know I love Christmas, but sometimes I feel like by the time it really is Christmas, we've already overdone it. This week's been really chilled."

"It has." Julie arrives by my side. "I feel like it's done me a load of good."

She does look calmer; happier. More like Julie.

"That's good to hear, Julie." Sam steps forward and kisses her cheek. "And Luke's back tomorrow?"

"Saturday, I think. Tomorrow if he can but this client's being a pain. And he doesn't want to let them down, because they're a non-profit..."

"So they're taking advantage of his good nature?"

"Ha! Yeah. Seems that way. But I'm super chilled now, and can't wait for tomorrow morning. After that, I'll see everyone off then I am going home to bed."

"That sounds pretty amazing. I might do the same."

"Oh yeah, rub it in, while me and Soph are off to school and work!" Sam smiles.

"We have to take our rest when we can," I squeeze his hand.

"Shh…" Julie says, seeing that Lizzie has ascended onto one of the wooden seats. The gathered guests go quiet and we all turn to face her.

"Thank you, everyone, for what has been a wonderful few days." There are general murmurs of thanks to Lizzie, which she acknowledges graciously. In her poncho, her hair even frizzier than normal from the damp earlier in the day, her eyes are glowing in the light of the flames. She looks wild and wonderful. We can't take our eyes off her. "In the morning, we will celebrate the return of the light. I know some of you have done this before but from having

135

spoken to all of you during the week, I think this is a new experience for most of you. It's going to be a very special way to end this course, and send you back home with the blessing of the spirits. Tonight, we give thanks for our wonderful feast –" now people turn to Julie and cast thanks her way, "– and the most wonderful welcoming hospitality we have received at Amethi." Now eyes are on me. I find myself blushing but hopefully in the dark this is not visible.

"I am going to stay out by the fire all night," Lizzie says and there are a few gasps. I was not expecting that either, but nothing Lizzie says could surprise me. "If anybody would like to join me, you are very welcome to do so. But if you prefer the comfort of your beautiful beds, this is no problem. We will reconvene here in the morning at 6:00am. I will talk you through the celebration of the returning of the light, welcoming in the spirits of the east, south, west and north as the sun begins to rise. The fire will keep us warm, but make sure you have coats, woolly hats and gloves."

There are murmurs of excitement around the fire.

"Now, before we all go our separate ways, I want to sing you a song."

I can't look at Julie but I can sense her shaking beside me with scarcely contained mirth. From somewhere below her poncho, Lizzie produces a tambourine. There is silence for a moment, and a slight breeze steps up, whispers across our faces. Even Julie is still, and Lizzie begins to sing, keeping time with her tambourine. Her voice is clear and deep and she closes her eyes as she sings a song about the green man; the holly king, giving way to the mighty oak king on the solstice.

Sam puts his arm around me and smiles as I look at him, his other arm around his daughter. I feel Julie move closer to me and I look at the people gathered around the fire; these lovely individuals who have spent the last few days here, and Rosie and Vanessa. All of us rapt, listening to Lizzie's song. I feel a shiver of wonder and happiness and my mind goes, as it never fails to do these days, to the tiny being deep inside me.

As Lizzie finishes, her eyes remain closed for a moment, then she opens them, to a round of applause and a few cheers.

Shortly, people begin to head off to their beds, all stopping to thank Lizzie and then Julie and me. Embarrassingly, I feel close to tears. This seems like an incredibly emotional night – but for once the emotion is pure happiness. I am so proud of what Julie and I have done, and so grateful to Lizzie for this experience she's providing for us all. I hug her before I head off. "Are you really staying up all night?"

"Of course! And Vanessa's staying with me, aren't you?"

"Really?" I turn to Vanessa, then Rosie. "How about you, Rosie?"

"No chance!" she laughs, "I'm off home to my nice cosy bed. I'll see you in the morning." She kisses Vanessa and heads off to the car park. Sophie walks part of the way with her then goes back to our house while Sam, Julie and I clear and wash up the cups.

"Are you two going to be warm enough?" I ask Vanessa and Lizzie. Nobody else has taken up Lizzie's offer of pushing through till dawn.

"Of course!" Lizzie looks cosy as anything in her poncho, but Vanessa seems to be shivering despite her long winter coat.

"I'm bringing you some blankets, just in case."

"OK," Vanessa looks slightly relieved. I wouldn't be

surprised if I find her snuggled up on one of the sofas in the communal area, when I come back in the morning. Lizzie, however; I don't think anything would send her inside on this special night.

Julie is staying in one of the spare rooms and we've already set our alarms for 5.00 am. I am going to help her get all the breakfast things ready. Sam and I take it in turns to hug her then we say our goodnights and head home, shutting the door on the darkness.

In the morning, I wake before my alarm. It is 4.53am. I switch the alarm to 5.30 so Sam can have a little more sleep, and tiptoe out of bed, shivering slightly and taking a sneaky look through the curtains. There is not a light to be seen, although I know that just around the corner the fire will be flickering. Will Vanessa have made it through the night?

I dress quietly and quickly in the bathroom, making sure I put on my thermal layers first, then I go downstairs, cursing the creaky step, although nobody else stirs. I come out of the house to see Julie exiting the door just across the gravel area.

"Julie!" I hiss, and I am struck by the urge to giggle. I feel like we're back at school.

"Hi!" She waits for me. "Let's do this!"

We walk around the corner as quietly as we can and there, by the fire, are Lizzie and Vanessa, both with their eyes closed. Vanessa is slumped on a wooden seat, her feet propped up on a tree stump. Lizzie, however, is sitting straight and her eyes suddenly flick open. It startles me.

She smiles. "Welcome."

"Hi, Lizzie," I whisper. "Can we get you a drink?"

"No need." With a stick she lifts a tin kettle from above

the fire. "I've got that covered."

"What's in it?"

"Wild strawberry leaves, apple, orange, mallow blossom, sunflower blossom, some berries… would you like some?"

"I'm not sure." I would, normally, but I do feel I should be careful, being pregnant. None of those things sound like they'd harm a baby but I don't know that for sure.

"I'll have some, please, Lizzie," says Julie, and Lizzie finds a small tin cup, pours some out.

"That is really good," Julie says and I look at her closely but I think she means it.

"Next year," I say, "I'll try some."

"Perfect," says Lizzie.

Julie and I head into the kitchen and warm up the ovens to freshen the loaves of bread, and open jars of fruit preserve. There is yoghurt and granola, and an assortment of fruit juices. All tea and coffee is decaf. "We should have thought of a solstice tea," I say.

"That stuff of Lizzie's is really good," says Julie. "We'll do it next year."

"This is ridiculous! Can you believe this is us, doing all this? Sometimes I feel just like I did when we were fifteen. But now we have this amazing business, and people want to come and stay here. They're even willing to pay for it! And we're planning ahead to next year, and…"

"I know!" Julie laughs. "And you're about to become a mum," she adds gently.

"Shit." Tears start to trickle down my face. "It's too much. I'm too lucky."

"No. You are just as lucky as you deserve to be."

"But you deserve it too," I sniffle, inwardly kicking myself for being such an idiot.

"We'll see. Let's hope so. Come on, you're meant to be happy."

"I am happy," I sob.

"Then pull yourself together, and let's celebrate!" She hugs me briefly and gets back to work.

When all is laid out in the communal area, we head outside. Already, there are a handful of guests around the fire.

"Morning!" I say. "Go on in and help yourselves if you're hungry, thirsty, whatever…"

"Maybe just a drink for now?" suggests Lizzie. "Keep the food for after the sunrise; I want to keep us warmed up with a bit of yoga so empty stomachs might be good."

My own stomach rumbles at this moment but I don't think anybody hears it.

Sam and Sophie arrive, followed by Rosie, who gently wakes a slightly bemused-looking Vanessa. Once all the guests are gathered, we are ready to begin.

Julie and I stand next to Lizzie.

"Good morning, everybody," Julie says. "Thank you so much for leaving the cosy comfort of your beds to joins us this beautiful – although slightly dark – morning."

The sky is still night-time navy, stars sprinkled generously across it, and the moon is looking down on us as we gather by the fire. The damp grass glitters in the light and, suspended between a couple of upturned tree stumps, illuminated by the fire, a round-bodied spider sits fatly at the centre of its web.

The fire is not huge but it is crackling healthily, and Sam adds more logs, which are welcomed into its embrace, first smoking gingerly then beginning to glow before the flames take hold.

I look around the circle of gathered, expectant faces. "I'd like to add my thanks," I say, "to all of you for what I hope you will agree has been a really special few days. And particularly to Lizzie, for all the hard work she has put in, and for leading us in this celebration."

There is a small smattering of applause and Lizzie raises her hands. "I am delighted to be able to do this," she says. "There is no need for thanks. Now let's begin." She looks around the group, at all of us in turn. I follow her gaze and smile at Sam and Sophie, standing huddled together on the opposite side of the fire to me.

Lizzie continues, smiling. "This is the longest night of the year. Now is the time to celebrate the return of the light. To gather with friends and welcome back the sun."

She pauses. We keep our eyes on her. Even Julie is still and, if I'm not much mistaken, reverent.

"I would like to invite the spirits to join us in our celebration," says Lizzie. She bends to the ground, picks up an incense burner on a long chain. Lights the incense and wraps the chain around her hand to shorten it. She walks around the fire, swinging the burner gently, so that we all smell the incense as it passes us by. "Let this incense cleanse this space, and all of us gathered here," Lizzie says.

She stops when she comes full circle and I realise my head is bowed, as though I am in church. A swift glance up reveals that most of the others are the same.

"Look up!" says Lizzie. "It is time to greet the spirits."

I glance at Julie. Will she be sniggering? She doesn't look at me. She is watching Lizzie. Whether she is mesmerised or trying not to laugh, I'm not sure.

"Turn, friends, to the east," Lizzie says, positioning her own body so we all know which is the right direction. "Now nod, to show your respect to the spirits."

We do as we are told. I think I can see the slightest lightening in the sky.

"Now we do the same for the spirits of the south... and the west... and the north."

We do as we are told, solemnly. The slightest breeze dances about us, blowing a few stray holly leaves around our feet. Lizzie lights a small candle, holds it out for somebody to take. Julie steps forward and takes it.

"This red candle represents the root chakra. Safety, survival and nourishment from the earth." Lizzie takes another candle, lights it and holds it out for Vanessa to take. "This, orange, candle represents the sacral chakra. Emotions, creativity, sexuality. It is linked with water." She goes on to light and hand out five more coloured candles: yellow (the solar plexus; intellect, personal power and will); green (the heart; love, integration and compassion); blue (the throat chakra; truth, communication, creative expression); purple (the third eye; inner wisdom and extra sensory perception) and finally, white (the crown chakra; spirituality and consciousness).

"And now, we stand together to face the sunrise. We open our hearts and let the light grow within us."

Following Lizzie's lead, we turn almost as one and unmistakably, to the east, the sky is far lighter. We cannot see the sun yet but I know that a mile or two away, it is pushing above the horizon, casting its first light across the sea. I picture gulls rising up; gannets and cormorants warm in their nests, feeling the sun on their feathers and waking, stretching their wings. Here at Amethi, the day is beginning for our garden birds, too. I hear a blackbird chattering. The distinctive song of a robin. The air is cold but the warmth of the fire touches my skin.

Lizzie, after a few moments' silence, walks round the

group, giving each person a slip of paper and a pencil. "These are for your wishes," she explains. "You should each think of something you would wish for; something meaningful, and write it down here. This is your own, private wish, and you should tell nobody else what you have written. Fold the paper up and we will take it in turns to add our wishes to the fire, where the paper will shrivel and burn but the meaning of your words will be carried up into the air, rising higher, towards the light."

I clutch the pencil in my hand, unsure exactly what I want to write. There are so many things. Most obvious is the health of the baby. But what about everybody else in my life? I'd like Mum to be truly happy. I'd like Sophie and Kate to be OK. I'd like Julie to become pregnant. I'd like us to have a bigger house! This last one I dismiss instantly. This is not about material things.

I hear the scratching of pencil on paper all around me. I need to decide. Taking a moment with my eyes closed, I hope for guidance. Then I open my eyes and begin to write. I fold the paper, awaiting my turn.

As each person steps forward, we others are quiet and respectful. The ceremony has taken on a sombre air and I am struck by the fact that everybody here, no matter how outwardly sorted they may seem, will have something big they would wish for. I observe their faces as they watch the papers burn. Julie casts hers into the flames and I am sure I know what she is asking for.

It is my turn next. I look up and meet Sam's eye. We smile at each other.

Sophie looks nervous and unsure, scurrying quickly back to her place. Sam is next and he steps forward, dropping his neatly folded paper in and watching as it is consumed by the fire. As the logs pop and sizzle in the heat, and sparks fly high into the early morning air, I think of the diverse wishes, of eighteen people gathered together, flying up into the burgeoning light of the day. Looking around the group, I realise I am not the only person in tears.

Gradually, the sun becomes more dominant in the sky, banishing the stars, although the moon watches from a respectful distance, dim against the colourful morning sky. The mood at Amethi lifts with the sun and Lizzie invites us all to perform a series of sun salutations with her.

After this, we thank the spirits for their help, turning from north to west to south to east, stopping for a moment in each position to express our gratitude.

"Although we are bidding farewell for now to these spirits," says Lizzie, "remember that they, and the gods and goddesses, are always there if you are in need."

We are still for a moment and I feel the touch of the sun on my skin. It is slight, but it is there, and I close my eyes, think of everybody gathered here, and everyone I love. The breeze breathes across my face and, when I open my eyes again, I see Lizzie is watching me, smiling.

Sam and Sophie have to be quick, wolfing down breakfast before going on their way. Sam is dropping Sophie at school then heading off to work.

"That really was worth getting up early for," he smiles and kisses me.

"It was, wasn't it?" I hug him. "I wish you didn't have to dash off, though."

"Me too, but it can't be helped – but I'm off next week."

"Can't wait," I kiss him. "Have a good day, Sophie!"

Already in the car, she waves at me.

I head back to the communal area, where I tuck into

144

three helpings of breakfast. I have not felt this hungry in a long time. I even find myself wanting a cup of tea and, taking a cautious sip, find I am no longer completely repelled by it. This is a blessing in itself.

After the guests have left, along with Vanessa, Rosie and Lizzie, Julie and I clear everything away. I am tired now, but somehow still energised.

"That was great," I say.

"It really was. And you know how cynical I am but I found it really moving. Especially the wishes."

"Me, too. I guess we've all got things we'd like to be different."

"Yeah, OK, Jerry Springer. On that final thought, I'll finish drying up and go home to bed."

"Ahhhh… bed," I smile.

"Go on, pregnant woman, I've got this covered."

"Are you sure?"

"Yes, now go before I change my mind!"

Although it is the kind of crisp, blue-skied winter day when I really should be walking on the beach, or along the coastal path, I am grateful to shut the front door behind me, traipse up the creaky stairs, and climb into my bed.

16

I feel a bit groggy all day of the solstice; perhaps it's just the anti-climax after the end of another incredibly busy week. It's hard to switch off at all when we have a yoga or writing retreat going on. And as much as I love the social side of work, it is also quite exhausting to be constantly 'on'; outgoing, sociable and accommodating at any given moment.

Perhaps, though, it is just the after-effects of the early start. Or, maybe, the work of Lizzie and her spirits. It really did feel like there was something deeper working its magic when we were gathered together. And after we had all gone our separate ways, I slept soundly for a solid three hours.

I spend the afternoon in the toasty, fire-warmed lounge, reading a copy of Carol Ann Duffy's *The Christmas Truce* – a long-form poem about the football match between the Allied and German soldiers during the First World War. How is it that again and again we need to be reminded to celebrate what we have in common, instead of making capital of what might set us apart?

It's a beautiful little book and when I've finished reading it I sort through the various papers which have gathered on the coffee table, dig out my other 'Christmas' books: *On Angel Wings* by Michael Morpurgo; *Cat on the Hill* by Michael Foreman, and of course *Father Christmas* and *The Snowman* by Raymond Briggs. I arrange them side by side, then in a fan formation. I pat my stomach lightly; *I can't wait to read these to you.*

Sophie is staying at Amber's tonight so it's just me and Sam, and I'm looking forward to an evening in with him. At half-past six he arrives carrying a takeaway curry and I realise that I am famished. As I tuck in to poppadoms then a samosa, and then chilli paneer on puri – the baby giving a little kick at the spiciness – I realise that I have no feelings of queasiness at all, for the first time in what feels like a very long time.

We watch *Die Hard* and retire early to bed, both of us ready for a good sleep.

"All set for tomorrow?" Sam asks drowsily, smudging a kiss across my cheek and wrapping his arms around me.

"Yes, at least I think so. Tree's coming first thing then we need to get all the decorations down and…"

"Sorry!" Sam laughs. "Don't think about it now. Let tonight be all about sleep."

"That sounds good to me."

I've left the curtains open and, despite my fatigue, I lie awake for a while, hearing Sam's steady, deep breathing beside me; looking up at the clear winter sky; thinking of the story of the Christmas star.

In the morning, I am woken by Sam bringing me breakfast in bed.

"I can't believe I didn't wake up when you did," I say, sitting up and rubbing my eyes.

"Ah, well, you were extra tired. Sorry you can't have tea," he says, presenting me with a tray bearing a plate of scrambled eggs on toast and a cup of hot water with a slice of lemon floating on its surface.

"I think I'm OK with tea again," I say.

"Now you tell me," Sam says, mock-sighing and heading for the door.

"Don't go especially, not for me…"

"You don't mean that, for a minute."

"No, you're right. I mean, if you really insist on me having one…"

"I'll be right back."

I realise I feel refreshed; energised, even. Could this be the beginning of the second trimester wellness? Maybe it's a gift from the spirits we invited to the solstice celebration. Whatever, I am so happy to feel like this. I eat my breakfast and I get out of bed, singing in the shower before I dress. I love the extra-high waistbands of maternity trousers; they're so warm. Everyone should have a pair.

My tummy is expanding at some pace now; I could still be mistaken for just having a larger tummy than normal but when I look at myself in the mirror, naked (not something I do too often, I hasten to add), I can see the changing shape of me.

Downstairs, Sam has the fire going and is sitting drinking coffee in the lounge.

"That smells good! Coffee smells good!" I exclaim.

"Do you want one?" Sam says, jumping to his feet.

"No, thanks, I'd better not – this baby isn't used to too much caffeine. Anyway, you should sit down and relax. You had a long day of work after our early start yesterday."

"I'm fine! And only Monday left to go at work, which is bound to be very quiet and everyone'll leave early cos it's Christmas Eve. Then I'm not back in till January. And, as if that wasn't enough, we've got our week off a few days later."

"You are excitable," I smile.

"I've every reason to be," he pulls me in for a hug and a kiss.

I still have to work today, though – all our Christmas

148

guests will be arriving for the week, and the tree needs to be up before they get here, even though it won't be decorated until later.

Julie is coming and Sam is primed to help. While I wait for the delivery, I go around to each holiday let, hanging a holly wreath on each door, humming to myself as I go, imagining the forthcoming week of good cheer each one of these places is about to host. I also check each house, which Cindy has made beautiful and festive, and make sure each has a hamper of Christmassy goodies on each table. I leave a card next to each hamper, issuing an invitation to the tree-decorating party later, but being careful to stress there is no obligation. This is their holiday. They may not feel like being sociable.

Bang on time, the same delivery man who brought us the wreaths arrives. He unloads the tree and asks me to sign for it, his face and manner entirely devoid of any Christmas spirit.

"Merry Christmas!" shouts Sam, arriving in time to see this paragon of festive cheer clamber back into his cab. "Come on," he says, "Leave that to me. There is no way I'm letting my pregnant wife drag a tree through the yard."

"I'm not your wife yet," I remind him.

"To all intents and purposes, you are," he says. "Unless that sounds like me trying to claim ownership of you. That's not what I meant at all."

"And that's not what I thought you meant. I think it's romantic," I kiss him.

Julie arrives, in the little red car, while we are still kissing. "Oi, you two! Save that for the mistletoe!" She climbs out, brandishing a bunch of the stuff. "From David," she says. "He popped by after he'd been to the Christmas market. Martin and Tyler were in the car; Martin looking very unimpressed and Tyler barely visible between the branches of a tree nearly as big as that one. God knows how he got it in the car."

"David has more than enough Christmas spirit for everyone," I laugh.

"Maybe he nicked that delivery bloke's," suggests Sam. "Now, come on. I'm glad you're here, Julie. Alice was trying to carry this tree round the corner on her back."

"I was not!"

"Doesn't matter. Julie's here now, you just trot ahead like a good little lady."

"It's a good job there's a tree between you and me right now."

I don't feel any less able to do things like carry Christmas trees but I do realise my body's changing; muscles slackening, skin stretching… calcium being secretly sucked away from my bones and my teeth, by this tiny little being I'm carrying around. So I do need to be careful. But I don't like not being able to get stuck in.

Nevertheless, I do as I am told and I lead the way, offering helpful advice to Sam and Julie, who have not got clear vision through the branches. "This way… no, not that way. Left, no, sorry, I meant right. I do apologise, Sam, it's my little lady's pregnant brain going all fluffy. Silly me. Did you bang your ankle?"

Eventually, we get it to site, where the tree stand is positioned, on the gravel area near the entrance to the kitchen and the office; this is the best place for the tree to be visible from the majority of the properties.

"Now we've got to get it in that!" says Julie.

"Let's just take a minute," Sam breathes heavily.

"How did we manage it last year?" I ask.

"We had Luke to help us," says Sam, turning to Julie,

"Where is that husband of yours when we need him?"

"It's a good question," Julie says, slightly glumly. "He'll be back this afternoon. We don't need him, though," she insists, pushing and pulling the tree to try and work out the best way to get it upright. "Should we get the netting off before we put it up?"

"That is going to be pretty prickly," I say. "I'm sure we did it once it was erected last year. I'll go and get the ladder."

"No!" my best friend and boyfriend shout at me in unison.

"I'm sorry, Alice," says Sam, "but you do need to let other people do these things when you can. We will get the tree up, then I will go and get the ladder. You could put the kettle on…?"

I huff slightly at this, muttering to myself as I head off to our house. Behind me, I hear Sam and Julie in fits of giggles as they try to get the tree up and into the stand.

By the time I've emerged with a tray of tea and biscuits – "I am allowed to carry this tray, am I?" – the tree is up. Sam goes to get the ladder and I put the tray on a table.

"Alright?" I say to Julie, putting my arm around her.

"Oh, yeah, just had another fight with Luke."

"What about this time?" I am a bit worried about how often Julie seems to be arguing with Luke these days.

"The usual. Well, not quite. They had their work thing last night and of course Sinead was going and I probably said something stupid about it."

"Probably?" This is so out of character for Julie, who I have never known to be insecure before.

"Yes, well, I had suggested he come home last night, seeing as he's not working today. I knew he had his night out. And god knows he's worked hard enough for it, but I

151

gave him a hard time and asked him if it was because Sinead was going to be there."

"Oh, Julie," I sigh. "You do know there is no way Luke would cheat on you?"

"Yes, I do, and I don't blame him for being so pissed off. And he said he had to work in the early hours of the morning, to catch a client in the US before the Christmas break. Some problem with their site, or something. I'm an idiot, I know. I just feel a bit lonely at the moment."

Tears spring to her eyes and mine mirror them. Being lonely is not something I would associate with Julie.

"I'm so sorry. At least he's coming back today, and then you two have got some time together. Make sure you relax when you can. I know you're still going to be here quite a lot. So get that holiday booked, too, then you can really relax together."

"I will." She hastily dries her eyes at the sound of Sam's return.

17

The tree secured in its place – despite a fresh wind blowing in from a seaward direction, threatening to knock it down again – Sam, Julie and I retire indoors for a very quick lunch before the coming week's guests begin to arrive. Although Julie and I will be working this week, we have reduced the number of nights when Julie will be cooking – which past experience tells us suits our holiday guests anyway; people tend to want to spend uninterrupted time together over Christmas – and I have asked people to let me know two weeks in advance if they need any days out arranging, tables booking, etc., which works frees me up and at the same time is a necessity, given how busy everywhere is at this time of year.

The number of requests I've received have been minimal, although I did have a bit of a struggle getting the Evans family on the 'Polar Express' train service, which runs on a track further upcountry. That was booked up months ago, but thanks to my nice little network of tourism partners in Cornwall, which is beginning to extend into Devon, I was able to find some late availability spaces.

Aside from that, I've booked a couple of tables at the Cross-Section, which was not too difficult, given Sam's friendship with Christian, and some tickets to the Eden Project's Christmas Festival – which looks amazing. That is one downside of working in this business; making arrangements for all kinds of things I'd love to do, and never having the time to actually do them myself. Hopefully, eventually, Amethi will be earning enough money for Julie and I to take on an employee or two and gain a bit more time for ourselves.

We sit at our kitchen table, squeezed into the three seats there.

"I feel like one of the three bears," Julie says. "I think we need to extend this place before your baby turns up!"

"It is definitely going to be cosy when there's four of us," Sam says.

"Ah, you'll be fine," Julie says, and a thought flits through my mind that it's easy for her to say, with just her and Luke sharing that huge four-bed house in town. But I know she'd rather be living here, with a baby on the way, and I kick myself for being so mean-spirited.

"We'll make it work," I say determinedly.

"Of course you will!"

"Here's to a happy Christmas," Julie says suddenly, raising her mug of tea.

Sam and I lift ours to join it.

"Happy Christmas!"

The guests arrive full of Christmas cheer. The Evans family are first to arrive; two young children, their parents, and one set of grandparents. They are rosy-faced and full of enthusiasm as they get out of the car, the children immediately racing each other around the car park.

"Max! Winnie! Watch out. And don't mess up the gravel, or you'll be out here raking it all back into place!" Mr Evans says, turning to me. "Sorry about that."

"It's no problem; my dad enjoys raking it all nice and smooth again, anyway. They're keeping him busy! Welcome to Amethi."

"This place looks amazing," Mrs Evans comes to join us. "What do you think, Mum?"

"Just beautiful," the older woman climbs elegantly out of the people carrier. "We stopped in town as well, didn't we? Had a little walk by the sea… you can probably tell from my red cheeks!"

"Nothing like a bit of sea air," her husband joins us, too. "Now then, you must be Alice. I'm Derek, we spoke on the phone."

"Of course. Nice to meet you, Derek." I haven't missed his wink; although Mr Evans booked the holiday, Derek called to secretly arrange the Polar Express train ride.

"You spoke on the…?" Mrs Evans asks.

"Yes, yes, just wanting to make sure there are enough bathrooms for us all. You know what I'm like during the night. Up and down like a jack-in-the-box, isn't that right, Pam?"

"That's one way of putting it," Pam says drily.

I lead the way and show them to their house; they *ooh* and *aah* in all the right places, as they spot the huge Christmas tree on the way over, and the Christmas hamper in the kitchen, then the pile of logs stacked neatly by their fireplace. "We have a woodpile, tucked away behind the communal area, which I will show you whenever you're ready. Please just help yourselves, and let us know if you need anything. I live on site, with my partner Sam and his daughter, Sophie."

"And would I be right in thinking there's another one on the way?" Mrs Evans asks quietly.

I look down, examine the small bump outlined by my fitted top. "Yes! I didn't know it was obvious, yet."

"It's not, at all. I just happened to notice the way your hand was resting on your tummy, which is what I always did when I was pregnant."

"I didn't even realise I was doing that!"

"Enjoy your last peaceful Christmas," she says ruefully, but smiles widely at her two. "What do you think, kids?"

"We love it!"

"Good, now let's go and help Grandma and Grandad unload the car."

I leave them to it and go up to the office, from which I can hear any more arrivals. I turn the heater on and enjoy a few minutes' peace, pulling my boots off and resting my feet on Julie's chair.

In time, all our guests have arrived; all seem happy, and ready to enjoy their week. In the meantime, it has started to drizzle and I hope that it's a passing rainstorm, as decorating a soggy tree in the cold Cornish rain doesn't seem quite so full of festive cheer, somehow. All comes good, though, and by half-past three, the rain has passed, just in time for our party guests.

First on the scene are David, Tyler and Martin. I kiss the men and stoop down to cuddle Tyler, who squirms and runs away.

"Ty! Don't be so rude!" Martin says.

"You can't blame him," says David. "It is Alice."

"And you shouldn't be so rude, either," Martin gently cuffs his husband's arm.

"It feels like I haven't seen you for ages," I say, leading the way to the communal area, where we have a vat of mulled wine and a non-alcoholic mulled cider on the go. The table is covered with trays of food that we have actually ordered in. I refused to let Julie do any more work for this party, after our heavy week.

"Do you want a drink, Tyler?" I ask the little red-haired tornado, who has spun in through the door.

"No!" he shouts, and runs off outside again, Martin hot on his heels.

"Any news?" I ask David, just as Julie comes in.

"About the adoption?" he asks. "No, nothing more, really – it all looks like it's going to happen, though. I can't believe it. I never thought I'd have children, and now I'm going to have two!"

"That is so great," I say, wishing I'd timed the conversation better, for when Julie was out of earshot.

"Julie, what time's Luke getting here?" is my poor attempt to change the subject.

"Should be any time in the next hour." She could sound more excited about it. I feel David's eyes on me but I don't look at him. Luckily, this is the moment we hear Bea's voice calling from outside.

"Hello-o?" She is with Bob, and Jonathan. We go to greet them all, and Tyler kicks Bob on the shin.

"Ow, you little…"

"Tyler, say sorry to Uncle Bob," says Martin sternly.

"No!"

"Please excuse our delightful toddler," David says.

"Don't worry about it! We were probably all the same at that age."

"No way would Mom have let me get away with that," Bob mutters but Bea gives him a look.

"Come on in, get a drink," Julie says, and they do as they're told, Jonathan following Bea and Bob like he's their teenage son.

"What's up?" I take the chance to ask him. I feel like I haven't seen him very much lately. He annoyed the hell out of me when we first worked together, but that's a long time ago. It seemed like he grew up when he and Lydia got together, but then she dumped him for a career in London, where she is doing incredibly well. I can't help feeling sorry for Jonathan, being left behind.

"Ah, nothing," he smiles. "Thanks for inviting me, the place is looking lovely."

"We needed somebody tall to put the star on top of the tree. That's the only reason we invited you."

"I knew it."

"Seriously, if you'd rather be out in town, with your mates, I'm not going to be offended. Or on a hot date," I raise my eyebrows annoyingly.

"Round here? I don't think so," he says glumly.

I keep my counsel. Get him a beer from the fridge, knowing he is not a mulled wine type of person. When I get back, he's having a laugh with Sam, so I leave them to it and take myself off for a quick wander around Amethi. It's nearly dark already and the air smells of the recent rain, mixed with the smoke emitting from most of the chimneys. Some of the houses have their curtains drawn and the windows glow softly in the winter darkness. As I tread slowly and deliberately across the gravel, I can hear muffled laughter and happy conversation from within the holiday lets. It gives me a warm feeling and I pull my coat around me, smiling.

Soon enough, my parents arrive, then Amber's parents appear, Amber and Sophie chattering behind them. I convince them all to stay, for a little while, at least. Paul and Shona have sent their apologies, but have to attend some terribly important event in London. Shortly after, Stef and April; Stef carrying Reuben, who is burying his face in Stef's long blond hair, and April holding Annabel's hand. We are just waiting for Luke.

"I'll phone him," Julie says. "See where he is."

She takes the phone outside and I see through the window that she looks annoyed. She stomps back in. "Let's begin without him," she says.

"Is everything OK?"

"Yes." Through gritted teeth. She softens slightly. "Fine. He just got held up. He's on his way. I just thought he'd be here by now. But no, work got in the way. Again."

"But you know what work's like, I'm sure he wouldn't choose it to be like this."

"No, you'd think not." Julie helps herself to a large cup of mulled wine and bangs a spoon on an empty glass. "Welcome, everyone," she has somehow managed to switch on a smile which would convince anyone but me, "and thanks for coming to our Christmas party!"

"Mind if we join you?" The Evans family and grandparents are standing just outside.

"Of course not, you're very welcome!" I usher them in. Tyler gravitates towards the children.

"Yes, come in," Julie says. "We need as many people as possible to get this tree looking Christmassy! Do you think you kids are up to it?"

"Yes," Winnie Evans says shyly.

"No!" shouts Tyler, and everybody laughs.

Carrying boxes of outdoor lights and hundreds of sturdy baubles between us, we head outside. There are now just the tiniest glimpses of light in the sky. Sam gets a ladder and he, Bob and Martin begin to wind the lights around the tree. With the help of another stepladder, Jonathan and Julie are able to start taking the decorations we pass to them. The wind from earlier has stepped up a notch, making the job of hanging the decorations all the harder, but it feels like this is lifting the spirits of my friends.

Sam has decided to bring the fire to life, at the other side of the gravel, and some of the guests have gravitated that way. Meanwhile, Tyler, Reuben, Annabel and the two Evans children are darting in and out of the communal area, laughing wildly as they do so. Sophie and Amber have disappeared across to our house.

"We'll be back for the lights going on, Dad," Sophie promises Sam. "Text me when it's happening."

"Sure, because I've got nothing better to do," Sam grins and ruffles his daughter's hair.

"Thought not!"

"You should have invited Josh," I hear Amber saying.

"No way, he'd think this is really lame," Sophie says.

I smile to myself. I think we need to meet Josh properly.

Bob takes it upon himself to keep everybody's glasses and mugs topped up. I stick to the mulled cider, and Dad, Martin and Bea keep me company. I can feel the alcohol fuelling the mood of the others.

"Let's get some music on!" David says. He's been chatting with the Evans grandparents.

"Great idea!" says Julie. "I'll get the speaker." She goes inside and I see her topping up her glass again. I decide to keep a watchful eye on her. She sees me, and half-shrugs. "Just getting this set up," she says, bringing the speaker outside and connecting it to her phone. "Any requests?" she asks the general gathering.

"*Fairytale of New York!*" shouts Sam.

"So obvious," Julie tuts but sets it playing, then goes around asking people for their favourite Christmas songs to add to a playlist.

"Shall we put the lights on?" I ask Sam. "It seems like the right time."

"I agree. Shame Luke's not here."

"Yep, I think we need to keep an eye on Julie, too; she's enjoying those drinks a little bit too much."

"We can't tell her what to do, though."

"No, nobody can tell Julie what to do," I agree. "We'd better just be ready to catch her if she falls."

Sam pulls me around the side of the building.

"What are you doing?"

"Just grabbing a moment," he says, sliding his arms around my waist. "While everybody's distracted. I feel like I haven't told you how much I love you today."

"Only today?"

"No, I mean I haven't told you it today. But I could go off you, you know, smartarse."

"Sorry." I turn my face upwards to kiss him. His cheeks are cold from the winter air, but his mouth is warm and welcoming. I close my eyes.

"I love you so much, Alice." Sam moves his mouth close to my ear, pulls me to him.

"I love you, too." I wrap my arms around his neck and bury my face into his shoulder, dimly aware of the party going on just round the corner, but happy to let it fade into the background, just for this moment.

"Lights! Lights! Lights!" The chanting is growing louder. It is led, I realise, by Julie.

Uh-oh.

"OK, OK!" Sam laughs, putting his hands up. "I just need to let Soph know."

"I'll get her, it'll be quicker."

I hurry home and open the door, shout up the stairs. "Girls! It's time for lights-on!"

"Coming!"

I smile up at Sophie and her friend as they hurry down the stairs, suddenly not too cool for our little Christmas party. I can see they've been doing each other's make-up. Hopefully it won't be too visible in the darkness.

We arrive back at the tree, where everybody is gathered around.

"They're back!" Jonathan shouts to Sam and there is a countdown.

"Five... four... three... two... one!"

The tree is alive with lights, and Sam arrives by my side, slipping his arm around my shoulder and kissing the top of my head.

"Merry Christmas, everybody!" Bob shouts. "Hey, stick that one on the radio, Julie."

"Radio?" she teases. "Surely you mean the wireless."

"Yeah, yeah," he grins good-humouredly, then grabs Bea by the hands and they begin to dance. I see Sophie and Amber roll their eyes at each other but the Evans grandparents join in, then David and Martin, too. I look at Sam.

"No way. Sophie might never speak to me again."

Instead, he goes to tend the fire, joined by Dad. I see them chatting away and I smile, then head inside, where I take a seat near the open doorway.

"Are you OK, Alice?" Jonathan appears by my side.

"I'm fine, thanks," I say. "Just a bit tired. How are you? You seemed fed up earlier."

"Yeah, well, I guess I am. I don't know, Alice. I think I've had enough of being here. Everything seems to be closing in on me. It was OK when Lydia was about."

"I know." I put my hand on his. "But this is the best place in the world!"

"Yes, it is. If you're sorted. If you've got the job you want, and a girlfriend or whatever, but I haven't got either." He swallows. "And I do really miss Lyd, you know. And I love the Sail Loft, but this last year I've been getting bored. Itchy feet, I suppose."

"I get it. I really do. You're the same age now that I was when I moved back down here. Your problem is, you're already here – so while it was exciting for me, for you it's the opposite. But what are you going to do?"

"I don't know. Go travelling again? I'd love to open a restaurant, but I can't see how I could do that. Not here. Everywhere's so expensive. And there are already so many great places to eat. I feel like I need something a bit different, like what you've got here. But I think I might want to be somewhere bigger than here. Look around you, Alice. What do you see?"

I do as he says. All around are families; or older, established couples. The children seize this moment to whirl past us, chubby toddler Annabel giggling as she follows the older children. I smile to see Winnie Evans take her by the hand.

"All the people I love. Or most of them." I smile at him. "But I can see what you see, too."

"Seriously, most of my friends have left this place, or else they're settling down. Buying houses, getting married. Even having kids." His eyes linger on my tummy. "I don't resent them, but I can't see it happening for me. Not here."

"But… this is the best place in the world!" I say again.

He smiles, and puts his hand on my knee. "It is, for you, and maybe it will be for me again one day."

"You're talking like you're leaving," I say.

He shrugs. "Maybe."

"Look, let's meet up one day, have lunch, a proper chat. It's hard to talk now."

To prove the point, Julie stumbles in. "We're out of mulled wine," she hiccups. "What's next?"

"I bought you a bottle of whisky for Christmas," Jonathan says. "Sorry to ruin the surprise."

163

"That is very thoughtful of you," she slurs. "Bring it on!"

I want to tell them to stop, but I know I can't. "Don't drink too much!" I grin.

"Guide's honour," Julie makes a poor attempt at the Girl Guide salute.

"Hmm." I stand and go outside, leaving my two friends to cheer each other up.

The tree is holding its own against the increasingly strong wind. "I might let the fire go out," Sam tells me, "I'm a bit worried about the embers blowing somewhere they shouldn't."

"Good idea," I say.

He and Dad decide to slosh some water on the flames, sending sizzling steam and smoke into the air. It blows around us, then settles at a low level, wreathing the bottom of the tree. Soon, the rain begins again and we all hurry into the communal area, while the Evans family head home.

"We'd better be going, too." David kisses me, a tired Tyler resting against his shoulder.

"No problem," I say. And soon enough, the party breaks up.

"Where's Jonathan?" Bea says. "We need to be going, too."

I look around. I can't see him. Nor can I see Julie. "I'll go and look for him."

I walk to the door of the kitchen. Push the door a little. It is nearly dark inside.

"Shh," I hear Julie's unmistakeable voice. I switch the light on, revealing a very guilty-looking Jonathan and Julie, standing close together, a half-drunk bottle of whisky on the side. I turn, and leave the room.

"Alice…" I hear Julie's voice, but I am filled with anger and I can't look at her right now.

"Jon's going to make his own way back," I say to Bea.

"Is everything OK, Alice?"

"It's fine, thank you, Bea. And Bob. Thanks so much for coming. I hope you have a lovely Christmas." I recover myself enough to say goodbye properly, pushing thoughts of Jonathan and Julie from my head.

Mum and Dad are the last to leave and just as I see their tail-lights disappear between the line of trees, I hear another car getting closer. I know that expensive-sounding engine. It's Luke.

What should I do? Do I go and tell Julie? I am torn, between anger and loyalty.

I decide to go and tell her. By the time I get to the kitchen, Julie and Jonathan are already outside. He is having a cigarette, she is leaning against the wall. Holding her head.

"I shouldn't have drunk all that whisky," she says.

"No, you shouldn't. But now you need to pull yourself together, because Luke's here. Poor bastard," I mutter.

"Alice, you've got it wrong…" Julie begins lamely but I am already on my way back to the car park, plastering a big smile on my face, ready to welcome Julie's husband as he deserves.

"Luke!" I say, as he gets out of the car, and I hug him, then realise he has a passenger. For the second time in as many weeks, I am wrong-footed, by the same surprise visitor appearing in the car park.

"Hi, Alice."

Sam's mum steps out of the car.

18

Before I have the chance to process the sight of this unexpected arrival, the back door of Luke's car opens and out steps a young woman I've never seen before.

Sinead? I think, feeling like my head is spinning.

"This is Janie," Luke grins, then his smile drops. "Sam's sister! Are you OK, Alice?"

I realise I've stumbled slightly. Luke comes over to steady me.

"Sam's got no idea!" he says. "Karen and Janie wanted to surprise him." I notice Luke is looking at me very deliberately. He knows what Sam's relationship with his mum is like.

"Yeah, Janie got in today," Karen takes up the story. "Eurotunnel to London. We just turned up at your flat this morning, didn't we, Luke?"

"Yes, you did."

"Should have seen his face!" Karen cackles.

"Well, I was on a work call…"

"Work!" she scoffs. "It's Christmas!"

Luke looks at me slightly helplessly. I think of discovering Julie and Jonathan in the dark in the kitchen. If I'm not careful, Sam's mum and sister turning up isn't going to be the only surprise he has today. He looks tired. I put my hand on his arm. "I'm glad you made it," I say, then turn to Janie. "And Janie, it's really good to meet you."

"Hi," she says, shyly, and I immediately warm to her. "I hope it isn't too much trouble, us turning up like this."

"They're family!" Karen scoffs. "Of course it's not too

much trouble. Now come on, you need to see this place!" She marches ahead, Janie casting an apologetic look my way.

"I'm so sorry, Alice," Luke says quietly. "I didn't know what to do. And they made me promise not to tell anyone. Was Julie really mad I didn't make it in time? We had to go and get Janie's luggage from a locker, and she'd lost her key, and…"

"Don't worry," I say. "Don't worry at all. And Sam should be happy to see his sister… shouldn't he?"

"Oh yeah, Janie's a sweetheart," Luke says. "It's just Karen who's a, how shall we put it, a *character?*"

I want to race ahead and warn Sam, but evidently Karen has got their first. "Hello Samuel," I hear her say. "Look who's here!"

"Mum…?"

I turn the corner to see Sam carefully extricating himself from Karen's embrace. "And Janie!" This said with more enthusiasm. I can't help but smile to see him hug his sister. She hugs him back and then they stand together, his arm around her shoulder and a grin on his face. Maybe this wasn't such a terrible surprise.

"Luke!" I hear, along with the sound of feet skidding on gravel. Julie arrives in some kind of style, and throws her arms around her husband. "You're back. I'm sorry I was such a bitch."

"It's OK," he says carefully.

You don't know the half of it, I think, looking for Jonathan but he is nowhere to be seen. I realise somebody needs to take control of this situation.

"Come on, everyone, let's get the kettle on." I lead the way to the communal area, ignoring the muttered complaints of "No booze?" from Karen.

"Why don't you and Janie go and get Sophie?" I say to Sam. "She'll be so excited to see her aunty."

"And her gran," Karen interjects.

Behind her, Luke and Julie walk hand-in-hand, Julie holding Luke's arm with her other hand, to steady herself, and also as if she can't really believe he's here. I can't think about what might have happened with her and Jon. I just have to deal with the here and now.

But there is Jonathan, seated just inside the doorway of the communal area. He looks like the tail end of a heavy night out. I find myself feeling sorry for him.

"Are you alright?" I whisper. "Sam's mum and sister have just turned up. *With Luke*," I say meaningfully.

"Oh, right, great. Hi, mate," he says to Luke, standing to shake his hand.

I'm staggered by both his and Julie's ability to behave as though nothing happened.

"I'll get the kettle on," I say, heading towards the kitchen. "Coffee all round?" I don't wait for an answer.

By the time I return, Sam, Janie, Sophie and Amber have arrived and everyone is sitting around the huge wooden table. Sophie and Amber are looking at Janie as though she's Ariana Grande. In the light, I can see Janie is very striking – with Sam's blue eyes but her mum's very dark hair. She also has a ring through her nose, and dark eye make-up. It suits her.

"Here we go," I say, delivering the tray to the table. "I'll just go and get some mugs."

"I'll help," says Sam, and he follows me through to the kitchen.

"Are you happy?" I ask.

"Yes, well, I'm so excited about seeing Janie again. It's been five years, at least."

"She seems lovely."

"She is. But do you mind, them turning up like that?"

"It was a bit of a surprise," I admit, "but they're your family. God knows you spend enough time with my parents!"

"But your parents are easy."

"Family's family," I shrug, then, a thought occurring to me, "Where are they going to stay tonight?"

"I don't know," says Sam. "They can't stay here. There's no room. Don't worry, though, Alice, this is not your problem."

"No room at the inn," I laugh.

"Oh my god, but you're the pregnant one. Should I have got you a donkey?"

"I would love a donkey! But I suspect we have more than enough to think about right now."

We hurry back, with the mugs, and some milk and sugar. Sam pours coffee for everyone. I sip my water.

"So, where are you staying, Karen?" Julie asks, leaning happily into Luke.

"Ooh... I hadn't really got that far," Karen says. "I was hoping we might be able to use one of your holiday lets."

"Sorry, they're all full," I say, relieved to have a genuine reason not to allow her to stay at Amethi. I feel like she's the type of person who might never leave.

"Alice and Julie are up for some tourism awards," Sam says proudly. "You'd be lucky to find a free week here between now and Easter."

"But you said nobody stays in January...?" Karen says hopefully.

"Sorry, we're doing a deep clean then," she says quickly. It's as though Luke's presence has sobered her up; brought her back to earth. I flash her a grateful look.

"Oh, right, well, not to worry. I'm sure we'll find somewhere. It is the season of good will, and all that."

I look at Janie, who is staring into her coffee, her cheeks slightly flushed.

"You can stay at ours tonight," Luke says, and Julie turns to look at him. "Just tonight," he says firmly, to her and to Karen. Julie thinks better of being annoyed, and returns to leaning against him.

"What will we do after that?" Karen asks plaintively.

"I don't know, Mum. You should probably have thought about it before turning up unannounced," Sam says sternly. "And dragging Janie here, too. Janie, if the worst comes to the worst, I am sure you can sleep on our settee for a few nights." He looks quickly at me, raising his eyebrows for approval.

"Of course you can," I say, and Janie sends a grateful smile my way.

"What about me?" asks Karen.

"I don't know. I'm sure we'll sort something out," sighs Sam. Karen looks like she is going to sulk. "It'll be OK, Mum," Sam's tone softens. "You won't be out on the street."

"Do you want to see my room, Janie?" Sophie asks eagerly and Janie readily agrees.

"She's lovely," I say when they've gone and both Sam and his mum look proud.

I get up to stretch my legs, one of which has become restless and twitchy.

"We'd better get going," Luke says.

"Could I get a lift back to town with you guys?" Jonathan asks Luke. Between him and Sam's mum, I don't know who has more of a nerve.

"Of course, as long as you're not going to be sick."

"No, I think that coffee's sorted me out."

"Then no worries. Come on." Luke stands and Julie, Karen and Jon follow suit.

"I'll get Janie," says Sam.

I walk with the others to the car. Karen takes the front seat, which leaves Jon and Julie to get in the back.

"Why doesn't Janie go in the middle?" I say. "She's the slimmest of the three of you."

"What are you trying to say?" Julie asks, hugging me. "Nothing happened, you know," she whispers in my ear.

"It's none of my business," I whisper back and before she can reply, she sees Luke looking across the top of the car at us. Julie just hugs me tighter. "Don't say anything, I'll explain as soon as I can."

"Sure." I kiss her cheek and she sinks gratefully into the car, shifting across to the other side. This is not a car made for three full-sized adult passengers in the back, but it will have to do. Jonathan stands by, waiting for Janie.

"It's nice to meet you, Alice," she says before she gets in.

"You too, Janie. I'm sorry we're all so tired tonight. I hope we get a chance to spend some proper time together in the next couple of days."

She smiles, and turns to hug Sam. "It's so good to see you," I hear her say and then she gets in, Jonathan gallantly holding the door open, then wedging himself in next to her. I close door, and he presses his face against the window, trying to make me laugh. I'm not in the mood.

As the car disappears down the drive, Sam puts his arm around me. "Come on," he says. "That's enough excitement for tonight. Let me make you a cup of hot chocolate and carry you up to bed."

"As tempting as that sounds, how about I go up to bed and you carry the hot chocolate upstairs?"

"It's a deal." He stops, turns me to him. Kisses me on the lips.

"What's that for?"

"Just for being great. My mum and sister turn up like that and you welcome them in. Even Mum."

"What else could I do?" I ask. "And anyway, it is lovely to see you and Janie together. I could see immediately how happy you were."

"I miss her," he admits. "I try not to think about it, but she's my sister. And poor Janie's been stuck with Mum for longer than I was."

"Well, she's welcome here any time. Let's make sure we make the most of her being back in Cornwall."

We walk, arms around each other, slowly back to our house. All is quiet when we get in but then I hear the unmistakeable giggles of Sophie and Amber. I think of Julie and me at that age. We were just the same. I'm sad to think of Julie at the moment. I know she's in a state. I wish I could help, but I'm also annoyed at her. I want to know what happened with her and Jonathan. I suspect it might be a good job I walked in when I did.

That is all for tomorrow, though. I pull off my clothes and wriggle into my pyjamas, then sink gratefully into bed, falling swiftly into a deep sleep so that I don't hear Sam come up the stairs and place the hot chocolate softly on the bedside table. I stir ever so slightly as he kisses my forehead. "I love you," he whispers and, eyes closed, I just smile, and fall back to sleep.

19

There are two days until Christmas Day and walking through town lifts my spirits. Despite the murky grey clouds hanging threateningly overhead, the streets are alive with last-minute shoppers, and holiday-makers, bundled into warm coats, scarves, hats and gloves. Couples hanging onto each other's arms.

The old cobbled street may be full of different shops these days but the buildings are the same as ever and it's easy to imagine the place a hundred years ago; people walking with paper-wrapped bundles; ordering their Christmas turkey from the butcher's; children pressing rosy cheeks against a toy shop window. It's a scene borrowed from a film or a story book, of course, and I'd love to know what life was like back then, for the people who lived in this town. Did the fishermen get Christmas Day off work? Would the average family here have been able to afford a turkey for dinner? What would they make of the town now, with its fudge shops and bakeries interspersed with expensive clothing retailers and restaurants? They may be shocked but this is life now, and as I make my way through the steady stream of smiling, festive shoppers underneath the strings of pretty Christmas lights, I can't help but fill with Christmas cheer.

I am on my way to meet David, for lunch. I called him this morning and immediately he could tell something was not right.

"What is it, Alice?"

"Oh, it's something and nothing. Well, it's a few things, actually. It's... can I meet you? I just need to talk to somebody."

"Yes, of course... as long as Martin doesn't mind." I heard a muffled conversation between the two of them. "That's fine," David's attention returned to me. "And actually, I can get his present while I'm out. Pop into Boots for some aftershave or something."

"I heard that!" Martin's voice in the background.

"Have you not got his present yet?" I asked, incredulous.

"Of course I have," he whispered. "Just keeping him on his toes."

At the door to Joe's, I stop and look in. David is already there, which is lucky, as there are no free tables. The bell rings when I open the door and David looks up and smiles.

"Alice," he stands and kisses me, his eyes on my face, looking for signs of trouble. I see him glance at my belly.

"Thanks for meeting me, David."

"What, and miss the chance of a lunch without somebody refusing to eat their food, then chucking the plate on the floor? You're not going to do that, are you, Alice?"

"No!" I laugh. "At least, I don't think so. I'm sorry to only ask you out for lunch when I need somebody to talk to. We should do this more often, just because we want to."

"We should. But we probably won't. We're busy, and very important, people, remember?"

"You're right."

"Now, what's up?"

I go on to describe how Karen and Janie have arrived, unannounced, just in time for Christmas. How Janie and Karen are now staying at an unspecified 'friend' of Karen's.

"No!" David says. "So how long are they back for?"

"That's the thing. I don't know. Karen's been back for nearly two weeks and is showing no sign of returning to Spain. But at least she's got a place to stay. Apparently, the friend's away for a few weeks so she's house-sitting."

"Sounds a bit suspicious! Hasn't she got a job to go back to?"

"Not a regular one, no. And Sam says she's just broken up with some bloke she was seeing so she doesn't seem to have much reason to go back there any time soon."

"And Janie?"

"Janie is lovely. And she's working at an IT company in Spain, in Barcelona. She is definitely only here for a week, and then she has to get back for New Year's, and work."

"Maybe Karen'll go back with her?"

"I hope so."

"So how can I help?"

"I don't think you can," I say. "And really, that wasn't what I wanted to talk to you about. It's Julie…"

"Go on," David doesn't seem overly surprised.

"… and Jonathan."

I watch David's face, as the words register with him. "Julie, and Jonathan?" he exclaims.

"Shh!" I look around, luckily not recognising anybody else in the café. "Yes, well, maybe."

I describe how I'd found them in the kitchen, at the Christmas party. We are interrupted by David's cheese and onion toastie arriving ("Don't tell Martin, we're meant to be on a diet.") and I order the same again, and an orange juice.

"So they were kissing?"

"I think so."

"You think so? Did you see them?"

"No, but they were in the dark, very close together, and looked extremely guilty when I walked in on them."

"Maybe you got there just in time?" David suggests. "Have you asked Julie what happened?"

"I haven't had a chance to. She's been with Luke ever since. She did tell me nothing happened."

"Well, there you are, then."

"But she's been under a lot of stress lately. And Luke's been away a lot. And she thinks he's interested in somebody he's been working with."

"Luke?" David nearly spits out his coffee.

"I know."

"He adores her! As if he'd risk losing her by doing something stupid. Why does she think that?"

I realise I can't say any more. It's not up to me to reveal that Julie's been checking her husband's messages, and I swore I wouldn't tell anyone. I feel bad enough talking to David about my suspicions now, but I know I can trust him, and it's not like I can tell Sam. He's Luke's best mate.

"I don't know," I say.

"So you think she got drunk and did something stupid with Jonathan? I mean, I can think of worse people to do something stupid with…"

I look at him sharply.

"Sorry," he says. "Why don't you ask Jonathan?"

"I don't know. He was pretty down himself that night. And it's not really my place to ask him, anyway. Julie, I should be able to ask anything. I've known her forever, but it's a bit different with Jon."

"There was a time when I thought you two would get together, you know."

"Me and Julie?"

"No, you idiot. You and *Jon*."

I can't say the thought never crossed my mind – once I'd got over what I thought was his arrogance, and when things had gone wrong with Sam – but then Lydia and Jonathan became serious, and I knew where my heart lay, really.

"Nah, never crossed my mind," I say now.

"Really? With somebody that gorgeous?"

"Really," I say firmly.

"OK, I believe you. Thousands wouldn't. But anyway, back to the matter at hand. You want to know what to do about this thing you think you saw?"

"Yes."

"Nothing. Do nothing."

"But if Julie's been unfaithful to Luke..?"

"What? A little kiss in the kitchen at a Christmas party? Is it really worth risking a marriage for?"

I am silent.

"If Julie tells you about it, that's up to her," David says. "Or Jonathan, for that matter. But it sounds like they were both in a bad place, and maybe they just did something really stupid and instantly regretted it."

I mull it over, offering a smile to Joe as he brings my juice and toastie over.

"Alice, you have very high standards, and I don't know if any of us are able to live up to them. Maybe Sam," he concedes. "But people do stupid things all the time. It's obvious to anybody how much Julie and Luke love each other. And you and I both know they're struggling at the moment, trying to get pregnant. If you step in and say what you saw – or thought you saw – you can only make a difficult situation worse. If you suspect there's something still going on, then that's a different matter, but it seems very unlikely to me."

"And you'd be OK if Martin did that to you?"

"God no, I'd kill him!" We both laugh.

"David, I could kiss you," I say.

"Steady on, I'll settle for another coffee," he smiles. "Seriously, Alice, just let it go. You look worn out, and you've got enough to worry about with Sam's mum loitering around, by the sound of it. Just forget it. And enjoy this special Christmas!"

What's that saying: *a problem shared is a problem halved?* I feel like it couldn't be more true than it is now. It's like David's given me permission to enjoy myself and I feel my shoulders relax, as I sit back and look around the crowded, steamy-windowed café, bedecked with tinsel and fairy lights. David smiles at me.

"Happy Christmas, Alice."

After lunch, I head up to Mum and Dad's. I don't want to leave town yet; it may be quiet and peaceful back at Amethi, but just now I am loving the bustle of town. As I walk up the hill, I remember doing this when I lived here, and that terrible Christmas when Sophie went missing. That seems a lifetime ago. I thought Sam and I were over for good. Now look at us.

"The house looks very festive," I say, kissing Dad as he opens the door.

"Alice!" he looks pleased to see me. "We were just talking about you."

"I should hope so. I'm your only daughter. What else is there to talk about?"

Mum appears, smiling. "Of course, you are our only topic of conversation. Actually, it wasn't you. Your dad is getting excited about buying presents for our grandchild next Christmas. Scalextric has been mentioned."

"I'm sorry to disappoint you, but he or she will only be six months old next Christmas! I think we're a few years away from Scalextric yet, Dad."

"Hmm. We'll see. Are you stopping for a cuppa?"

"I'd love one," I say, still enjoying the novelty of being able to enjoy tea again. Mum ushers me into the lounge, where the fire is blazing in the hearth and *Carols from King's* playing through the speaker system. The tree in the corner bears all the decorations I remember from my childhood. I unbutton my coat, cheeks glowing in the sudden heat.

"Doesn't look very Christmassy out there," Mum says, looking through the window.

"Not weather-wise, no, but it feels like Christmas. The star on the church tower… the shop windows… I love it!"

"You miss the town, don't you?"

"Yes, and no. I love the peace and quiet at Amethi, and the wildlife, too. But yes, I do love this place."

"We're looking forward to you staying over," she says.

Christmas Day promises to be a hectic one, beginning at our place with Sophie, then going to Kate's for Christmas Dinner Number One, and on to Mum and Dad's later in the day for Christmas Dinner Number Two.

"I can't wait," I smile.

"And what about Sam's mum? And sister? What are they doing?"

"I don't know," I admit.

"It's up to them," Sam said this morning. "I don't mean to sound harsh, particularly with regards Janie, but we didn't know they were coming. They can't just turn up and expect us to fit everything around them."

I feel bad, though. I've asked Bea if she knows of any last-minute cancellations in town, for dinner, but everywhere is chock-full and there are already waiting lists a mile long.

"Why don't you invite them here?" Mum suggests.

"Really?" Guiltily, I realise I don't want to. I have been looking forward to finishing the day with my parents, and I really don't want anything getting in the way of that.

"Yes, really. It's Christmas, Alice, and it's Sam's family."

"I don't know if Sam would want them to…"

"Alice," Mum says warningly. "I'm afraid this is what Christmas is about, and I am sure Sam's mum will want to spend Christmas with him if she can. I am guessing she won't be able to go to Kate and Isaac's…"

"No, it would be a bit of a squeeze," I concede.

"Whereas we have plenty of space. Too much," she laughs. "Come on, it may not be your ideal Christmas, but let's be generous. Make somebody else happy on Christmas Day."

"You haven't met Karen," I say grimly, but I know Mum's right. And I am sure Sam will love being with Janie, if not his mum. "Thank you, Mum."

"I'd better just check with your dad, too."

"What's this?" Dad asks, appearing with a tray of tea and shortbread.

"Sam's mum and sister. I was saying we should invite them for Christmas dinner."

Dad looks like he shares my feelings. But he knows my mum too well.

"OK," he says, without a great deal of enthusiasm.

"Phil, come on, this is what Christmas is all about."

"I thought it was about presents and nice food and watching TV."

"Hmph. You're better than that. We are all better than that. Everyone should have somewhere to go at Christmas. Anyway, they might already have plans. They might say no."

I already know that is never going to happen.

20

Christmas Day dawns bright and crisp and… no, it doesn't. It dawns grey, and cold, and misty, but we don't care. Sophie bounces into our room with her Christmas stocking, at a very reasonable 8.00 am. She also has stockings for the two of us.

"These are your main presents from me," she tells us, beaming. I can tell she's proud of herself, and possibly more excited about watching us open them than she is about opening her own.

At the feel of the long, woolly sock rustling with paper-wrapped parcels, I feel a familiar frisson of excitement and the memory of childhood Christmases comes readily.

Sophie really has put a great deal of thought into these presents. I have a range of skin oils, which she says will be great for preventing stretch marks – how is it that she even thinks like that? – and some beautiful soaps, a bar of dark chocolate for making drinking chocolate, as well as a bag of chocolate truffles, some hand cream, a pair of soft fingerless gloves, a tiny teddy bear, and a white Toblerone.

"My favourite!" I say, opening the immediately recognisable triangular package.

"I know!" she says proudly.

Sam is opening his Chocolate Orange at the same time. He has also had some gloves, though his are waterproof – "For when you're working at the beach" – and a little reference guide for British wildlife, along with some miniatures of whisky, and some men's skincare products.

"Sophie!" he says, pulling her to him. I see her eyes close

as her head rests on his chest and I feel my heart strings pull. She is at such an age, moving ever further from the little girl she was, but that little girl is still there.

"You are brilliant, Sophie," I say. "Thank you so much. Now, why don't you climb under this duvet and you and your dad have a little rest while I get breakfast on the go?"

"I was going to do that," Sam says.

"No, don't worry." I feel like they could do with a little bit of dad-and-daughter time, and anyway, I quite enjoy mornings in the kitchen. I whip up some pancake batter and, spotting one of our resident robins in the garden, grab a small piece of bread, opening the door and letting some of the mist whirl inside.

The robin cocks its head slightly but does not fly away.

"Here," I tear a tiny piece of bread and toss it to the ground. The robin considers it for a moment then hops across, picking up the bread in its beak then flying off a little way. Just in case I decide I want the bread back.

The bird feeders need refilling, I see, so I top them all up, emptying the water dish and refreshing it from the outside tap. Although it is damp and grey outside, it is nowhere near cold enough for the taps to have frozen. It feels more like autumn than the bleak midwinter.

Nevertheless, the open door is making the kitchen cold. I close it behind me as I come back in and turn on the stove, warming the frying pan for the pancakes and filling a separate pan with milk for hot chocolate or coffee. The little kitchen soon feels warmer, though I am grateful for my slippers' protection against the cold red floor tiles.

Quickly nipping into the lounge, I switch the tree lights on. Back in the kitchen, I bring fruit salad from the fridge, a bottle of maple syrup and a jar of pecan nuts from the cupboard, and a case of tiny pastries from the bread bin, then I begin the pancake-making. I have long since given up trying to flip them. Sometimes it works, but it's such a waste when it doesn't.

With a pile of steaming pancakes centre-stage on the table, I call Sam and Sophie downstairs. They rapidly descend, Sam switching on the radio so we have Christmas carols to accompany our breakfast. It feels nice, it feels cosy, and I feel ravenous.

With full stomachs, and still in our pyjamas, we move into the lounge. The pile of presents below the tree is modest, and most are for Sophie. She loves the top, and her earphones. "Thank you, Alice!" She flings her arms round my neck.

Sam has bought her some CDs and books, and a voucher for the two of them to go out on a dolphin-spotting boat, "When the weather's better."

"Thank you, Dad!"

When I give Sam his gift, he smiles. He shows Sophie. "Must be because I'm such a *fun guy*."

"Da-aaad," she groans and looks at me.

I shrug, "He's your dad."

"Yeah, but you're *choosing* to marry him."

"You've got a point," I laugh. "I got the same for Luke," I tell Sam. "I thought you might enjoy going together."

"I'm sure we will," he kisses me. "Thank you, that sounds brilliant. Though I hope they don't expect us to share a tent, I don't think there's going to be *mushroom* after all that food."

"I could change my mind," I say to Sophie.

It seems wrong not having the fire lit, but as we're going to be heading off to Kate and Isaac's in the late morning, it seems a bit pointless to get one going. Instead, we put on the TV and Sophie and I snuggle under some throws while Sam clears the kitchen. We watch *Frozen* and pretend not to cry. Then it's time to get dressed and get moving. I am glad to see that Sophie has done the same for her mum and Isaac as she did for me and Sam, with stockings packed full of gifts for them.

"Come on," I call up the stairs to Sam. "We have to go!"

"I haven't given you your present yet," he says.

I can't pretend I haven't noticed, but I didn't want to make a big deal of it. He appears at the top of the stairs, his laptop in his hands.

"Sorry, it's not wrapped up – I've been waiting for confirmation of this, and it's only just come in, so I haven't even had a chance to print it out." He walks down the stairs carefully, hands me the computer. On the screen is a picture of a bedroom with floor-to-ceiling windows, and a backdrop of a sunset sky, reflected just outside in... what... a pool?

"What's this?" I ask, excitement rising.

"I am taking you to Thailand. Phuket, to be precise. We fly two weeks today."

"We...? What...? We're going... there? You and me?"

"Yes!" he laughs. "We deserve a break, and it may be a long time before we have the chance to go anywhere like this again. It's just for ten days. I've been looking for a deal for ages, and I was just waiting to make sure we'd got it. And we have!" He is grinning from ear to ear.

My mind starts whirring. "What about Sophie?"

"I'm staying at Mum's."

"What about this place?"

"It's January, your down time, remember?"

"Oh. My. We're really going there?"

I look at the screen again, flick through the pictures.

More rooms like the first one. Crisp white linen on huge beds. Open doors leading onto verandas. Blue skies. Palm trees. The hotel has four different pools. Five different restaurants. A health spa. It is just the kind of opulence which might have me feeling guilty, but right now, as I open the door and my tired eyes take in the damp, cold day, I feel like it is exactly what I need.

The most difficult thing is keeping my excitement contained, and keeping my mind in Christmas mode, rather than gushing on about the holiday that lies ahead of us. I would never have chosen that holiday and Sam knows it, and it's not really his usual thing, either. But he is right; once the baby comes along, anything like that will be completely out of the question.

Nevertheless, Kate very generously lets me babble on for a while. It's her fault, she asked me about it.

"I can't believe it. I… can't… believe it. It seems totally out of the question that we might ever go somewhere like that. And I would normally say it's not really my kind of thing, but you should see it, it's amazing, I think it is possibly exactly my kind of thing! But we're so lucky, I know we're so lucky, to be able to go somewhere like that."

Kate has not had a holiday for years. She used to take Sophie away up the coast for a week in a caravan, having saved vouchers from one of the papers, but they haven't even done that for a while. And now, starting up the new venture with Isaac, I guess it might be another few years until she is able to think about taking a break.

"You are lucky, but you work hard, both of you. And it's not like it's something you do all the time. You deserve it, Alice, so don't even think about it."

"You are lovely, Kate, thank you."

I hug her and all these thoughts go through my mind, of our initial friendship, and then when I thought she was trying to sabotage my relationship with Sam. How things have changed, and how glad I am that they can.

As predicted, Kate and Isaac are over the moon with Sophie's presents to them. As Isaac opens his little horde, including some yoga socks – "For the winter" – and vegan chocolate bars, I can see he is really touched. I catch his eye, and smile. *See, she does love you.*

We enjoy a lovely, relaxed and unorthodox Christmas meal of curry, poppadoms, samosas and bhajis. Jacob gurgles away in his little seat until Isaac picks him up and holds him while Kate eats. She goes to take the baby but Isaac insists: "No, you eat first, and take your time. There's no hurry." I catch her eye and smile.

Instead of crackers – "All that plastic crap" – Isaac has made beeswax wraps and tied them around specifically chosen gifts for us all. Rose quartz for Kate, as he says it represents unconditional love. Kate looks quite emotional.

I have a carnelian crystal, which Isaac says can help provide emotional support for female reproductive issues.

"She's already pregnant," Kate says, "I don't think Alice has got any issues in that area!"

Isaac looks slightly embarrassed.

"It's lovely, thank you," I put my hand on his.

"They all take some looking after, if you want to do it properly, but these are just symbols, really," Isaac says.

Sam has black obsidian, to help keep him grounded – though to my mind, Sam is one of the most grounded people I could imagine – and Sophie has a bracelet of chrysocolla crystals. "It's meant to help women with communication, self-expression, and education. This is the goddess stone, Sophie," Isaac says almost shyly. "I'd love it if you would like to wear it, and remember, even if we're in Devon and you're here, we are never really far apart. Especially you and your mum."

I don't think there is a dry eye at the table – apart, perhaps from Jacob's – as we contemplate the year ahead.

We leave Sophie at Kate's and go to Mum and Dad's.

"Alice! Sam! Come in!" I see relief on Dad's face and, as I hear Karen's voice in the background, I think I know the reason for it.

Mum is much better at this kind of thing than Dad, who I know will resent having extra, unfamiliar, house guests on Christmas Day. We pull off our shoes, boots and coats, and follow Dad through to the lounge.

"Sam!" Karen exclaims, and rises to kiss him. She may have had a wine or two, I suspect, but she looks happy and relaxed. Janie stands, too, and greets her brother more quietly. I kiss them both, then turn to Mum, trying to assess the situation from the look on her face.

"Happy Christmas, Mum." She looks happy enough.

"And to you, Alice, and you, Sam." She kisses him while Dad, perhaps just glad of some male company, is trying to usher him through to the dining room to select a beer. I sit down next to Karen, and she puts her arm round me.

"How's the mum-to-be?"

"I'm very well, thank you." I really do feel good. It may be the first Christmas in some years since I've not had a drink, and by this time I am usually ready for a sleep, or at the very least to slump on a settee and watch TV. Today, I feel energised. I tell them about our day so far.

"Sophie's really growing up," Karen says admiringly.

"She is. And she's really enjoying having you around, and seeing Janie. I think you're her new idol, Janie."

Sam's sister blushes.

"You are! You're young, and cool, and have a great job. And you live in a foreign country. Sophie can't stop talking about you."

Janie just smiles. Karen steps in.

"Talking about being around for a while," she says, "I've been thinking about that. What with you and Sam having the baby, and Sophie growing up so fast, I think I might stay."

"Stay?"

"Yes!" she laughs. "In Cornwall. Turns out I kind of miss the old place."

21

When Sam heard about his mum's plan, he did his best not to let his face fall, but I could see it, and it was obvious Karen could, too.

"No need to look so excited about it, son!" Her laugh was not one hundred percent convincing.

"It's just a bit of a surprise, I suppose," I countered.

"That's an exciting prospect," Mum said. "Do you know where you might live?"

"I've got a few ideas," Karen said. I had visions of her trying to squeeze into our little house as well. "Somewhere in town, I think."

"What about you, Janie? Are you thinking of staying?"

"No, I've got my job to go back to. I've got another five months left on my contract on my flat, as well."

"Won't you miss the sunshine?" I asked Karen, the sun choosing that very moment to break through the clouds, lighting up the window and causing the wet street to glisten.

"Cornwall's not too badly off," Karen laughed.

"But why, Mum? Why now?" asked Sam.

"Like I said, you're about to have another baby. And Sophie's growing up. I don't want to miss out anymore."

I can understand this, and I could see Mum and Dad were sympathetic, too, but beside me, Sam was tense. I put my hand on his knee. Decided to try and change the subject.

"Sophie did Christmas stockings for us, didn't she, Sam?"

Mum took up the mantle. "Did she? She really is a sweetheart. Make sure you remember to take her present from us, won't you?"

"Of course."

The conversation unsteadily guided away from Karen's plans, for the moment at least, we went on to open our presents and enjoy a Christmas dinner, this one more traditional than the lunchtime curry. It was not the most relaxed meal I've had and at the end Janie's phone pinged. She picked it up apologetically, but her expression brightened as she looked at the screen. "I hope you don't mind if I get going soon," she said.

"Got a date?" Karen asked.

"No!" Janie said hotly. "Sue, thank you so much for dinner; and you too, Phil. It's been lovely. Can I help you clear things away before I go?"

"No, love, that's fine. And you're very welcome," said Dad, who I could see had taken a shine to Sam's sister. "You get going. We'll sort this lot out."

"Well, thank you again. And for the presents. The scarf is lovely."

Karen rose to hug her daughter. "See you back at the house."

"Yes, see you later, Mum. Happy Christmas."

"Happy Christmas, darling."

She was off like a shot into the night, no doubt relieved to have an excuse to get out of there.

Sam and I helped Mum and Dad clear everything away while Karen sat at the table, helping herself to wine: "I don't know where anything goes, I'll be more hindrance than help."

With a pot of coffee, and a tea for me, we played a few

games of cards, but soon the long day caught up with me. I tried to stifle a yawn.

"Are you tired, Alice?" The eagerness with which Dad said this did not escape me. "Maybe you'd better get going. I'll walk you back to your place, Karen."

It was smoothly done, and there was no getting out of it; not that Karen tried to protest, anyway. She seemed content, even jubilant, as she said her goodbyes. I tried not to mind her putting her hand on my tummy without asking. "Merry Christmas, little one," she half-slurred. As she followed my dad out of the house, I heard her exclaim, "It's so good to be home!"

Mum, Sam and I sat quietly for a while, focused on the flames licking the soot-blackened fireplace.

"Shall I make some tea?" Mum eventually broke the silence.

"That sounds great, thank you."

She went into the kitchen, leaving Sam and I to talk.

"So…"

"So," he echoed, still staring at the flames.

"Your mum..?" I suggested.

"Yeah. Shit."

"Do you think she means it?"

"I don't know. I guess so. I did think it was weird she'd stayed so long. Last time she was over, it was for about three days, then she was off back to Spain, saying it was too boring here."

"Maybe she'll come to that conclusion again?" I offered hopefully.

"Yeah, maybe, but from what Janie said, I think Mum's kind of burned her bridges in Spain."

"Really?" Why had he not mentioned this before?

"Yeah, apparently she and her bloke – Steve – were best mates with this other couple, only it turns out that Mum and the other woman's husband were a bit closer than friends."

"Oh."

"It's so fucking embarrassing, Alice, having a mum who behaves like this. And next to your mum, too. I couldn't imagine two more different people," he laughed bitterly.

"Well, yes, OK, but Mum isn't perfect."

"What?" Mum appeared at the door, a tray in her hands and a teasing smile on her face. "I'm not?"

"We were just talking about Karen," I told her.

"Ah, yes, I wondered how you felt about that, Sam. Will it be nice to have her closer?" Mum asked hopefully.

"I doubt it," Sam mumbled.

Mum poured the tea, and Sam told her what he'd told me about his childhood. She didn't say a word; just listened, and thought.

"Well, I can't say I'm surprised that you're not delighted, Sam. But is there any chance she's changed? She realises what she's been missing, with Sophie, and now a new grandchild on the way?"

"I think you're being generous," Sam said, "and I don't think I can be."

"No," Mum said thoughtfully, "it is definitely easier to be generous from a distance."

At that moment, we heard the key in the door and Dad came through, rosy-cheeked and full of energy.

"I needed that walk," he said, "I took a bit of a detour down past the harbour. There are people spilling out of the Mainbrace and the boats look so pretty with their masts lit up. Look, why don't we all go down there? Just for a quick one? I know it's not been the ideal Christmas day, and a bit of sea air might just do us all good."

"Dad, that is an excellent idea," I could have kissed him. I did. "Sam?"

Sam nodded. "Why not? It is Christmas."

Mum prodded the fire a bit, placing the guard carefully in front of it, and we gathered our coats and boots, pulling on hats, gloves and scarves. Dad was right; getting out of the house was exactly what we needed. I held Sam's hand with both of mine, pulling myself close to his side, and Mum took Dad's arm. We walked down the hill, towards, exchanging Christmas greetings with everyone we passed.

Down at the harbourside, the tide was in, the effects of the merry lights of the boats and the pier doubled by their reflections in the gently swaying water. The Mainbrace was packed to the brim with jolly drinkers.

"Will you be alright out here?" Dad asked.

"Yes! Of course," I said. "We'll just lean against the wall, and keep an eye out for any free seats."

"You should have one of those Baby on Board badges," Sam said, "they'd be fighting to give up their seats for you."

"I don't think I'm at that stage yet," I said, happy to see his smile. "But I'll be making the most of it in a couple of months, don't you worry."

Mum followed Dad into the pub and they were soon lost amid the packed room. Sam leaned on the wall and I moved in front of him, putting my hands on his knees. He put his hands on my waist, pulled me close, kissed me gently. "This time next year…"

"I know! Don't," I shivered involuntarily. "I can't wait."

"Even if Mum's here, sticking her nose in?"

"Even then."

Sam turned me gently round, pulling me back so I could

193

lean on him, his arms round my waist and hands on my tummy. As we waited for Mum and Dad to return, I relaxed against him. The only man I have ever been in love with. And I thought about his hands, and how only centimetres away from them was the tiny little person I was longing to meet. Growing every day.

All around us were people enjoying being together, on this one day a year that we allocate for family time, and being with loved ones, and putting problems far from our minds. In the pub, somebody was playing the piano for a good-natured, if not aptly chosen, rendition of *Silent Night*.

We waited for Mum and Dad to return, to toast this special occasion with them, wrapped in the warmth of the good feeling surrounding us; looking out across the harbour, to the deep inky depths beyond and up above, to the star-strewn sky.

All is calm, all is bright.

22

The following week is quiet, workwise. Julie has been at Amethi a couple of times to cook, but I have missed her both times. The first of these, Sam and I had been invited to Andrew and Becky's. I really missed Julie then.

With both Becky and me being pregnant, the conversation was naturally baby-focused, and I couldn't help imagining what Julie would be thinking if she was there. How that kind of talk excludes others, and how painful that might be if you can't get pregnant, or have lost a baby. But it was good to talk to somebody in the same position as me. Their due date is about three weeks before ours and already they're a couple of steps ahead.

"We've been looking at nursery furniture," Becky said. "I know it sounds daft as the baby's going to be in with us for the first few months so it's ages till we'll really need it."

"Becky loves interior design," Andrew laughed. "Sometimes I think she only wanted a baby so she could design its room!"

"I haven't even started thinking about all that stuff," I said, wondering if I'd been remiss. But what nursery, anyway? There is literally no room in our house for a nursery.

"I don't blame you," said Andrew.

"No, I wish I was more chilled about it; like you, Alice," Becky smiled.

Am I chilled about it all? I liked that idea, even if I was only giving the impression of being chilled. I suppose, although the baby is the most important thing in my life, of course, there still are so many other important things going on, and I have to try and compartmentalise it all.

"I'm bored at work," Becky admitted. "So I spend the day trawling websites, if I can get away with it!"

"I must admit, Mum and I have bought a few things for this little one… just clothes. And I really enjoyed it!"

"I wondered when you were going to mention that to me," Sam smiled, and I realised I still hadn't told him.

"You've seen them?"

"Of course! There's not much room in our house to hide anything. I was looking for my walking socks and saw the bags of stuff. It is pretty cute," he admits. "Reminds me of Sophie, too."

"Of course! You've done this before, Sam," Becky smiled. "We'll be able to come to you for advice."

"I don't know about that; it's a long time since then. I feel like I've forgotten everything."

"It's quite scary, isn't it?" Becky turned to me. "How do we know what to do?"

"I don't know!" I think back to the conversation I had with Mum about this, some time before I was pregnant. *You do your best, and you learn as you go along.*

"I'm really glad we're going through this together, Alice," Becky said when we were leaving.

I hugged her. "Me, too." And I meant it. She's a lovely person, easy to get along with, and motherhood is a hugely daunting prospect. "Thanks so much for a lovely evening. Let's keep in touch, and get together again soon."

"Definitely."

As Sam and I walked back to the car, I couldn't help thinking of Julie again, feeling like I was being disloyal. I went straight to the kitchen when we got back to Amethi but she had already gone.

The second time I missed seeing Julie up at Amethi was when Karen invited Sam, Sophie and I over.

"Where is this place?" I asked Sam, looking at the address.

"It's just up the coastal path, along towards the estuary. Mum said it might be better to park at the station and walk up. I think it's one of those little private roads. Where the posh houses are!"

"OK." I was driving, and Sam was nervously clutching a bottle of wine. I hated seeing him like this; it felt wrong to be nervous about seeing your own mum.

"And whose house is it?" I asked, even though I was aware Sam didn't know. I just wanted to keep the conversation going.

"Some friend from way back," he said absently.

I was glad to park the car and have the few minutes' walk. I had been along that path before, many times, and admired the huge houses tucked away up there. I was not prepared, however, for the place that we came to.

"Is this it?" I asked. The house was modern and white-washed, with a balcony wrapped around the front and sides. It reminded me a little of Paul's house, further down the coast – where design and gadgets are key.

Sam checked his phone. "Yep, this is it. Who the fuck does Mum know with a house like this?" he murmured, out of earshot of Sophie.

"We'll soon find out. We can do some investigations. There's bound to be photos up, and other clues. We'll be like PIs."

"Ha."

I squeezed Sam's hand, and strode up the path with him, Sophie holding onto his other hand. We might as well just get on with it.

Karen opened the door before we reached it. "Sam! Alice! Sophie!" Kissing us all. "Come on in. Isn't this place something else?"

"Er, yeah, you could say that," said Sam.

"Whose is it again?" I chanced.

"Oh, an old school friend's. He's away over Christmas and New Year, and said I could house-sit for him. Aren't I lucky?"

"Just a bit!"

She ushered us in and up the stairs, into an open plan living area. "It's a reverse design, to get the most of the view."

I turned to see a window running the width of the room, doors either end leading onto the balcony. Framed either side by the tall old trees was the sea.

"That is stunning," I breathed.

"Isn't it? Just a shame I can't stay forever!"

"Yeah, about that..." said Sam, but I cut him off, thinking it wasn't the right time.

"We bought you some wine," I said, taking the bottle from Sam and handing it over.

"Ooh, lovely, thank you," said Karen. "Now, I know you're vegetarian, Sophie and Alice, and, of course, Alice is pregnant, so I looked up some suitable recipes and we're having Spanish tomato soup and then a vegetarian paella. I hope that's OK."

"I'm vegetarian, too, Mum," Sam said.

"Really?"

"Yeah, for about four years."

"It sounds lovely," I said, quite touched that she had gone to some trouble, and hoping to dilute the tension.

"I'll just call Janie. It was her who made the soup, actually. Why don't you take a seat, and help yourselves to bread, and oils. And olives. I thought I'd give you a little taste of Spain!"

"That's really nice. Isn't it, Sam?"

"Oh yeah, great, thanks." He sounded unconvincing, to say the least.

"Janie!" Karen called down the stairs and soon Sam's sister appeared, coming in to kiss us both.

"It's nice to see you," she said, sitting next to me.

It's weird, and I don't know if it's just because I'm pregnant and subconsciously preparing for motherhood, but I felt what I can only describe as maternally protective towards Sam's sister. Or maybe like a big sister. I'm an only child, so I don't really know.

"I guess you're heading back in a day or two?"

"I wish you didn't have to go," Sophie sighed on Janie's other side.

"I know. I have to go back to work, though," Janie said.

"Will you come back?"

"Of course!" Janie laughed.

"Maybe when the baby's born?" I suggested.

"Definitely, if not before."

"You're always welcome to stay with us, if you don't mind the settee."

"She can stay with me." Karen placed bowls of soup in front of Sam and Sophie. "When I find a place."

"Of course," I said. "But as long as you know you're welcome to stay with us too, Janie."

"Thank you," she smiled. Karen returned with three more bowls of soup, for me, Janie and herself. She sat on my other side, a space between her and Sam.

"This is delicious, Janie," I said, piercing the silence.

"Oh, thank you. It's pretty easy, though. There are so many tomatoes in Spain, and the heat makes them…"

"Oh yes, the tomatoes," Karen cut in. "And the orange trees, and lemons. It's like heaven."

"Then why aren't you going back there?" Sam asked.

I shot him a look but he was deliberately avoiding my gaze.

"You know why, Sam," his mum laughed lightly. "It's time I came home."

"Home," he laughed himself. "It's been a while since this was your home, Mum."

"But once a Cornish girl, always a Cornish girl. Your Sophie is, and Janie is, too, and your baby's going to be – Cornish, I mean. Boy or girl. Sorry to say, Alice, even if you spend the rest of your life here, you'll never be real Cornish."

"Well, the baby will be half me and half Sam, so I guess it isn't going to be truly Cornish, either, then."

"It's a load of old bollocks anyway. Sorry, Soph," Sam said. She shrugged, not in the least bit shocked. "Alice might not have been born here, but she fits in perfectly. Just being born somewhere doesn't mean you have god-given rights to a place. And anyway, what does it matter where you're born? It's who you are, and how you act, that's important."

The temperature was rising. Janie spoke up. "I don't feel Cornish. I've lived two-thirds of my life in Spain. I went to school there. I work there. I speak Spanish, and most of my friends are Spanish."

"Yes, well, I was only saying…" said Karen.

"Well don't," Sam exclaimed. "Alice is my fiancée, soon to be the mother of my child; she runs a business here; she works with loads of other businesses, has loads of friends here, and she loves this place more than you can imagine. You come back after years away, you have no idea what's going on in our lives. You somehow get to stay here, in this, this *mansion*, without paying a penny for it, and you feel you've got the right to cast judgement on who should and shouldn't be here. Who is and isn't Cornish."

"I was just making conversation, Sam," Karen said quietly.

"Don't give me that. There is no such thing as 'just' with you, Mum. There's always a motive – hidden or not. What are you doing, coming back to Cornwall? Don't think you can just step straight back into my life, or assume you have the right to spend time with Sophie, or the baby, just because you happened to give birth to me."

"Sam…" I looked at him across the table.

Karen put her napkin down. Pushed her chair back. Stood and left the room.

The four of us sat in silence.

"Go and see her," I said.

Sam did as he was told. I heard his footsteps echo his mother's down the stairs.

"Mum," I heard him say, and the click of the door closing after him.

I looked at Janie, and Sophie. They both looked shocked.

"They've got a lot to talk about," I said, picking up my spoon and taking another mouthful of soup. I finished the bowl. The eldest of the three of us, a mother-to-be, I felt I should take the lead. "Here, I'll wash these up."

In the end, the three of us cleared everything away. The paella sat keeping warm in the oven. It smelled delicious, but it would have seemed a bit insensitive to tuck in.

"So when are you going back?" I asked Janie conversationally, as though nothing was going on.

"Tomorrow."

"Well, I meant it, about coming to stay. You are so welcome, any time. I could see how happy Sam was to see you."

"Just not Mum."

"No, well... no." I could be nothing but honest.

Sophie took a place by the window. "Do you think we can go soon, Alice?"

"I don't know," I sighed. "We have to wait for your dad."

"I'll go and see how they're getting on," offered Janie, looking at her phone. "I have to go out soon, anyway."

"It's great you've still got friends here."

"Yeah," she said, putting her phone in her pocket.

"All the more reason for you to come back and visit soon!"

Janie went downstairs, knocked softly at the door, and Sam was soon back with us. He looked sad, but his eyes appeared to be dry.

"Shall we go?"

"OK." I stood, and Sophie did, too. We took our coats from the hooks, where Karen had left them, and went downstairs.

"Shall I say bye to your mum?"

"Just give her a shout," he said, so I called my thanks to her. There was no reply.

"Mind if I walk with you?" asked Janie.

"Of course not."

When we reached the car, we took it in turns to hug Janie. Sophie had tears in her eyes and I put my arm round her while Sam hugged his sister.

"Sorry I ruined that," he said.

"You didn't. I know why you're angry. You have every right to be. I'll see you soon, OK? Bye, Alice. Bye, Soph."

We watched her walk towards town then quietly we got back into the car and headed home to Amethi.

23

On New Year's Eve, Bea and Bob were hosting a party at the Sail Loft, for their paying guests and their friends and family. By this point I was shattered, as was Sam, and we opted out. There was also a small part of me that didn't particularly want to be in the same place as Jonathan and Julie, despite David's excellent advice.

"I hope you don't mind, Bea," I said on the phone. "I think I need to sleep, and to start the New Year refreshed and energised. I don't think I'll make it to ten o'clock, never mind midnight."

"That is fine, Alice, I promise. But we must get together soon, before you go on your holidays."

"OK," I said, "though they're not far off now."

"I know – how exciting! I bet you can't wait."

"Warm sea, golden sands, sunshine, all-you-can eat buffets and four swimming pools? What makes you think I'm looking forward to it?"

Bea laughed. "I'll give you a ring in a day or two, and we'll get together. Happy New Year, Alice."

"It's not here yet, Bea," I said. "But happy New Year to you, too."

"It's going to be an exciting one."

"Just a bit."

Sam cooked pasta and made sticky toffee pudding for dessert. By nine o'clock, I felt full to the brim and, sitting with Sam's arm around me in our cosy little lounge, I began to doze off.

"Why don't you just get an early night?" Sam suggested, kissing my forehead tenderly. "I won't be far behind. I might just watch the end of this." We were only about ten minutes into *The Intouchables*, which I've seen a couple of times before anyway.

"I think I might, if you don't mind."

"Of course I don't mind. Go on. We'll get a good sleep tonight, although it might get a bit noisy when the minibus brings the rabble back."

All of the guests staying with us decided to pool resources and asked me to book them a minibus into town, so they could enjoy the celebrations there. Streets flooded with people in fancy dress, bursting their banks and spilling out onto the harbour beach, where a DJ is usually stationed, keeping the crowds entertained until the big pre-midnight countdown, and beyond.

It's a really fun way to see a New Year in but I was happy to stay home, stay quiet, and contemplate the year ahead. As I plodded up the stairs slowly, the cooler air away from the fire woke me a little, but I knew that I'd be asleep almost as soon as my head hit the pillow. I brushed my teeth, put on my pyjamas, and looked out of the window, to say farewell to the old year. I could just see the top of the Christmas tree, lights aglow, the rest of Amethi in darkness. The sky was clear and I decided to leave the curtains open so that when I got into bed, pulling the duvet up over my shoulders, all the way to my chin, I could see a handful of stars. I focused on just one, until it seemed to disappear from view, then I relaxed my gaze and I could see it again.

In the quiet stillness of the night, I thought I could hear the music travelling up from the town. Carrying across from the harbour and over the land. I thought of that place that I love, and all the people I love who were there in that moment. Mum and Dad were planning on going to the Sail Loft, then on to their neighbours'. David and Martin were also not intending to stay too long at the party, for fear that Tyler might implode. Jonathan was going to be at Bea's, as were Julie and Luke; even Paul and Shona, and a few of the local business people I know. I should have gone, really, but I have to 'listen to my body', so everybody tells me, and I just didn't have the energy to be sociable.

I closed my eyes, thought of the sea. Imagined a hot summer day, walking out along the coastal path. Stopping to rest on sun-warmed rocks. Sneaking into that little tumbledown shepherd's hut, where Sam and I once sheltered from a storm. Picking my steps, and my route, carefully, hearing the sea crashing into the rocks far below, waves moving in, and moving out, until I fell asleep.

As Sam predicted, the returning party-goers were quite noisy and either the sound of the taxi doors slamming, or their voices as they called goodnight and happy New Year to each other in what they imagined were hushed tones, woke me. I couldn't help smiling at the sound of them. The whole purpose of Amethi is to make people happy. These people sounded happy. Sam, by then in bed next to me, did not wake. I moved close to him, the cooler air on my face contrasting with the cosy warmth of the bed.

The baby gave a little wriggle inside me and I thought of how big, or small, it is now. I get weekly emails from some mum website I signed up to, keeping me up-to-date with the baby's progress. At seventeen weeks into the pregnancy, the baby is the size of a pomegranate, just over five inches long, and weighs about six ounces.

I moved onto my back, saw that the sky was no longer

clear; a cloud glowing from the light bouncing off the moon. One by one, I heard the holiday let doors close; some more quietly than others. I was awake again, and alert, but all was well. *Happy New Year*, I tried to transmit the message to my baby. "Happy New Year," I said to Sam, turning slightly so I could kiss the back of his curly-haired head. He didn't stir.

And now, the first morning of the New Year, it feels like the whole of Amethi is nursing a hangover. Sophie is at Amber's, and Sam and I stay in bed for a while, revelling in the peace.

Eventually, I head down to the kitchen, looking for juice and toast. I spy my phone on the side and pick it up, to find I have seven text messages to answer.

David: **Happy New Year, Sam, Alice and Bump. Let's hope it's a great one. Love D, M & T xxxx**

Mum: **Happy New Year, Alice, love Mum and Dad. We hope you had a nice restful New Year's Eve xxx**

Sophie: **Happy New Year, I love you xxxxx**
I am touched by this. I quickly reply, *I love you too! Happy New Year, Sophie. Hope you're having fun xxxx*

Stefan: **You missed a great party, you should give Bea a ring. Happy New Year x**

Paul: **Happy New Year love Paul and Shona xxx**
This strikes me as a 'send to all' kind of thing.

Jonathan: **Happy New Year, Alice and Sam xx**

Julie: **Happy New Year to the best friend a girl could ever have. Hic. Only joking, I haven't drunk that much. Looking forward to seeing you in the afternoon for planning and all that good stuff. Love you xxxx**

I put the kettle on then reply to all the unanswered messages. I remember a time when my phone was almost the first thing I thought of after the New Year chimes had rung out. To send good wishes for the coming year to as many people as I could. Now, the phone is an afterthought, but I'd have been gutted not to have received any messages this morning so it's a good job other people are more thoughtful than me.

I do feel slightly sad that I missed Bea's party, but I am sure there will be plenty more of them. Buttering the toast, I hum to myself and then carry the tray upstairs, trying to stop the teapot from sliding off.

"Here we go." I put the tray on the end of the bed then carefully crawl back under the covers.

"This is the life," Sam says. "Can you believe we're going to be in Thailand in a few days' time, though?"

"I actually can't." It really hits me for the first time that Sam and I are going to have a proper holiday together. "Wow!"

"I know! I can't wait. But," he looks at me apologetically, "I am going to have to put in the hours at work between now and then. In fact, I was thinking I might go into the office today. Would you mind?"

"No, of course not. I mean, for your own sake I'd prefer it if you didn't but it's all for a good cause."

"The best," he says, kissing me then reaching for the plate of toast.

By midday, Sam is out and I'm getting ready for Julie to come over. I head to the communal area, laptop under my arm, a load of papers nearly spilling out of a box file. This next year is going to take a lot of planning. I need to ask Julie about Mum getting involved. She has said she's OK with the idea, but I want to be absolutely sure about this, and we need to decide exactly how it should work.

Then there are the yoga retreats, which are all almost fully booked, and the writing courses. We have supplier contracts to renew, renegotiate, or find alternatives to. Also, a budget that our accountant has helped us with, which we now need to go through in detail.

I roll out a huge year planner, which will give us a visual idea of what the next twelve months are going to be like. I look from January 1st to June 24th. I am just six squares away from my due date.

"Hello!" Julie appears in the doorway.

I go to her and we hug. "Happy New Year!"

"And the same to you."

"Sore head?"

"Really not too bad. Luke's currently comatose on the settee, though."

"Poor Luke."

"Poor Luke, nothing! He's a big boy, he knows what's going to happen if he drinks beer, champagne, then more beer… then red wine… then whisky."

"Well, if you put it like that…"

"Where's Sam?"

"He's at work."

"You two are like a power couple."

"We're just trying to get ready for Thailand."

"This time next week, you'll be packing!"

"I know! I can't wait. Have you and Luke got your holiday sorted?"

"Yes," she says and something uncomfortable stirs inside me. I know that voice, that expression.

"And..?"

"Let's get the kettle on, and I'll tell you everything." Julie looks slightly nervous now and that uncomfortable stirring becomes a clench of fear. What's going on?

"So. You know Luke's been having a hard time at work?"

Julie is sitting at one end of the table and I am at a right angle to her, cupping my mug of camomile tea in my hand. The steam rises, carrying its comforting aroma to me.

"Yes. Well, no. Did I know that?"

"He's been working away so much, hasn't he?"

"Yes." It's true, he's been in London far more over these last few months. Which is part of the reason Julie formed that fear about Sinead. I hope that it isn't something to do with that.

"Well, what I hadn't quite realised was how much it's been driving him mad. I've been thinking all sorts of things... well, you know what I've been thinking... and through it all, he's been desperate to pack it in. Or at least have a change. He says he hates the travelling, and he hates being away from me."

Julie looks happy as she says this and, while I am pleased for her, I can't help thinking of her and Jonathan in the kitchen, in the dark, at the Christmas party.

"So he's decided... *we've* decided... things have to change."

"That sounds like a good thing," I say cautiously, still wondering where this is going.

"Shit, Alice, I don't know how to say this so I'm just going to say it."

Here it comes. I don't know what, but I know I'm not going to like it.

"We're going to India."

"You're what?" I put my mug down on the table and look at her. "What do you mean? On holiday?"

"No, longer term than that…"

My mind fills with questions. "What… you're going to live there? What about this place? What about your house, and Luke's business? What about me?"

The words hang in the air for a moment while Julie looks at me, her face creased with concern. "Let me tell you everything. I have a plan. *We* have a plan, Luke and me. And first of all, it is not forever. It's this charity project that Luke's been involved with – the one Sinead works for, actually." Julie doesn't meet my eye and I sense she'd rather I just moved on from that, as she apparently has. "Helping these kids," her eyes are shining now, "who have been working – *working* – in factories. Little kids, rolling cigarettes, can you fucking believe it? Because their families can't make a living from the land anymore, and there is no provision for them. Do you know how old the youngest kids are?" I don't say anything. "Seven. Seven years old. Rolling cigarettes. It's called bidi rolling. Anyway, this project is about providing healthcare, and education, for these kids. And Luke's been offered the chance to get out there and actually work for them. I want to go with him, and volunteer. There are lots of ways I can help, too."

"I'm sure," I say, dumbfounded. Can I really be angry that she wants to leave to do something that sounds so good?

"You know how I've been, this last year, about getting pregnant. I think I've lost my mind a bit. And Luke, too, but we didn't talk to each other enough. Anyway, we've decided to go for it and so, to come back to your question about a holiday, we're not having one. We're going to travel in India when we can. I don't want to leave here, or leave you, Alice, but it really feels like this is the right thing to do, for me and Luke."

I look from her to the table: the year planner; the box file. My ideas. Our plans. What does Julie's news mean for all this?

"But it's not forever," she says, "and I've already got you a chef." She smiles, although has the grace to look slightly unsure of this.

"Have you?" I cannot think what might be an appropriate thing to say.

"Jonathan!" she announces proudly.

"Jonathan?"

"Yes. Do you remember I asked him ages ago, if he'd cover for me here if I got pregnant? Well, I'm not pregnant, but the principle's the same. He's been quite fed up at work, you know."

"Yes, I know." I bristle slightly, thinking, *He's my friend. Of course I know.* Tell me I'm not jealous of whatever happened between them? I do a quick search of my feelings for Jon, but find nothing more than, right now, irritation. That he and Julie have been making these plans without me.

"He's going to come and see you later," she says. I don't reply. "Are you angry, Alice? I don't blame you if you are."

"I'm shocked. That's what I am. I wasn't expecting this."

She puts her hand on mine. "And of course I'm not expecting to draw anything from the business this year."

211

"No." I hadn't even thought of that side of things.

"And this time next year, we'll be back. Ready to start again. Ready to meet your baby!"

My baby. It will be six months old by then. Is she really telling me she won't see my baby till it's six months old?

"Oh, Alice. I'm sorry."

We hug and hold each other for some time. It gives me a chance to let it all sink in. Julie is leaving. I don't want her to go. And I want her to be here when my baby is born. To be part of its life. But that's selfish, I know. She has been more than generous in supporting me in this pregnancy. I know how difficult it's been for her.

"You're my best friend," I sniffle.

"And you're mine," she says into my hair.

A thought occurs to me. "What about our night away? In April?"

"I was thinking about that." She pulls back. Takes my hands. "I wondered if you'd take Becky, instead? I wish I could be there, Alice, but I can't come back just for one night, no matter how much I'd like to. Or take your mum."

"And Luke; his night away with Sam?" I already know what her answer is going to be.

"He could take Andrew," she suggests. "They get on really well, don't they? It might be good for you both, to spend some more time with people who are in the same position as you."

Who are you to say what's good for me and Sam? I think but instead I say, "OK. Well, I mean, it sounds amazing. An amazing opportunity for you and Luke. I think I just need to take some time to get my head round it."

"I know. Of course. Do you still want to go through all this?" She waves her arm towards the planner and papers.

"Well, yes, of course," I say strongly, and a bit meanly.

"I've still got to keep this place running."

"And you will. With your mum, and with Jon. You'll hardly notice I'm not here."

"I don't think so, somehow." My voice sounds strangled as I swallow back a sob. Then I think of something. "Shit, what's Bea going to say about Jonathan coming here?"

"Ah. That's the other thing." What is this leading to? "You need to talk to Bea, really, but I can't not tell you." *Spit it out.* "She's moving to America. Going with Bob, so he can be closer to his kids. And she's selling the Sail Loft."

24

It takes the rest of the afternoon for us to go through all the plans, and I draw up two lists as we go, the first detailing everything we decide and the second all the questions which spring to mind. Julie's absence will affect so many things. We are business partners, and there are legal implications. What if there's a problem, with a building, or a guest – a medical emergency, or an accident… or a death? What if somebody tries to sue us? I would rather not be shouldering this responsibility without Julie, particularly with a baby on the way.

In her absence, Julie wants to sign all decision-making over to me. "I kind of have to; I don't know how easy it will be to get hold of me. Is that OK?"

It'll have to be.

"And you've got your mum to bounce ideas off. Sue will be great. And Paul."

But it's not their business. It shouldn't be their responsibility.

"Jon can keep things covered on the catering side. You know he's done a great job at the Sail Loft. He's going to give you a call to discuss things."

Great. And when did she start calling him Jon, anyway?

It may not sound like it but I am doing my best to be positive, and supportive. It's just that there is a little part of me that can't help thinking this is typical. We have committed to this business and now Julie has changed her mind. She's always been more frivolous than me, which is really how we ended up coming back to Cornwall in the first place. I should be grateful to her for that, and I am.

But now, faced with the prospect of running this place without her, I am angry.

We run through all the items we have both noted down and contact our accountant and solicitor to arrange a meeting in the next week, so we can keep things above board, and work out how and what to pay Jonathan, and Mum. After that, I find I have nothing to say.

"I guess I'd better get going, then," says Julie.

"OK."

"Alice…"

"I'm fine!" I smile unconvincingly. She goes to hug me but I move aside. "I'll see you tomorrow."

"OK." She fishes her car keys from her pocket and I watch her trudge, head down, across the gravel, vanishing into the dark of the cold winter afternoon. Then I run home for cover, unlocking the door and slamming it behind me. I go into the lounge, lie on the settee, and I cry.

"Alice?" It's Jon's voice at the door. "Are you in there?"

Although it is dark outside, I haven't put the lights on.

"Just coming." I push myself up, run my fingers through my hair and wipe my face on my cardigan. Switching the light on, I walk the short distance to the front door and open it.

"Hi," he says, looking at me intently.

"Hi." A pause. "Want to come in?"

He does, quietly, and I shut the door behind him.

"Bit dark in here, isn't it?"

"I hadn't noticed." Why am I acting annoyed with him? It's not Jonathan who's leaving. In fact, he's saving the day by stepping into Julie's shoes. I have a quick internal word with myself. "I'll get the fire going," I say. "Come in."

He hangs his coat and scarf on the banister, takes off his

shoes. "Julie said she's spoken to you."

Again, I experience an irritation that the two of them seem suddenly to be such good friends. All these little conversations behind my back.

"Yep," I sigh. "She did."

"Oh, Alice," Jonathan says, and he puts his arms round me. "I'm not so bad."

It makes me laugh, a little. "I know. And I am so grateful you're doing this. But I can't believe she's going."

"It's not forever, though. And I think I can understand why she's doing it."

"Me too," I admit. "But Julie going… and Bea selling up, too. I don't think I'm built for dealing with so much change." *Not to mention Sam's mum moving back to Cornwall; oh, and the small matter of having a baby in six months' time.*

"I know Bea wanted to tell you herself," he says. "And I have known about it for a while. Bob's wanted to get back to see his kids, did you know he's going to be a grandad?"

"No! So Bea's going to be a grandma. I bet she's thrilled about that."

Jonathan grins. "Yes, she didn't seem too happy at my suggestion they call her Granny. It's part of what's been getting me down, though. I told you I was bored, which is true, but I couldn't see any opportunities, either, and not knowing who might take on the Sail Loft… you know the restaurant's not a huge money-spinner anyway. There's every chance they'll just want to switch the place back to a standard B&B."

"Hotel," I correct him with my best Bea impression.

"Oh, yes, sorry. Hotel."

"But aren't you going to be in the same boat here?"

"Well, yes and no. I like the idea of working a bit differently, and it's only for a year. I hope it might shake things up a bit for me, give me the opportunity to make a few plans of my own."

"Then you'll leave, too."

"I might! But I might not. And anyway, Julie will be back by then. Plus, you're going to be a mum, Alice. You won't care if I'm here or not. You'll only have eyes for your baby!"

I smile again. Grateful for Jonathan's positivity.

"Come on," I say, leading the way into the kitchen. "Let's get a cuppa, have a proper chat about working together again." The prospect isn't so bad.

"Great." He gets out his phone. "I'm just going to text Bea, let her know you know what's going on. And that you're OK. She was a bit worried you'd be upset." He types out a message. "I'll just use your bathroom, if I may." He puts his phone on the kitchen table.

I sit, waiting for the kettle to boil, and a message flashes up on Jonathan's screen. I shouldn't look, but it draws my eye. It's from Bea.

Great. I hope Alice is OK. Have you told her about you and J, too?

So something did happen between Jonathan and Julie! I knew it. I hear the flush in the bathroom and the water pipes come to life. My heart is beating fast. Jonathan's phone screen goes dark. Hopefully, he won't know I've seen anything. *Don't say anything… don't say anything,* I tell myself. *It's none of your business, Alice.*

Just a few years ago I'd have been on it, if not to Jonathan then I'd have been quizzing Julie, trying to find out what's been going on. We fell out about Gabe, her ex, and how I thought she was messing Luke about, that first

217

summer back down here. She wasn't married, then, though. But it's not my relationship, and it's not my place to say anything. If David is right, and it was just a moment of madness, of two sad people comforting each other, then perhaps it really is best left to sink away into the past.

As Jonathan comes down the stairs, I busy myself at the counter, making a fresh pot of tea, noting how he looks at his phone then shoves it into his jeans pocket.

"So you're alright, Alice? About everything?"

"I'm going to have to be," I turn, a smile painted on my face. "Unless there's anything else you want to tell me?"

"No, no, I think we're good," he says.

You little… I think, but David's voice comes to mind again. And I think about Julie and Luke, and how they're heading together into this new opportunity.

I lift my cup of tea in a little salute. Jonathan joins his cup to mine.

"Happy New Year," I say.

"Happy New Year!" He takes a sip of the scalding tea. "Ow! That's a bit easier when it's cold and fizzy." But he lifts his cup again. "To an exciting year, of new beginnings!"

25

The sea seems so alien, so warm and still and turquoise. Like a spa pool, compared to the passionate, restless Cornish waters. But absolutely, unbelievably lovely. It's our sixth day in Phuket and I feel like I have truly relaxed. As though the ten days should start now that I have finally disentangled myself from thoughts of home. Instead, I am fighting the feeling that the scales have already tipped; we are over halfway through this holiday and soon we'll be going back to it all.

Now, I know that is not the way to think. It's very negative, and unproductive, but it's hard to explain just how welcome this break has been, and still is, for both Sam and me. Despite my genuine belief, as described in *Staycation* magazine, that it is not necessary to travel halfway across the world in order to enjoy a holiday, right now I cannot think of anything more perfect.

Sam is lying semi-supine on one of the beach loungers, his paperback open on his chest, while I am wading into the gentle sea. Tiny shoals of tiny fish dart out of my way as I walk through the perfectly, unbelievably, clear water. It spills across my thighs as I stride further out across the gently shelving sand, until the tops of my legs are submerged and the material of my maternity tankini begins to glisten across the round hump of my tummy.

The smells and the sounds of this place are different, too. There are no greedy gulls screeching from the rooftops, waiting to snatch pasties and ice creams. Very few people, considering the expanse of beach. If this were high season in Cornwall, there would be deckchairs and wind breaks, beach tents and kites, all crammed as tightly as possible across the sand. The sea would be teeming with surfers, although they'd be destined for disappointment in this sheltered bay.

Here, a few people laze, like Sam, on the beach loungers, while a couple walk hand-in-hand along the shoreline. There are palm trees at the top of the beach and round the hotel, as well as banyan trees, with their low spreading branches and populations of enormous red ants. The birdsong here is so different, too. Chattering, repetitive chirping, as well as some more familiar sounds, similar to the songs of the robin and the blackbird. At the pool near the back of the hotel, where the complex meets the tropical forest, the sounds are rich and varied. I could close my eyes and listen for hours.

This place is incredible.

I lie on my back in the water; so salty that floating is almost effortless, and there seem to be no currents to pull me away. I look up, check my position in relation to Sam. I'm still in line with him. I lay my head back in the water, feeling my hair spread out. The sun is high at this time of day and I know I will have to seek shelter soon, but right now, nothing could be more perfect. My rounded tummy rises through the surface of the water. I feel the baby wriggling.

Underneath me, the tiny fish play, and up above me the sun beats down on the sea and the land. In Cornwall right now, my parents and my friends will be just waking up. It's hard to imagine them, but impossible to forget.

In the week before we left, Isaac made the move up to Devon, leaving Kate in the flat, which they are trying to sell, but are stubborn in their refusal to sell to anybody who will use it as a holiday rental or second home.

"We'd get more for it, and it would be snapped up, even though it's well out of town, but I'm not doing it," Kate said.

"I think that's great. But aren't you going to miss Isaac?"

"Of course we are, aren't we, Jacob?" She lifted her ever-growing baby up to look her in the eye. He giggled. "But we'll get more time with Soph, won't we?"

"I'll look after her, Kate. Not instead of you," I hastened to add. "But I'll make sure she's OK."

"I have no doubt about that," she said sadly. She paused. "Do you think she'll hate me for leaving, like Sam hates Karen?"

"No. I don't. In fact, I know she won't. You've let her decide what she wants to do. You haven't just upped and left. And you'll see her every two weeks."

"Every two weeks… it's nothing. Sometimes, Alice, I really don't know if I can do this. Maybe I don't want the flat to sell, so I can stay here."

"But you need somewhere larger anyway," I reminded her, "or you will as Jacob gets bigger."

"Yeah, well, you'll be in the same boat soon," she said.

"I know. Don't remind me."

We had waved Isaac off and I was proud to see Sophie hug him tightly then go to her mum, who had tears in her eyes and her baby in her arms. We went inside with her, Sophie playing with Jacob while I chatted with Kate.

Kate and I sat quietly for a while, both contemplating our separate challenges over the forthcoming months. Jason Wilberforce, my sales manager at World of Stationery, would have advised us to call them 'opportunities'. I think 'challenges' is generous.

Sophie is living with Kate and Jacob in the flat while we

are away. She is sharing Kate's bed with her. This could never work in the long-term, but I think they are both glad of the chance for this mother-daughter closeness before they are separated.

I also had the meeting with Julie, the accountant and the solicitor, to get things as watertight as possible while Julie is away. She has waived her right to decision-making if I am unable to make contact with her, which seems to be both a blessing and a curse. I feel a heavy weight of responsibility.

Luckily, Mum can see I'm worried and she's been up at Amethi a lot, asking Julie and me questions and beginning to build up a picture of how it all works. I will at least have her to consult with when it comes to any big decisions.

"But Alice," Julie said when we left the meeting, "how bad can it get, anyway? You'll always make the right decision, but if something goes wrong, it goes wrong. We can put it right, and it is not going to affect our friendship. Nothing can do that."

She was looking directly at me as she said those last words, but I only met her gaze briefly. I couldn't agree with her, although deep down I knew she was right. We have had plenty of ups and downs in our friendship, but they have only ever made us closer.

I know we can get through anything and, having had time to accept that she's going away, I have gradually been able to genuinely see her point of view, and feel less like I am being let down.

It is not all about me, after all.

I'm beginning to look forward to working with Jonathan again, as well. I don't know what Julie would have done if he had said no. I like to think she wouldn't have gone. But that's irrelevant. He said yes, and she is going. And I have to admit I'm feeling quite mature for not having asked either of them what happened in the kitchen on the night of the Christmas party. I'm trying not to feel put out that Jonathan has clearly confided in Bea, as well.

Sam went to see his mum and apologise, although he says that he still feels justified in everything he told her that day. I don't know exactly what happened, but I know he told her how he felt about her just pitching up and expecting to be welcomed with open arms. She had cried, apparently, and said she was sorry, for everything, which just made Sam more mad.

"She's the parent in this relationship," he'd said angrily. "And when she left here, I was barely seventeen. She wasn't bothered about me then, so I don't buy it that she's the slightest bit bothered now. Unless there's something in it for her, of course."

I'd let him rage a bit, blow off some steam.

"Anyway, she said she wouldn't stay. In Cornwall. I think she wanted me to beg her to change her mind, but I didn't say anything. And we left it at that."

So who knows what's going on with Karen?

As I lie on my back in the sun-soaked Andaman Sea, I let these thoughts wash over me, imagining each gentle wave dissolving my worries and carrying them away.

After a time, I begin to feel too hot and I right myself in the water, which is still only just over waist-deep; head back to shore, where I can see Sam has dozed off. The sun is hot on my skin, and the sand underfoot, as I walk up the beach. I spread my towel flat over the lounger next to Sam and I sit and drink from my water bottle before lying down on my side, facing him, listening to the music from the radio in the bar a hundred yards away, and letting the heat and the utter relaxation lull me to sleep as well. When I wake, I swim again and Sam joins me. We float on our backs, holding hands, then bump closer together and end up embracing amidst the gentle waves.

"You'd never do this at home!" I say.

"And neither would you." He grins, kissing me so I taste the saltwater on his lips.

"This is just like that scene in *The Beach*," I say.

"Yeah, a lot of people say I remind them of Leonardo DiCaprio."

"I'm sure they do. And I'm a dead ringer for Virginie Ledoyen."

"Except we're both slightly more attractive."

"Obviously."

Hand-in-hand, we head back to our loungers, wrap towels around our waists and pick up books and water bottles, then we head back to the hotel room. It is not quite as pictured on the website; that was one of their exclusive villas, but still, it has a balcony with a sea view, and an en suite with an enormous bath; more than big enough for the two of us. We peel off our swim clothes and sling them into the sink; get in the shower together, rinsing away the salt, then fall onto our huge, luxurious bed.

"I can't believe we've only got four d…"

"Don't say it!" Sam silences me with a kiss. I'm happy for him to do so. With the reassuring whir of the ceiling fan, we move together, forgetting our worries back home. For the moment, there is only us.

The remainder of the holiday follows a similar routine: get up; eat breakfast; swim in one of the pools, or the sea; doze; swim; eat; doze; swim; repeat. By the time our tenth day comes around, it feels like we have always lived like this.

We eat in the poshest of the five restaurants that last evening, at a table by the open glass doors, where the decking runs down to meet the beach. It is dark by half-seven here, and the darkness comes quickly, though not before we are treated to a spectacular sunset. The night birds screech and the insects burr as we walk, after dinner, on those soft white sands, still warm from the day's sun.

"This time tomorrow…" I say.

"Don't say that!" Sam laughs. "And definitely, this time next week, don't say, 'This time last week…'!"

"OK. I know it's futile."

"Yes, it is, and besides, we have a lot to look forward to." His kind blue eyes are on me and his hand travels gently down to my pregnant tummy. I put my hand on his.

"Thank you, Sam."

"What for?" His voice is soft.

"For… this…" I gesture around me. "For the holiday, and for being with me." There is a lump in my throat and I curse myself for being too emotional.

"You don't need to thank me for anything." He kisses me and I put my arms around him, moving closer. Putting my head against his chest so I can hear his heart beat. I think of that other heartbeat, the baby's, and I wish I could hear it now, too.

I know Sam is right. There is much to look forward to.

26

By the time the day of the awards ceremony comes around, Julie and Luke have been gone for over four weeks. In their absence, our table of twelve has changed so that now Sam and I will be sitting with Paul and Shona, Cindy and Rod, Bob, Bea, Lizzie, Sophie, Josh and Karen. That's right – Josh, and Karen.

Mum and Dad can't come now, as they have offered to care-take at Amethi.

"This is my chance to get my teeth into it!" Mum said. "Without you to tell me everything I'm doing wrong."

"Mum!" I laughed. "I wouldn't have to do that if you did it right."

"Ha."

Jonathan has stayed at Amethi, too, as he needs to provide continuity for the food. Dad might be able to whip up a mean breakfast, but I don't think he's quite up to covering for dinners.

The rest of us have travelled to Bristol for the awards, all staying at the same harbourside hotel. The nerves kicked in the minute I woke this morning. In reality, they have been chuntering along inside me for weeks, especially since Julie left. She was excited to go, but when it came to saying goodbye she was in tears.

"It's only a year," I said, "don't be such a drama queen."

"Sorry," she managed a grin.

"I'm going to miss you so much."

"I can't believe next time I see you you'll be a mum."

"All being well, "I reminded her.

"All being well."

Sam and Luke watched us, their own goodbye slightly less emotional, but nevertheless I knew Sam was going to miss his friend.

"Think of it like me being in North Wales," he had said to us all. "That was three years I spent up there."

"Yes, but I can't just get a train to India," I pointed out.

"And you had study breaks," Julie reminded him. "We're not going to have any of them."

"Alright, alright, don't accept my pathetic attempt at making this easier!" Sam hugged Julie and I managed to extricate my hand from hers in order to go to Luke.

"Make sure this is an amazing year," I said to him.

"I will do everything in my power to make it so." He wrapped me in a bear hug and I felt how much I would miss him, too. He is far and away the best thing to have happened to Julie, and he feels like a brother to me. I'm so glad I never made anything out of whatever happened between her and Jonathan. David was absolutely right.

As we watched them go along the drive and disappear between the trees, Sam put his arm around me. "OK?"

"Yep," I managed, but I couldn't look at him. I wriggled out from under his arm. "I just need a little walk. When I come back, I'll be able to talk."

Without looking back, I turned and strode towards the wildflower meadows, treading carelessly across the brown, broken stems of last year's growth. As soon as I was out of earshot, I let the sobs come, and I kept on walking, to the woods, taking shelter in the bird hide. There I sat, on the slightly damp wooden seat, contemplating the year ahead without my best friend. How could she leave me when I was about to go through the biggest change of my life? But that was one of the reasons she could leave me.

It would be hard to see me go through something she wants so badly and, while she is never a jealous person, I know she was pre-empting the pain. As it is, I can keep her updated from afar and it may seem slightly less real, or immediate, or agonising.

"We're not stopping trying," she had told me, "but at the same time we aren't really trying, as such. We've got this year away and I don't think getting pregnant would be ideal, or having the baby in India, and it's kind of a relief to have a reason not to get pregnant."

I wondered if not stressing about it might make it easier to get pregnant but I wasn't going to voice that thought to Julie.

"When we're back, if we aren't getting anywhere, then we'll go and see somebody. A doctor. Find out what the problem is."

By then, my baby will be six months old. I felt strongly that I didn't want to take that next step without my friend by my side. That she should be pregnant; we should become mums together. But life is never going to work out like that. Instead, I'll have to forge ahead, be brave, and hope that she is able to join me on that road very soon.

Just two weeks later, Sam and I went for the twenty-week scan. We had the same sonographer as before; still, she barely acknowledged Sam's presence, but this time it just made us grin at each other. Anyway, who cared what the sonographer was like? We were able to see the baby so much bigger than it had been at twelve weeks; its head still looking oversized, but its fingers now clearly defined, and we could see the details of its spine.

"Do you want to know its gender?" We didn't.

"Very well. Everything seems to be in order."

She ran the handheld device firmly around my tummy,

while pointing out the various details, describing them briefly then putting the scanner back in its cradle and removing her gloves. We were dismissed. The assistant helped me clean the gel from my tummy then showed us out. Despite the lack of warmth from the sonographer, Sam and I practically skipped out of the hospital. It was just the tonic I needed in the wake of Julie's departure.

All of this runs through my mind as I lean my forehead against the window, high up on the eighth floor, looking down at the busy market which runs alongside Bristol's harbour. The awards ceremony is in this hotel so all we have to do is get changed, and make our way down for pre-dinner drinks at 6.30pm. It's easy, but in a way it makes it harder; I have more time to sit and be nervous.

Sam is in the shower and I go through what I would like to say, should we win any of the awards. Having to go up to accept them without Julie, feeling her absence strongly. But I really don't expect to win anything, so this is probably a waste of energy. But this is going to be a great experience, and exposure for Amethi, as Shona has said more than once.

Sam emerges from the bathroom, a towel wrapped around his waist. "Your turn."

"Maybe I'll have a bath."

"Why don't you have a shower? It'll be quicker. We haven't got that much time, you know."

I glance at the clock. It's 5.45pm. "Shit. When did that happen?"

"Time flies when you're having fun. Now go on, hurry up."

"Alright, alright," I smile. "It's OK for you. You can just relax and enjoy the evening. I've got two worries: if we win anything, having to accept the award, and make a speech; but if we don't win anything, I'll be gutted."

"You're damned if you do, and you're damned if you don't."

"Seems like it."

"You'll be fine, and if you do win – and I can see no reason that you wouldn't – you just have to smile nicely, say thanks very much, and I owe it all to my amazing fiancé."

"Of course. Thanks; that's all settled, then."

I wash my hair twice in the shower, reluctant to get out and face the music. But I mustn't be late, I know that. Eventually, I turn off the water and tread wet footprints into the bedroom, drying myself off in front of the mirror and casting a critical eye at my expanding belly.

"Urgh. I hate getting dressed up anyway, and now I have to deal with this."

"You will look beautiful. Plus, the bump gives you an interesting conversation piece."

"Oh yeah… *do you know what sex it is… when's it due?* Like I'm not asked those questions every bloody day."

"People are just interested. It's nice."

"I know. Sorry, the nerves are making me grumpy. I'll be so glad when it's all over and we're back up in this room. You look lovely, by the way."

Sam is dressed in black tie, as specified on the invitation, and he's even had a shave and managed to tame his unruly hair.

"Why, thank you." He kisses me, running his hand across the bare skin of my tummy. "Now, get dressed and let's go. The sooner we're down there, the quicker you'll settle into it."

Downstairs, the bar is already humming with conversation, packed out with women in evening dresses and men in black suits and bow ties. We spot Paul and Shona, standing near one of the windows. Outside, the night has fallen and the docks are lit up, the bars across the water already busy with Saturday night drinkers.

"Alice, you look lovely," Paul says, kissing me.

"You do!" Shona exclaims. She is dressed in a long, slinky silver dress, and predictably looks amazing.

I kiss her on the cheek while Sam and Paul shake hands.

"I'm so nervous!" I say.

"I'm nervous for you," Shona looks around the room slyly. "I've been trying to find out who's being touted to win and I think you're in with a good chance for both."

"I don't know if that makes me feel better or worse."

"Take a deep breath, Alice. You're here because you deserve to be, so hold your head up and remember you have just as much right as anybody else to be here."

"Thank you."

"It's such a shame Julie isn't here."

"I know. She'd be in her element."

We are soon joined by the others and I begin to feel more at ease, surrounded by people I know and love. Shona manages to strong-arm the event's photographer into taking photos of me, on my own, and with Lizzie and Cindy. "You're all part of the team!" she says.

Should I drag one of them up on stage, if I win something? I am not sure Cindy or Lizzie would be up for that. Would Shona come with me? I tell myself it's silly to think like that; we're not going to win.

Karen comes to me, tells me I look lovely.

"Thank you, Karen." I hug her. I think she's been making a real effort since Christmas. She's working as a cleaner for a holiday letting agency, and living in a small flat in town; little more than a bedsit really, while she decides on her next move. "I'm really glad you could come tonight." I realise I mean it.

"Me too. You and Julie are amazing. I wish I'd been more like you at your age. Or now, even," she laughs.

"I don't know about that."

Nearby, Sophie and Josh stand silently, overawed by it all. We had asked Amber if she wanted to come, but she had a family party, and when Sophie had asked about Josh, I could see Sam wasn't keen. But it's nice for Sophie to have somebody her age here, and I am sure she will be happy Josh has seen her in her new dress. She looks beautiful, and she's starting to look so grown up. Josh's mum, Sharon, has hired a tuxedo for him, and she's driven him up here; he'll be sharing a room with her tonight. I felt bad that she couldn't come to the awards but, "Are you kidding? An evening to myself in a hotel? I'll get room service; maybe use the pool while all you lot are at the awards; I guess it's going to be quiet."

Sophie's going to stay in with Sam and me tonight, then tomorrow Sharon's taking her and Josh to the science museum before bringing them both back to Cornwall.

I smile at the two teenagers. It makes me feel stronger, trying to put somebody else at ease. "Are you two OK?"

"Yes, thanks, Mrs…"

"Alice!" I smile at Josh. "I'm not a Mrs, anyway."

"And Alice isn't my mum," Sophie reminds him. He goes red.

"Don't worry about it! It's so good you two are here, it makes me feel a bit less nervous."

"You don't need to be nervous, Alice," Sophie says. "I bet you win both the awards."

"Thank you, Sophie, but I think that makes me feel more nervous!"

"Sorry!" she laughs.

After half an hour or so, of drinking the free orange juice – I allow myself one small champagne as well – it's time to go through for dinner.

"I need the loo," I tell Sam.

"Of course you do. Go on, I'll wait here, by the table plan. But be quick!"

I cast a critical eye over myself in the over-lit mirror in the ladies'. It's time to do this. In three hours it will all be over.

Deep breath. Nice and slow. In one nostril and out the other.

I should have asked Lizzie to do a yoga session with me to chill me out.

Sam holds out his hand, smiling, and we walk into the event room, among the last to settle ourselves into our seats. I pour a glass of water.

"Steady on," Sam says, "or you'll be needing another wee."

Ah, the romance of it all.

The compère is excellent. Warm, and funny, putting everyone at ease. But then it's time to eat – the awards are after the dinner.

"Why don't they do them first?" I ask Sam.

"I don't know. This is the problem at weddings as well. When we do eventually get married, let's do speeches first, like Luke and Julie did."

"It's a deal. Oh, I wish she was here."

"I know."

I do my best to eat my dinner; tomato soup followed by an excellent salad with roasted cauliflower, itself followed by a summer pudding, which is out of kilter with the season. I hardly make a dent in it. My heart's in my mouth. I pick and push at my food and I know I'm going to be hungry later.

Eventually, the tables are cleared. Shining silver coffee and tea pots are brought around, along with more carafes of water and wine, and trays of gold-wrapped mints. Silence falls across the room as the compère resumes her position on stage.

"Good evening again, ladies and gentlemen. I trust you all enjoyed your dinner. I'd like to extend all of our thanks to the excellent chef, and waiting staff, and would ask you all to join in a round of applause."

We clap obediently and she moves smoothly on to reading the details of the first award, for Business Travel, along with a short description of each of the shortlisted entrants. I know that the first award Amethi is up for – Best Young Business – is third on the list, and I am grateful for not having to wait too long, but as the second award, Best UK Travel Group, is announced, I feel my palms clenching and my teeth gritting.

"Breathe," Lizzie mouths at me and smiles. I try my best, but I don't think I can.

We are up against some stiff competition and I hardly hear the words the compère says about Amethi but I'm dimly aware of a few lines: "… run by two thirty-somethings, so a genuinely young business…." (a few light laughs at this); "in its third year, and receiving rave reviews from the like of *Staycation* magazine…"

I wait, with bated breath, for the announcement, and my mind is a whirl of disappointment and relief as the award goes to a Dorset-based vineyard and hostelry.

"Not to worry, Alice, you were up against some stiff competition," Paul says, a couple of spaces away on my left. Bea is opposite and she offers a consolatory smile.

Three more awards go by until it's the Women in Business category. I don't feel quite so nervous now that we haven't won the first award, but at the sound of the name Amethi, the clenched teeth are back. Again, I try to breathe. I feel an unfair wave of resentment towards Julie, for having let me deal with this on my own.

Except, I'm not on my own. I have all of these people around me. I glance at Cindy and Rod, who are making the most of the free wine and the rare night away from home. Cindy gives me the thumbs-up, just as I hear the words, "And the winner is… Cornwall's Amethi."

Shit. Shit, shit, shit, shit, shit.

I stand, look around. That stage looks a long way away. Without thinking, I take Bea's hand. "You're coming with me."

"What?" She looks surprised, but she stands, her napkin falling to the floor.

We walk, hand in hand, to the stage, up the steps, over to the compère. She smiles and hands the award to me. "Well done."

I hold the award, move to the microphone. The lights are glaring and it's hard to see more than a few smiling, expectant faces, which in a way makes it a little bit easier.

"Thank you," I say, aware my voice is faltering. "I'm expecting somebody to come and take this off me, tell me I've misheard and it isn't ours after all." A little scattered laughter. It gives me heart. "I'm sorry to say that my wonderful business partner, and best friend, Julie, isn't here to accept this award with me. We have dreamed of having a place like Amethi for years and have many people to thank for playing a part in its success. Some of them are here in this room. Paul, Shona, and of course Cindy and

Lizzie." I pause at Lizzie's name. Breathe. "And you may be wondering who this is standing next to me. Well, this is a very important person – *woman* – who has been an inspiration to me and Julie, since we were teenagers. Bea Danson, owner of the Sail Loft Hotel, who built up her business single-handedly and gave us our first jobs in Cornwall. Then she gave us jobs a second time, when we came back. So I'd like to say thank you, Bea; this award is partly yours, and Julie, I wish you were here tonight to accept it with me. Finally, Sophie – I can't see you, but this is for you as well! For whatever you want to be in life."

It is over in moments, and I just hope I've made sense. I turn to see Bea smiling at me, her eyes dewy with tears, so I think it went OK. She hugs me and then we are gone, off stage, back to our seats. I sink into mine, shaking, the award on its side on the table. Sam puts it up straight. "You forgot to thank me."

"I..?"

"I'm kidding!" He smiles. "You were great. I videoed it and sent it to Julie."

"Thank you," I say.

At last I can relax, give my full attention to the remaining awards, and feel overwhelmingly proud at what Julie and I have achieved.

27

March comes in like a lion with a thorn in its paw, and stays that way. The sea is an outraged mass of blues, greens and greys, and the sky almost universally an oppressive grey. Snatches of blue are rare and as for the sun, who knows where that's got to? The trees at Amethi wave angrily in the winds that regularly rampage across the bare land, and I feel sorry for our guests, who have been hoping for some early spring sunshine.

I love the wildness of it all, though, and, lucky me, I will still be here when the sun finally decides to show itself, and spring arrives in force. The holiday-makers seem relatively happy to trundle around town and go for walks along the coastal path, as long as it's not so windy that they'll get blown over the cliffs.

"It's just nice to get away," Mrs Thorpe says, "and to be cooked for."

Jonathan is doing Julie proud, and seems to be enjoying his work here. "It's so different to the Sail Loft, and I don't have to churn out breakfasts every day. I think it might have been that which was really doing my head in."

"I love doing breakfasts!" Dad, who has come up to help tidy the gardens, chips in.

"You say that after five years of it," Jonathan grins.

"Dad's a creature of habit. It might suit him very well." He's been sweeping up the leaves, even though I keep telling him it's a thankless task. He clears the paths and the car park, only for them to look exactly the same again the next day.

"One menu, four or five different choices… it's easy!" Dad grins.

"Another word for it is boring," grumbles Jonathan.

"Well, hopefully that's not going to be a problem here," I say, "and you'd better get on, or we're going to have some very hungry guests later."

"Alright, alright," Jonathan says. "I don't remember you being this much of a slave-driver at the Sail Loft."

"I definitely was."

I leave Dad to it and go into the kitchen with Jonathan, to make sure he's got everything he needs.

"How's life, generally?" I ask. "Is this place really making you feel better?" I am aware that it was more than work that was getting him down. He does seem a lot happier, though. It's nice to see.

"Yeah, I'm really enjoying this! My only problem now is finding somewhere to live. I told you the landlord's selling the flat..?"

"Oh, yeah. Is it on the market already? At least you can stay at your parents' if you need to."

"That is definitely a last resort," he grimaces. "No, I need my own space. I don't want anything long-term, because I don't know what's going to happen when Julie's back. I still think I need to go somewhere new. Get out of Cornwall; for a while, at least. But everything here's on a minimum of twelve months' rent. I was wondering about Kate's flat. You said she was having trouble selling it. Do you reckon she might be up for renting to me for a few months? She must be wanting to get up to Devon. I could look after it, let prospective buyers in, that kind of thing…"

"I don't know. Do you want me to ask her? But what if it sells while you're living there?"

"If you could mention it to her, if you get the chance, that would be great."

That could solve Kate's problem, but then we will be hit with the reality of Sophie and her mum being two hours apart. Whenever Sam tries to talk to Sophie about this, she insists it's fine, but I don't know how it will be when it actually happens. Like many other things at the moment, we are just going to have to go with it. Deal with problems if and when they occur.

I resolve to speak to Kate later, when Sam and I pick Sophie up after dinner at Mum and Dad's. I can tell Dad's keeping something secret. When he's finished sweeping leaves for the day, he comes to find me in the office to say goodbye. "You still coming tonight, then? And Sam?"

"Yes, of course. Is there something you want to tell me?" He looks like he's bursting with news. He's never been very good at keeping secrets secret. He may not give away details, but it's normally obvious that there is going to be a surprise, of some sort.

"No, no, why do you say that?"

"No reason. We'll be there about eight."

"Half-six!" He looks crestfallen. "Your mum said half-six."

"Oh yes, sorry, my mistake." I can't help winding him up. It's clear he really wants us to get there as soon as we can. "Should we bring anything?"

"No, no, just yourselves."

When we arrive at Mum and Dad's, knocking on that all too familiar door, I hear other voices. "Is that Bea?" I ask Sam.

He listens. "Yep, or at least I think I just heard Bob's laugh."

239

"I didn't think Mum and Dad were inviting anyone else. This is weird."

"Alice! Sam! Come in!" Mum seems a little drunk, which is definitely not like her. I kiss her, handing over a bottle of wine – "Ohh, lovely!" – then pull off my shoes and go through to the lounge.

The fire is going and Dad is sitting, rosy-faced, on the foot stool in front of it, listening to something Bob is saying. They all look up and greet us.

"Hi, Dad. And Bea, and Bob…"

"Bea was telling us about your lovely acceptance speech, at the awards ceremony," Mum says, picking up a glass of red wine from the fireplace.

"Oh, yes, well…"

"It was lovely, Alice," Bea said. "It made me doubt whether I should sell the Sail Loft after all."

"I hate being the one to drag her away," Bob says and he starts singing, "Wild horses couldn't drag me away…"

"But you were so generous to come and live over here." Bea's eyes are shining as she looks at her husband.

Is everybody here drunk? There is definitely something weird going on. I look at Dad. He, at least, seems sober.

"Have a seat, Alice," he says. "You too, Sam. Here, let me get you a drink."

Dad returns with a lemonade for me and a beer for Sam. "Here you go, mate." There it is again, that knowing smile. The look brimming with excitement. I keep quiet, though.

"Your mum and I have got some news," he says.

"You're pregnant?" I ask, and everybody breaks into what seems to be nervous laughter.

"No, Alice, and I remember you saying that when we told you we were moving down here," Mum says, smiling. "You'd better get some new jokes. Go on, Phil…" she

240

encourages Dad but appears to be looking at Bea for permission.

Bea just smiles; inclines her head slightly.

"Well, you know Mum's been looking for a new line of work. As well as Amethi, I mean," Dad hurriedly says. "And you know I've been well, erm, trying to find things to fill my time since we moved?"

"Since you retired," I correct him.

"Yeah, OK, since I retired. Anyway, we've given it a lot of thought, and Sue and I have decided we want to buy the Sail Loft."

Silence. All faces turn expectantly to me.

"You're buying the Sail Loft?"

"Yes!" Mum looks at me excitedly. "I've wanted to start something of my own for years but I thought I was getting too old so I never really put much thought into it. But then there was the hospice job; it wasn't for me, and I realised I don't really want to work for somebody else anymore. And I'm really enjoying working at Amethi. I can see the appeal of the hospitality trade…"

It's too much for me. Too many words. I just look at my mum but I don't think what she is saying is registering.

Dad stands next to her. "Give Alice a moment, love. And we wanted to tell you, as soon as we'd got it sorted. It seemed silly to say anything before we knew it would definitely happen. And it's not going to affect Sue's work, supporting you at Amethi. We've still got Stefan and Lauren managing things at the hotel. The main difference will be a role for me, cooking the breakfasts!" Now I know why he was wittering on about that earlier. "And your mum can oversee the hotel and Amethi. We can do it all, I promise."

"Wow, I…"

"Do you mind, Alice?" Mum asks, looking concerned.

"Mind? No, why should I? It's just a lot to take in."

"Well, I do feel a bit like we've just followed you down here, moved into your house, and now we're taking over your hotel."

"Bea's hotel," Bob reminds her.

"Of course, I mean Bea's hotel. But when Alice worked there, it was always her place to me. And she might not want her parents coming in and treading all over her life."

"No," I say, my mind whirring and the baby seeming to respond. It feels like a twirling ribbon in my stomach. "I think I think it's great," I say slowly, looking at Sam.

"Well that's good news," Dad says, "because we've been to see the solicitor today, and the ball is well and truly rolling. Your mum's right that we don't want to tread on your feet but we aren't asking permission, either. We need something for us, Alice."

"I get that," I say.

"So tonight is a bit of a celebration, if you're happy to celebrate with us?"

"Of course we are," Sam takes the lead. "Aren't we, Alice?"

"Yes."

"And I just have to say again," Dad says, "this is not going to impact on the support we're going to give you at Amethi, and in helping look after our grandchild when you need us!"

"But it gives us a purpose here, Alice," Mum looks at me as if willing me to understand. "And a place in the community. So hopefully, over time, we won't feel such outsiders."

"It's a great idea, Mum," I smile. "And I can't think of a better place to take on than the Sail Loft."

It's odd, sitting in the lounge of the house I used to live in, which now belongs to my parents, who are about to take over the hotel I used to run. I suppose I'd assumed they were ready to wind things down a bit now, especially after Mum quitting her job and offering to help me with Amethi. I hadn't ever expected them to want to take on a business, and I have to bite my lip to stop myself telling them how much hard work the hotel is. They must know this already and if they don't, they are going to have to find out for themselves. I guess this is what they've felt like at times while I've been growing up. But they do have the luxury of a general manager, and a night manager. I feel like Dad's going to be challenged the most, making breakfast every day, and I know just how annoying some people can be when it comes to their breakfasts. But again, he'll find this out for himself.

"We won't have champagne just yet," he says. "I feel like that would be jinxing things. We'll keep it on ice until the papers have been signed."

"So when are you thinking that will be?" Sam asks.

"We're hoping for April or May," Dad says, filling up Mum's wine glass and smiling at her. I can't help feeling proud of them.

"I still can't really believe you're selling up," I say to Bea when we're washing glasses in the kitchen.

"I don't think I can, either."

"It must be really weird for you. I almost feel guilty that it's my parents taking over the place!"

Bea smiles. "I'm glad, it's going to people I think will love it as much as I have. And still do. But it doesn't feel real. Not after all these years."

"I bet Bob's happy. He'll get to see his family more."

243

"Yes, and I'll be leaving mine. Just when it looks like David and Martin will be having another child."

David is upset that Bea's leaving, but he doesn't want to put her off. "You will be coming back to visit, won't you?"

"Just try and stop me! In fact, the other part of all this is, I'm buying a flat in town, so I've always got a link here."

"Oh yeah?" I see what's coming and it's going to mess up Jonathan's plans.

"Yes, once your mum and dad made the offer on the Sail Loft, I went to see Kate, and I've put in an offer on her flat."

I laugh.

"What's so funny?"

"Oh, it's just crazy. I mean, I like it, but it's crazy. I knew when I came back here I was moving to a small town, but I had no idea that would mean everything moves in these little self-contained circles."

"It just made sense, to me, knowing that Kate needed a buyer, and that I wasn't ready to completely give up my place here. This is my home, and it always will be."

"So what will you do with the flat while it's empty?" I wonder if she'd let Jonathan rent from her.

"I've already got a lodger," she says.

"Bloody hell. So much for a slower pace of life in Cornwall. I don't think I can keep up. Anyone I know?"

"You could say that."

28

I realised the other day that my belly button's popped out. Every now and then, I can see a ripple pass across the surface, as my ever-growing baby moves inside me. It's a bit like an alien being. I love it.

Mum is up at Amethi more and more, while Dad has started working at the Sail Loft already, at first working with, and then taking over from, the agency chef Bea's had working for her since Jonathan came to us.

I am hearing from Julie on an almost daily basis now, after a couple of months of sporadic messages. She and Luke are in a flat at the moment, in a small city, and she has WiFi, so she's making the most of it.

Just been watching loads of Friends episodes. Can you believe it's already so long since we watched them for the first time? Remember your Rachel haircut?

I've still got it.

Ha ha! How are you? I miss you xx

I send her a picture of my belly.

Is that...? No!! That's gross. No offence.

None taken. I miss you too, like you wouldn't believe.

How's Luke?

He's great. He's loving it. I don't think he's going to want to come back.

Tell him he has to!

He knows. And he does want to come back, too. Think he's missing Sam!

Don't. Sam talks about Luke all the time.

Ah, that's sweet. I hope you talk about me all the time.

You barely cross my mind.

Give my love to your mum and dad, I still can't believe they're buying the SL.

**I know. Weird. But good.
But weird.**

Got to go now, lovely. We're sightseeing today. I'll message you later.

Do. And send me some pics.

I will. Love you.

I love you too xxx

Although it's great being able to message Julie so freely, in a way it makes it harder. I am reminded just how much I miss her. At first, I didn't want to talk to her; it was too painful and I preferred to just get on with things but, as she keeps telling me, she's already a quarter of the way through her time there. I don't want it to rush by too fast for her, but for me, I want it over with now. I want my friend back.

"I'm your best friend now," David said creepily, to make me laugh. "She'll be back before you know it, and it will be like she's never been away. Although, what's Jonathan going to do then?"

"I don't know," I sigh. "He's a bit stuck at the moment; he's only got another month in his flat, then he's effectively homeless. Or living with his mum and dad. I fear it's going to drive him away."

"It won't. He's committed to working at Amethi, till Julie gets back."

"Yes, but if he becomes miserable again, I can't make him stay, can I?"

"You worry too much. It's not good for you, or the baby."

"How are you so calm? It's only two weeks till you get your little girl."

It all seems to have moved so fast but David, Martin and Tyler are indeed about to become a family of four.

"I'm like a swan. Paddling furiously but just so graceful to everyone else. Oh, but she's beautiful, Alice. You are going to love her."

Once everything was confirmed, Martin and David were invited to a number of visits with Esme, and their social worker and hers. Once they had met her a couple of times, Tyler was invited, too. It's all so well thought-out and structured and David says their social worker's like part of the family now. As with Tyler, they are not telling other people anything of Esme's background; just that she is nineteen months old and she's going to be their daughter.

"I feel like she already is," Martin sighed.

I might be nervous about having a baby but I can't imagine how it feels for Martin and David, taking on a child who's had a rough start in life. What issues might she be bringing with her? I know they will be brilliant and I hope that Tyler copes with not always being the centre of attention.

"But that's normal for any kid with a sibling coming into their life," David said.

"They don't normally come already walking and talking, though!" Martin countered. "Can you believe she's talking already? She's not even two."

"Amazing," I said, having no idea at what age a child should be talking. I have so much to learn.

Sam and I have finally got round to picking up bits and pieces for the baby. Karen has actually been very helpful in this. Since Bea offered to rent her flat to her, she seems to have become happier, and more stable, somehow. She's still in the little studio flat for the time being, but she's making preparations to move, and visiting furniture sales across the county, selecting bargains. It seems she's got quite an eye for it, judging by the pictures she's been showing us. She's also been consulting with us as to whether we like the things she spots for the baby. This, according to Sam, is a new side to her character.

"She'd normally just buy something, and tell you how much you need it."

"Maybe she's mellowing."

"Maybe."

Sam has been keeping quiet when it comes to how he feels about Karen renting Bea's flat. When Bea told us, at Mum and Dad's, he went quiet. It was quite a lot to take in, alongside my parents taking over the Sail Loft, but what could we do? What could we say, about either thing? Really, it was none of our business.

It didn't stop us huffing to each other on our way home:

"Don't think Mum and Dad know what they're taking on. They've never run a place like that before."

"And does Bea really think Mum's going to take care of her flat for her? What if she decides to bugger off back to Spain?"

"We sound like teenagers, don't we?"

"Maybe. A little. But still, they should have spoken to us first."

"Should they, though? Isn't this really up to them?"

"I suppose."

"Are we going to want this little one telling us what to do? Or Sophie, for that matter?"

"She already does!" Sam smiled. "But I know what you're saying."

"They're all grown up now," I said. "We've got to let them make their own mistakes."

Anyway, so far, so good, with Karen. She's kept up the cleaning job, and seems to be enjoying it. "I might start my own cleaning business."

"One step at a time, Mum," Sam had cautioned. "Plus, there are a lot of established businesses here, you don't want to go pissing them off."

"Dad!" Sophie looked pretend-shocked at his language.

"Yes, Sam," I put my hand over my tummy. "Not in front of the children."

Sophie and Karen have developed a really easy relationship, which is lovely to see, and it might be just what Sophie needs when Kate goes up to Devon next month. Nobody is going to replace Kate in Sophie's life, but I feel like the more of us she has around her, the better.

Kate, meanwhile, is becoming more upset at the thought of going. I feel terrible for her.

"I don't think I can do it," she says.

"But you have to. I mean, you don't have to, but Isaac's up there, waiting for you. And Jacob. He must be missing you both terribly."

"But how can I leave my daughter?" she sobbed.

"She'll be OK," I said, putting my hand on her shoulder. Feeling useless. "We'll make it OK. And she knows where you are, and that she can join you any time."

"But I shouldn't have put her in that position!" Kate wailed.

I didn't know what to say. Kate is split between Isaac and Sophie, and Jacob, too. He should be with his dad and mum. But then so should Sophie. But it is physically impossible for both of those situations to exist.

"Sophie's fourteen now. I know, I know, not really old. But old enough to travel up to Devon on the train, and I know she's excited about that. Remember when she used to go up to stay with Sam, when he was in Wales?"

"I thought he was a selfish bastard for doing that," said Kate.

"Oh."

"Now he's going to be here and I'm not."

"It's going to be OK." What else could I say?

With all this going on, by the time my night away with Becky comes around, I am more than ready for it. Sam and I took Julie's suggestion, inviting Andrew and Becky along in place of her and Luke on our respective nights away, so Sam and Andrew are all kitted out for a night in the wild, while Becky and I have packed our maternity swimsuits and a good book each, and we're off to chill.

"See you tomorrow!" We wave the adventurers off, then turn to each other. It's weird. This should be me and Julie. But I'm quite looking forward to the chance to spend some time with somebody else who's expecting their first child, to compare notes and hopefully to get excited about it, too.

"I guess we should go, too." I look at Becky.

"Shall we get a McDonald's breakfast on the way?"

It's a good start.

When I walk through the doors of the hotel, I am reminded instantly of Julie's hen do – really, just a night away for the two of us. I wish I'd booked somewhere different now, but of course I hadn't known then that I'd be with Becky, not Julie.

"This place is lush!" Becky exclaims.

"It is," I agree. "And just what we need."

We go up to the reception desk and a member of staff, perhaps seeing our pregnant bellies, rushes around to take our bags.

"Thank you," I smile.

"We should tell them we're lesbians. Both pregnant courtesy of our gay friends, Sam and Andy!" Becky whispers.

We grin at each other and follow the man to our room.

"Oh. Twin beds," Becky says in a disappointed tone and I nudge her, trying not to laugh.

We change into our swimming costumes and robes, pick up our books, then head down to the pool, picking up some of the bright white towels and laying them across two of the loungers.

"I'm going to have a swim," I say.

"I might just lie here and read for bit."

"No worries." I pull my goggles over my head and then go down the steps into the beautifully warm pool. It is a relief to let the water take over, bearing my weight. It's been a while since I've been in the sea; it may sound silly, but I don't feel as confident now I'm pregnant. I am so scared of doing anything wrong; so responsible for this little life within me. Here, in the pool, I can relax.

It's not very busy; just a handful of other people share the water with me, most of whom are doing lengths. I follow suit for a while, with a leisurely breaststroke, then I push off the side and skim the bottom of the pool, bubbles shooting up around me and pushing through the columns of light that push up through the clear water. Breaking the surface, I swim to the deep end, pushing the hair out of my eyes, and I stop for a while, catching my breath, resting my elbows on the bar and letting my legs drift out in front of me. Becky looks engrossed in her book, which is resting on her belly. I am glad of her friendship and grateful to Julie for her wisdom in suggesting Becky come with me.

When I climb out of the pool, feeling that weight once more, I dry myself off, wrap the robe around me; it barely reaches around my stomach.

"I wonder how Sam and Andy are getting on," Becky says.

I glance out of the window. The sky is blue, but the clouds moving across it at a pace. It's not warm out there. "Sam'll be loving it. Still, I think I know where I'd rather be."

"Andy hates mushrooms," Becky says, laughing. "He didn't want to tell Sam, he was so chuffed to be invited!"

I laugh as well. "Oops! He's going to be hungry tonight."

"He's packed a few snacks in his bag, don't worry."

I've left Mum manning the fort at Amethi, with Jonathan. It wasn't easy to do.

"You're going to have to do it soon, love," Mum said. "Anyway, we managed when it was the awards ceremony, and that was with your dad to hinder us! You need to let things go a bit. That baby's not going to wait when it's ready to come out."

She's right and I know it, but it didn't stop me planning and noting down everything I could think of.

"That's some handover!" Mum smiled. "Now you need to go and relax."

And so I do. Becky and I laze by the pool, reading and occasionally having a dip. The steam room and sauna are out of bounds to us pregnant people, so it's a little bit frustrating, but still a much-appreciated break.

We eat a delicious dinner in the restaurant and by the time we've filled our bellies we are tired, and ready for bed. It is 9.00 pm.

"This is it, isn't it?" Becky says, mock-glumly. "It's Saturday, we've got a night away, and what are we doing? Going to bed earlier than we would do at home."

"Things have definitely changed, and I suspect this is just the start of it."

I sink gratefully into bed. It's quite an odd intimacy, sharing a room with somebody I don't know very well. But a good way to get to know Becky better, I suppose.

"Night," she says, turns onto her side, and is snoring within minutes. I hadn't considered this side of sharing a room with somebody. Still, as I read, my eyes grow tired, and a couple of times I have to stop myself from dropping my book. I tuck it under my pillow and turn off the light. I turn my thoughts to Sam and what he might be doing. Sitting by a fire? Probably. It's unlikely he and Andrew will have gone for an early night. Eating enough mushrooms for a family of ten? Possibly. I smile at the thought that Andrew was too polite to tell Sam he doesn't like mushrooms. I hope they're having a good time together. I have a feeling we're going to need some new-parent comrades in the months ahead.

My mind turns to Julie. What time is it where she is? It must be the middle of the night.

What I don't do is think about work. My mind tries to go there, but I am not going to let it. Mum will be in touch if there is an emergency and now I need to learn to let go a little. Because she is right, I will have to soon, and I am going to have to make this baby my priority.

I think of being by the sea, and of sunny days; imagine Lizzie's soft voice describing the scene.

You are lying on your back, looking at the blue, cloudless sky. The sun is just out of sight but you can feel its radiating warmth.

Lying on my back isn't an option these days but nevertheless, the soothing words seep into my imagination, which takes over my tired mind, and sends me into a deep, dreamless sleep.

29

Karen has built up quite a collection of nursery furniture for us, all currently in storage, along with the pieces she's bought for herself, as we have nowhere to put it.

"I was thinking I'd keep it in the flat," she says. "In Sophie's old room – and keep her bed there, too, in case she wants to come for a sleepover sometimes."

"It's going to be a bit of a squeeze, Mum," Sam said.

"You're one to talk! How are you all going to fit in that little house of yours?"

We are still none the wiser.

Sam's says defensively, "We'll sort it."

I have no idea how, but I admire his positivity.

"Well, until you do, I'll just hang onto this stuff, shall I?"

"You do that."

"Thank you, Karen," I say, to make up for Sam's gruffness. "We do appreciate it. You need to tell us what we owe you."

"I won't hear of it! I've missed so much of Sam's life, and I know you two want to get married one day. You keep saving for that if you can. Life's going to get even more expensive when the baby comes along, just you wait!"

"I do already have a child, Mum," Sam says sulkily, sounding a bit like a child himself.

"Come on, we'd better go," I say, standing and pulling him up. "Kate and Sophie will be waiting."

Tomorrow, Kate and Jacob leave for their new life in Devon. Today, Isaac is back and looking after Jacob all day, while Kate and Sophie have some time together. I feel slightly sick at the thought of how much of a wrench this is going to be for both of them. We've promised to meet them for dinner, at the Cross-Section, at Sophie's request.

By the time we arrive, they are already there, standing on the decking outside, looking over the estuary. It's a gorgeous day and the water is looking its best; glossy and shiny in the sunshine, rocking gently in the stillness of the day. A handful of gulls float on the surface, lulled by the motion of the sea.

"Hello, you two."

They turn as one and I'm struck by how similar they are in looks, and how Sophie is not far off her mum's height now. They both look sad, but manage to smile.

"Hi, Alice. Hi, Dad." Sophie comes over and hugs us both, but is quickly back by her mum's side, holding Kate's hand, as though she were a little girl again.

A memory comes to me, of my first meeting with these two. The seawater spilling from Sophie's bucket, waking me from my doze. An apologetic Kate. An enthusiastic Sophie, showing me her rockpool finds. How much they have both changed since then.

"Shall we go in?" Sam says.

Christian has reserved a table in the corner, windows on both sides. The sunlight is slicing through the other side of the room, but here in our corner it is cool and we can sit and enjoy the view along the estuary, or across to the town and the Island.

"So…" Sam says, because nobody seems able to talk.

"We'll miss you, Kate," I say, hoping to hold back the tears.

"I'll miss you, too, Alice. I wish our Jacob and your little one could be friends."

"They will be. We'll be seeing you, often, I hope."

256

In reality, we both know how busy we are going to be, with our babies and our businesses. Sophie will be free to travel up to Devon at weekends and holidays, but for Kate and me, these are the busy times. I feel very sad, all of a sudden, to be losing her friendship, despite the strains we've had between us.

Sam too looks sad and I try to imagine what this means to him. Any romantic feeling between him and Kate is long since gone, I am sure of that, but she has been a key part of his life for fourteen years now and that's not going to change. He and Kate had formed a neat arrangement, with Sophie always at the centre.

This has to be a happy occasion, though; for Sophie, if not the rest of us. We need to make this a positive change and let her see that we are all going to be here for her; whatever, whenever.

"Where's Isaac? And Jacob?" she asks.

"I thought maybe you'd like a bit of time with just me," Kate says.

"Yes, but we've done that. And now Dad and Alice are here, so shouldn't Isaac and Jacob be here, too? And Grandma Karen. And your mum and dad, Alice?"

This is unexpected.

"I'll call Isaac," says Kate.

"And I'll have a word with Christian," Sam says.

Both wanting to make their daughter happy.

Sam stands and goes over to the bar, where the barman lets him through. He comes back, smiling. "Christian says they can do some furniture rearranging. It's not too busy yet; he says if we don't mind it being a bit of a squeeze, we can pull up another table, fit a few more people around it."

He goes to move a nearby table but, "Don't you dare!" Christian calls. "You're a customer. We'll sort all that out."

"Call Grandma Karen, Dad," says Sophie.

"OK," he does as he is told, heading outside to the decking. I see him rubbing his head as he talks. Their relationship is never going to be an easy one, I think. But he smiles as he returns. "She's on her way. But she says she's bringing someone."

"Who?"

"I have no idea." I think of the mystery man whose house Karen was staying in over Christmas.

"What about Sue and Phil?" Sophie asks, standing and holding her drink while a waiter and waitress shift furniture. "Have you called them, Alice?"

"No. But your wish is my command," I say. I follow Sam's lead and go outside. The breeze strokes my skin and I look over the banister as I wait for my parents to answer. The shiny head of a seal appears, out where the water is deeper, like a glass bottle bobbing on the waves.

"Hello?"

"Hi, Mum. Are you busy?"

"A bit... I mean, no. Is everything alright?"

"Yes, all's fine," I reassure her, realising her immediate thought is the baby. "We're up at the Cross-Section, with Sophie and Kate. You know Kate's going tomorrow? Well, Sophie's asked if you want to join us. Isaac and Jacob are coming, too. And Karen, and she's bringing someone," I gossip.

"Ooh, who?"

"I've no idea."

"Yes, we'll come, won't we, Phil?" she calls to Dad, who has no idea what she's talking about. She quickly fills him in and I hear an answer to the affirmative. "We just need to change out of our gardening clothes, we'll be with you shortly."

I feel bad interrupting their peaceful afternoon; they've been quite stressed lately, as they approach the completion date on the Sail Loft. Maybe a little impromptu meal out will take their mind off everything, though.

The table now extended, we thank the staff and take our seats, leaving a space by Sophie for Isaac and Jacob, with room by Sam for Karen and her mystery man, and next to me for my parents.

Isaac is the first to arrive. Jacob is now a chunky seven-month-old, and looks happily and expectantly around as they walk in. He knows he's adorable. Sophie stands to welcome them both, quite the hostess. She brings them over, leading Isaac by the hand. She is pretty adorable, too, but I don't think she'd appreciate me telling her that.

Next come Mum and Dad. Sophie again forms a welcoming committee of one. I am so impressed with her and I know that, even with Kate up in Devon, this girl is going to be just fine.

It's another ten minutes until Karen arrives. I'm disappointed to see that she's alone. Sophie again goes across to the door. It's like she's the proprietor. I watch her hug Karen, then she sees something outside, lets out a little shriek, and jumps up and down.

Sam's head turns, in time to see Janie appear self-consciously in the doorway. A smile breaks out across his face. "Janie!"

He stands as they walk over, gives his sister a hug. "Mum! You should have said."

"Well, she only just turned up today. I had no idea she was coming. Then I thought it might be a nice surprise."

"It is that," he says, smiling broadly.

"The only thing is, we need another seat," Karen says.

Aha, the mystery man. At last.

"You said you were bringing one other person with you." Sam can't seem to help being irritated by most of the things his mum does.

"And I was," she blithely ignores his tone. "It's not me you've got to blame for this."

We look at Janie. Then look to the doorway, in time to see a slightly sheepish-looking Jonathan walking through.

"Well, this is a surprise," I say to Jonathan when we have a chance to chat, after the main course. We are out on the decking, and he's making me feel slightly faint, given how far over the banister he is leaning.

"Yeah, well, I didn't want to tell you, with her being Sam's sister. You know."

"I guess. But still… how long's this been going on?"

"Since Christmas," he says airily. "That party up at Amethi. Remember Luke gave me a lift back? We ended up sitting chatting for hours, after everyone else had gone to bed. She's awesome."

"I can't argue with that. But," a thought strikes me. "You and Julie… that night, in the kitchen…"

"Nothing happened!" he laughs. "We told you that! I could tell you didn't believe it. We were both just miserable, and drunk, and having a proper moan to each other. We left the lights off because we didn't want anyone to find us. But as if Julie would cheat on Luke. And as if I'd risk getting on his bad side. He's massive!"

The thought of Luke beating anybody up makes me smile. He may be huge, but he's one of the most gentle people I know. I realise how relieved I am that nothing did happen with Jonathan and Julie. But then I remember, and the words are out of my mouth before I think about what I'm saying.

"But that text…"

"What text?" Jonathan leans against the banister and looks at me.

"From Bea. I'm sorry, I wasn't checking your messages or anything. It just flashed up when you'd gone to the loo."

"I still don't know what you're talking about."

"It said, have you told Alice about what happened with…"

With J. It hits me. J for Janie, not Julie.

"Oh my god, I am such an idiot. I'm so sorry, Jon."

"You are an idiot, but I always knew that. Anyway, if it had been anyone I wanted to have an affair with, it would have been you," he grins mischievously.

"Yeah, right."

He hugs me briefly. "I'm happy, Alice."

"I'm so pleased that you are. And Janie looks happy, too. But what happens now? She's in Spain, and you're here… you're not about to leave us, are you?"

"No!" he laughs, revealing those beautifully straight white teeth. "At least, not yet. I am here until Julie gets back. I promised you I would be."

"Phew. What about Janie?"

"She's just back for a visit at the moment. It's still early days, Alice. We're going to see how it goes."

"I really hope, for both of you, that it goes very well."

We sit, our little party, at the table, while the sun sets. The plates have long since been cleared away, but we're having too good a time to leave, and I think Kate feels the same as I do; when we get up to say goodbye, it marks the end of her time in Cornwall. The start of her life without Sophie by her side. I want to prolong it for as long as possible.

I glance across at her from time to time; of everybody at the table she is the most quiet. I notice Sophie doesn't leave her side, but at the same time Sophie is talkative; animated; engaging with everyone. When did this girl become so mature?

I catch Kate's eye and I know she is not finished with today. As it turns out, the day is not finished with us, either. I sit back for a moment, place my hands on my tummy. *You're coming into this amazing group of people,* I tell the baby. I feel a hand on my shoulder. It's Dad.

"Can you come outside for a moment, Alice? And Sam, too? Think you can sneak away?" he urges.

I look for Mum and see she's not in her seat. A quick glance outside reveals she is watching the reflected sunset paint the waters of the estuary.

"What's up?" I say, wondering why all the secrecy.

"We wanted to ask you something," Mum says. "We were going to come and see you tomorrow anyway, but somehow this seems the perfect opportunity."

"We're thinking we might move," Dad says.

"What?" My heart drops into my stomach. "But you're buying the Sail Loft…"

"Exactly!" he grins. "We want to move into the Sail Loft. The house is too big for us. And we're going to be at the hotel so much of the time anyway. We're planning to extend the apartment Bea used, by a room or two. Maybe go up into the loft."

"I guess that makes sense," I say. "But what about the house?"

"That's just it," Mum is smiling, as if this should be obvious. "We wondered if you two… you three, including Sophie… four, including the baby, might want to move into the house."

"We can't buy that house," I say.

"No, we realise that. We did think about selling it, but I think it's better to rent it out," says Dad. "You were the first people we thought of!"

"If you'd like to," adds Mum. "You don't have to decide now. We just wanted to let you know it's an option."

I hardly dare look at Sam. Mum and Dad have just offered us the opportunity to move into the house I love more than any other. And back in town, as well. I know what I think, but what about Sam?

"I think that is an incredibly generous offer," he says. "We'd be mad not to. If Alice agrees?"

"Really?" I look at him now, see him smiling at me.

"Really."

"Shouldn't we think about it for a bit longer?"

"What is there to think about? I've been worrying ever since we found out you were pregnant, and Soph decided she should stay with us, about what we should do, where we could go."

"Have you? I thought you were quite relaxed about it."

"I didn't want to stress you out!" he says.

"But I've been worrying about it, too."

"You said it would all work out. I thought *you* were child out about it."

"Well, looks like I was right, doesn't it? There is one downside, though."

"What?" Sam stops smiling.

"The dodgy landlords."

We hug and shake hands, and then hug again. I can't stop smiling. *I am going back home*, I catch myself thinking. Images fill my mind, of the baby furniture Karen has bought for us, in what was Julie's old room… or perhaps up in my old room, at the top of the house, a gull keeping watch from above the window, the sea breeze blowing the curtain gently to and fro as the baby sleeps…

My daydreaming is cut short by the sight of Kate. We go back in, tempering our excitement. The space next to Kate is free. I go and sit by her.

"Alright?"

"I think so. I still can't believe I'm doing this."

"You're not doing anything wrong," I say. "Sophie will be fine."

"I know. It's not just Sophie – although of course she's the main thing. But leaving this," she gestures around her. "You're my family," her eyes fill with tears.

"And we still will be. Always." I look her in the eye. "And it's not like Devon's the other side of the world."

She laughs, wipes her nose. "I guess."

"Look, how about we wrap this up now, get going home? Why don't you come back to ours with us, let Isaac take Jacob home, and you come and spend a bit more time with Sophie, just the two of you?"

"That sounds good."

I pass the message round that it's time to get going; time to say goodbye to Kate, and Isaac and Jacob, for now.

Karen hugs Kate. "We'll keep an eye on Sophie for you." Kate has the good grace to accept this with a smile.

Janie is next. "See you, Kate. We'll come and visit you in Devon, if that's OK?" She glances smilingly at Jonathan.

"Definitely, if Alice lets me have some time off."

"You might have to ask Mum about that," I say, "I'll be on maternity leave soon."

"You'd better stay on my good side, Jon," Mum smiles. "Bye, Kate. Phil and I are definitely booking onto one of

your courses... don't look like that, Phil, it'll do you good."
She hugs Kate. "You'll be fine, and we'll be here, and
Sophie will miss you like you wouldn't believe, but she'll
be OK. Now stop feeling guilty, you've no reason to."

How does Mum always know what to say?

As we walk to the car, I look back along the estuary, the
sunset all but faded into the night sky; just the odd dark red
smudge remaining as evidence of the day that has passed.

I drive and Sam sits in the passenger seat, Kate and
Sophie in the back, their heads resting together. Back at
Amethi, Sam and I sit in the kitchen, while Sophie and
Kate have the lounge. The time ticks on and all seems
quiet. I remember the feeling when Mum and Dad
dropped me at university for the first time. I was terrified
of them going and at the same time I wanted them to go
so I would just have to get on with it. I feel the same for
Kate and Sophie now. They need to make the break, to
get started on their new future and to see, I hope, that it
really is going to be OK.

It's half-past twelve before there is a knock on the door
and a red-eyed Kate puts her head round. "I'd better get
going."

"I'll drive you back," Sam says.

Sophie appears and she hugs her mum from behind her.
She looks small now; a totally different girl to that
confident socialite from the Cross-Section.

Kate gently turns to her daughter. Puts her arms around
her. "I have to go, darling," she says, and I can feel every
ounce of her strength is in those words, keeping the tears
from dampening them.

"Let's wave them off," I say to Sophie, as brightly as
possible.

We make a very subdued party, traipsing across the

gravel and around the corner to the car park.

Sam hugs Sophie, then gets in the car, waiting for Kate.

"Bye, Kate. Take care. We will see you soon," I say firmly.

"Mummy," Sophie says, and she flings herself at Kate.

I want to turn away, to hide my tears. Kate hugs her daughter again and manages to squeeze out the words, "I'll see you next week. Be good, OK?"

Gently, she extricates herself from her daughter's embrace, looking to me. I step up, put my hands on Sophie's shoulders. Kate gets into the car, and I see Sam turn to her. She nods her head. Turns quickly to look at her daughter. Tries and fails to smile.

As the car moves away, I can just make out the shape of Kate, her shoulders crumpling as she gives into the grief.

I put my arms around Sophie and we stand in the darkness, an owl calling from the line of trees while the little girl leaning against me cries, and cries, and cries.

30

Sophie is subdued for some time after Kate has gone, but everybody makes a fuss of her. Amber's family take her on days out, and increase the regularity of sleepovers. Sharon invites her round for tea with her and Josh, every Wednesday. Sometimes she takes them to the cinema, too, but often they just go to the beach, muck about with their body boards with a big group of friends.

Bea and Bob take time out from packing for America to come and visit. I don't know if I can cope with any more goodbyes, but they both seem so happy that it's easier to feel positive about this one.

David, Martin, Tyler and Esme come at the same time. Esme is a little chunk of loveliness and so far, so good with Tyler.

"I'm a big brother," he tells me when he leaps into my arms from his car seat.

"I know," I smile, carefully placing him on the ground.

He runs to Sophie. "I'm a big brother!"

"Are you?" she asks, smiling, leading him across to the wildflower meadows to play hide and seek.

"She's a great girl," David says to Sam.

"I am, aren't I?" I smile.

"I said 'great girl', not 'great big'." David dodges out of the way.

It's true. I am enormous, or at least I feel it. And with the increasing heat, as summer moves into full swing, my feet are swelling unattractively.

Martin moves into view, Esme hanging onto him,

refusing to be put down.

"Another great girl," I murmur.

"She is. It's not easy, though," David says quietly. "And I think she prefers Martin to me. But we'll get there."

I admire his stoicism. How must it work, I wonder, to be able to create a bond from, essentially, nothing? I have had nearly nine months now, to co-exist with my baby. Always aware of its presence. Feeling its movements. Hearing its heartbeat. Both of us monitored and cared for, always together.

I watch David move off into the field, pretending not to see Tyler, whose giggling would give him away even if his bottom wasn't sticking out from behind a patch of giant daisies.

We sit outside the communal area, in the shade, drinking fresh lemonade made by Jonathan. Last weekend, Janie came back again and the two of them drove up to Devon with Sophie; her second trip up since Kate moved away. She was tearful when she returned, but already she seems to be accepting this new way of living; talking to Kate at least twice a day, both of them shaping their future, apart but together.

Bea sits next to me. "Are you all packed?"

"We don't have to take too much, we'll use most of Mum and Dad's furniture for now."

"I meant for the hospital!" she said.

"Oh, yeah, the hospital bag. All packed, and ready to go." Disposable pants. Urgh. I won't be using them, but I've stuck to the list like a good girl. Huge sanitary pads, the likes of which I've never seen before. But then nicer things. A new toiletries bag, which Karen bought for me. Nursing pyjamas. Most excitingly, the tiny babygros, which Mum bought on our shopping trip that now seems so long ago. Vests. Teeny, tiny nappies. A little hat and scratch mitts. Am I really having a baby? Me? It still doesn't seem real, but all evidence suggests that it is.

"And you're moving next week?"

"Yep. Nothing like a challenge."

"But how amazing to be back at David's. I'm sorry, I know it's not David's anymore, but it always will be to me," says Bea.

"I think it always will be to me, too! I will never forget the day Julie and I turned up on his doorstep. He was so lovely. And now look."

We both turn to see David and Martin sitting at the other side of the table, under a striped sun umbrella, Tyler on David's knee, Esme on Martin's. It would make a beautiful photo, but I haven't got the energy to get my phone from inside.

"Look after him for me, will you?" Bea's eyes are shining.

"Of course I will. And so will Martin. You know that."

"I do."

We sit quietly for a while. "Thank you, Bea."

"What for?"

"For everything. I meant what I said at the awards. How you inspired me, and Julie."

"Oh, don't be silly," she bats away my words.

"I mean it. You gave us jobs, and then you gave us jobs again, ten years later! I hated leaving the Sail Loft – or I hated myself for doing it, it seemed so ungrateful."

"It was absolutely the right thing to do," says Bea. "Forget any negativity about it, right now."

"OK!" I laugh. "I'll do as I'm told."

She nudges me. "You inspired me, you know."

"Really?"

"Yes. You had faith in relationships, which I never did.

But you and Sam found each other again and I thought, *I'd like a bit of that*. I hadn't quite intended to find somebody who'd drag me across the world to live in America, but that's life. Surprising."

"To put it mildly," I smile.

"Then let's thank each other, and look forward to seeing each other again in the not-too-distant future. You will be a lovely mum, Alice, I have no doubt of that."

I lean against her, unable to find any words. I may be missing Julie, but I am ever grateful for all these other wonderful people in my life.

***

Like the sea, life refuses to be still. Bea goes with Bob to his homeland, leaving a tearful David in her wake, Tyler kissing his leg in a bid to make him feel better. Mum and Dad move into the apartment at the Sail Loft, where once Bea lived, alone. They take a few items of furniture with them, making space in the house for the odds and ends we're bringing with us.

The move provides a new focus for Sophie, too, and Amber comes with us on the day, the pair of them giggling as they try to decide which room will be Sophie's. The main bedroom at the front – once David's, then mine, then my parents' – will be mine and Sam's, but we've said Sophie can choose from the rest.

I already think I know where she'll end up. My old room. Up in the attic. The mini-kitchen forms part of the appeal, but when I see her leaning out of the little window, just as I used to do, looking across the rooftops to the sea, I know she's found exactly the right place.

I wander the house happily; reacquainting myself with

it. Ambling heavily through the sunlight from the stairwell window. Opening the door into the sun-trap garden. We have all made our mark here over the years: me and Julie; Mum and Dad; David, and all those unknown people who came before him. This is an old house. I imagine it soaking up its history, forming a personality from its occupants over the years, standing tall and proud long before we came to it and, I hope, long after we are gone. Who knows how long we will live here? Mum and Dad will want to sell one day, I'm sure, and I doubt Sam and I will be in a position to afford this place. We just have to make the most of it while we can.

And what of our cosy little house at Amethi? There was an obvious answer to that problem. Jonathan. As well as saving him from having to live with his parents again, it means there is a member of staff on site, should any of the guests need anything. And I must admit that now I am away from it all, for the time being at least, I can breathe a sigh of relief.

Life, now, is about us. Sophie, Sam and me, and of course the baby.

And what happens when Jonathan leaves Cornwall, as he surely will? Janie is back in Spain and he's already missing her. Even if things don't pan out between the two of them, I know he is frustrated here. Like an energetic Labrador, pulling on its lead, desperate to reach the beach and be set free. Chasing gulls, barking at waves…

I'm getting carried away here and I'm not sure Jon would approve of the comparison, but I don't think he'd deny he is in need of freedom and adventure. We'll just have to cross that bridge when we come to it.

31

Three days to go.

"Don't count on it!" says Becky, from her hospital bed. "I thought this little one would be out way before now."

She spent two weeks after her due date passed, waiting, and waiting, and waiting. I spoke to her daily during that time, letting her rant at me. "Have I had the baby yet? If one more person asks me that, I'll go mad. Don't they think I'd let them know if the baby had been born?"

I made a mental note not to ask her that question.

"Seriously, Alice," she says now, her eyes not leaving the tiny bundle in the cot next to her bed, "I hope your little one's better at time-keeping. Typical bloke, I s'pose."

Jasper lies wrapped in a beautifully soft blanket, blissfully unaware of this criticism. Just the tiniest tips of his little wrinkly fingers are visible, clutching the shiny, silky edge. He has a baby-blue beanie on his head and his face is dark-skinned, a little bit blotchy.

"He is beautiful," I say and see the smile on Becky's face. She knows that it is true.

"I guess we'll be seeing you here soon, too!" a cheerful nurse says to me on her way past.

"I hope so." There is a part of me full of envy for Becky and Andrew, who have their baby, safely delivered, fully present and correct. But another part of me wants to savour every last minute of this pregnancy. Who knows if I will be lucky enough to experience it again? I lay my hand on my huge tummy. The baby moves, and I imagine a slick sea creature, slinking undisturbed through the depths.

272

What a shock it will be to emerge into the light; air on skin; sounds no longer muffled. No wonder babies cry when they're born.

Your time is coming, little one. And I can't wait to meet you.

Sam picks me up from outside the hospital, just as Andrew is walking across the grass to the maternity unit.

"Congratulations, Andrew!" I call.

"Oh, hey, you two!" He comes over, grinning. He looks shattered, and like he hasn't had a shave, or brushed his hair in weeks.

"Look at you, mate, what happened?" Sam says, leaning over from the driver's seat.

"You don't want to know, believe me." But he is still smiling. "Shit, it's incredible. Becky is amazing. My hero."

"And Jasper is gorgeous." I put my hand on his arm, reach up to kiss his cheek.

"A little boy! I can't believe it! Though I'd have been just as happy and amazed if it was a little girl. How are you getting on, Alice? Any twinges?"

"None yet, but we're still three days away from the due date."

"I hope it doesn't go over, like Jasper. I thought Becky was going to kill somebody."

"I imagine it's quite frustrating."

"Understatement of the century! Right, I'd better get this lot in. Becky gave me a long list, even though she had her bag packed weeks ago, and that was full to bursting."

"I guess you don't know what you need till it really happens."

"I think you're right, Alice. Now, take care, and get some rest. You're going to need your energy."

"Thanks."

"Bloody know-it-all first-time parents!" Sam calls as Andrew is walking away. Smiling, Andrew turns and gives him a one-fingered salute.

"You OK?" Sam asks, kissing me as I awkwardly half-climb, half-tumble into the passenger seat.

"This car's too low," I grumble.

"How was it?" he asks, looking at me. "How was Becky? Did she say how it all went?"

"I think you're more nervous than me. Anyway, you've seen it all before."

"And tried to forget it."

"Thanks for filling me with confidence!" I don't feel worried; not really. All along, I've thought that what will be will be. As long as the baby is safe and well, and Sam and I are able to look after it, then does it really matter how the birth goes? Becky didn't say too much about hers. I know it was a long time – sixteen hours – but she looks amazing now, even if she's tired. The glow of motherhood, or some such bollocks.

Sam drops me outside the house. I've found walking down the hill has been a bit of a strain lately. I'm worried I might fall and tumble head over tail all the way down the street.

I had wanted to go to Amethi, as I just… can't… let go… and had come up with a pathetic reason for it: "I need to pick up some files that I left in the drawer. Just some info for the writing course in November."

Sam clearly didn't believe a word of it. "You tell your mum what you need and I'll go and collect it. And shall I just check around and make sure everything's OK while I'm there?"

"Yes, please," I said. "If you don't mind. Actually, forget about the files. Perhaps just go and see how everything is."

"Sure. It's almost as though that was what you wanted the whole time."

I put the key in the lock and push open the front door into the empty house. It's immediately peaceful, just me and my baby, and I step carefully, gently, not wanting to break the silence, closing the door softly behind me.

I still can't believe I am back here again, and I greet the house like an old friend, which really it is. While outside temperatures are soaring, making this day the hottest of the year so far, it is cool in here. I look into the lounge, where the Moses basket sits at the side of the settee, near to the window. A pile of freshly washed babygros is folded on one of the chairs; never worn, but now extra clean and ready to be put away, waiting for their tiny occupant, who I am sure will waste no time in undoing all the careful work of cleaning them.

I feel restless. In fact, I don't feel great. But even though I know I should be sitting down, putting my marshmallow-like feet up on the footstool, the house is calling me, enticing me from this room to the next. I stop in the doorway, remember the Christmas when Sam and I were breaking up, after Sophie had gone missing. How he handed me a jewellery box and for the briefest moment I worried it was an engagement ring, which would have been everything I dreamed of and feared, all in one go.

My stomach feels heavy; full. Which of course it is. I feel like the baby could drop out of me any moment. If only it would be that easy. I wander into the dining room next door. See Julie being made up for her wedding. I stifle a sob at the thought of my friend. Sit on one of the straight-backed chairs and pull out my phone.

"Hello? Alice? Have you had it?" I think of Becky's frustration at this question, but to hear my best friend ask it, with such unbridled enthusiasm, makes my heart soar. The distance between us has made it easier these last few months, for both of us. Julie has had a different purpose to mine, which she's thrown herself into, and I have not felt guilt every day, as I might have done, flaunting my increasingly obvious pregnancy in front of her.

Instead, we have missed each other. Pure and simple. I long to see her again, but we are already six months – halfway – through her time away.

"Not yet," I smile. "I was just thinking of you."

"I was thinking of you, too. But I didn't want to ring in case you were in labour. Or in case you don't want people asking all the time if you've had the baby yet. Although I did just do that," she adds ruefully.

"I think that's acceptable! How are you, anyway?"

"Oh, great, thank you. It's night-time here. And it's the solstice today. I'm going to have to go soon, actually, we're going into the city for this crazy mass yoga session. I sent some details to Lizzie, she's desperate to get out here!"

"Ha! I don't think Isaac and Kate would be very pleased." Lizzie's up in Devon right now; the three of them have hatched this plan for a yoga-based summer solstice celebration; incorporating yoga on the hillside as the sun sets on the longest day of the year. I wish I could be there to see how it's all going.

"No, maybe next year. Wish you were here, Alice."

"In other circumstances, I'd wish that, too." I shift awkwardly on the chair, feeling hot and uncomfortable.

"How is it, being so heavily pregnant?"

"It's weird. And heavy. And my feet are huge. I've been swimming every day, just to take my weight off them."

"Can you believe you're going to be a mum soon?"

"No. I really don't think I can believe that."

"I'm so sorry I won't be there to meet your baby."

"You will, though, and it will still be a baby."

"But I'm going to miss out on so much."

"If you left India now, you'd miss out on so much there, too. I'll send lots of pictures."

"It's not the same. But you'd better."

"Promise."

We both fall silent. I don't dare ask about her and Luke. I know that if she was pregnant she would tell me. I just hope, so very much, that it goes right for them soon.

"I'd better go," she says. "I hate saying that. But Luke's waiting to go out."

"No problem." I imagine a dusty, busy Indian city, with cars beeping their horns, mopeds weaving in and out of queues of traffic. Probably entirely wrong and definitely based on what little I have seen of India on TV.

"Next time I speak to you... you might be a mum!"

"Maybe... but it could be a while yet. Becky had to wait two weeks. She had to be induced. In the meantime, I'm trying not to go to Amethi. Well, actually, I'm trying *to* go there. Sam isn't letting me."

Julie laughs. "My god, I miss that place."

"This time next year, we'll both be back there..."

"I thought you were going to say we'll be millionaires."

"I don't know about that, but I can't wait for us to be back together again, Julie. I love you, you know."

"I love you, too. And I miss you all the time. Even though we're having the best time out here. I wish I could share it with you."

We are both missing out on important parts of each other's lives, but our friendship is strong. No matter where we are, or what we're doing, nothing will change that.

"Have a good night," I say.

"Thank you, you too. Love you," she says again.

"Love you," I say, and the line goes dead.

I sigh and look around the room. Stand slowly up, feeling a twinge in my lower back. Wander into the kitchen and pour a glass of water laced with mint and cucumber.

"Keep hydrated," Becky had said to me. "Seriously, it will make a difference."

I drink the water in one go, top up my glass and go into the hallway. What a day! I should be down on the beach; in the sea. I don't have the energy or inclination. I am relishing this slice of quiet. *The calm before the storm.*

Up the stairs to the baby's room. Which used to be Julie's room. Karen has delivered and helped to set up all the furniture she bought us, and she's even made curtains; tiny seahorses, shells and starfish all over them.

"They are beautiful," I hugged her.

"Ah, well, I enjoyed it," she said.

She seems to have settled back into life here and is still working for the cleaning company; for now content to be employed, rather than try to create a rival firm. And she's softened, as far as I can tell – as has Sam's attitude towards her.

"It's never going to be like you and your mum," he said after we'd waved her off, "but it's kind of nice to have her about. Most of the time."

"And Sophie loves her."

"Yes," he'd said wryly, "and that's nothing to do with Mum spoiling her rotten."

"No, I'm sure that's just coincidental."

Sophie will always come back from Karen's with some new item of clothing, or a book that Karen's bought for her: "What can I say? Grandma's making up for lost time!" She is also almost always shattered, having stayed up late, watching films with Karen.

I look out of the window – *the baby's window*. The view is of the little sun-trap garden and the backs of the houses behind our street, tumbling parallel to ours down to the town. Between the two rows of gardens are the steep steps, which currently a red-faced man is doing his best to climb in the heat of the afternoon. It makes me tired just watching.

In Sam's and my room, I straighten the duvet on the bed, then sit for a minute, instantly crumpling it again. My back is really aching now, and there's a vague dragging sensation in my stomach. Kind of like mild period pains. The clock ticks quietly on the bedside table. How many seconds till the baby comes? *Don't wish your life away*, Dad would tell me, but I think he's almost more eager to see this baby than I am.

I peer out of our window, onto the street, remembering the early mornings I'd be walking up to the Sail Loft. Funny to think it's Mum and Dad up there now. It's been a 'steep learning curve' (as Jason Wilberforce would have said) but between Stef and Lauren, they've got things covered, and so far Dad has not tired of making breakfasts.

Although: "You could have told me people were so bleeding picky," he grumbled to me. "I did," I laughed. "More than once. You always said, 'They're on holiday, they're entitled to have breakfast how they want it.'"

"Did I? What an idiot."

"That's what I said."

I don't miss those early mornings, although I did used to love that feeling of being up before the rest of the town. Seeing the sun rise across the rooftops in the summer; in the winter, seeing the odd light come on in other households, imagining the lives within, as I trod my path up the steep street and across to the hotel.

"You'll have plenty of early mornings again soon," Mum said when I mentioned this to her.

"I think this baby's going to be one of those ones who sleeps from eight until eight. I've heard all about them." (One of the mums at the 'Bumps to Babies' group is always happy to mention this about her little angel, to the disgruntlement of the other mothers, whose dark-ringed eyes tell a different story).

"I'm sure it will," Mum just smiled.

Now I'm on my grand tour of the house, I need to complete it. I take the stairs slowly to the top floor, rounding the corner to the rooms that Julie and I once shared. Where our lives in Cornwall began.

Julie's room is full of Mum and Dad's stuff, and it's hard to get across to the window, but I determinedly pick my way through, just for the view. I startle a seagull when I open the window and it lifts indignantly into the air, squawking before it glides off to a safer spot a few houses away, ruffling its feathers as it settles.

The sea air fills my nostrils and lungs. I breathe in, close my eyes, hold my breath. Breathe out. Practise alternate nostril breathing, and wonder if Julie and Luke are right now doing the same thing, amid hundreds – maybe thousands – of Indian people and like-minded tourists.

Closing the window, I carefully retrace my steps between the boxes and bags, to the doorway, emerging into the little kitchen. Sophie loves having this at her disposal, though she really only uses the kettle and toaster. I walk past the door to the bathroom with the little porthole window, and I push open the door to Sophie's room. I feel a bit bad doing this, not wishing to intrude on her personal space, but there is something urging me on. This was, after all, once my room, where I woke that first morning aged eighteen, when David was our landlord and I had no idea what this place would come to mean to me.

Sophie has left the window slightly open and a breeze steals into the room, rippling the papers on the desk. I move to the chair by the window, carefully transfer her pile of clothes to her bed, and I kneel on the seat, my back to the room, opening the window wide.

Down below, some happy holiday-makers wander down towards town, footsteps and voices echoing off the walls and fading as they get further away. Above, the sun is still high, immersing the town, casting the kind of light that this place is famed for. A pull for the artists and writers and hippies who have flooded in, washing up in the nooks and crannies of this magical, meandering, cobbled old town, and coming to live as part of this centuries-old fishing community.

"Careful you don't fall out." Sam's voice makes me jump. I turn and there he is, smiling at me from the doorway. "Does Sophie know you hang out in her room all day?"

"I do not 'hang out in her room all day'," I say. "I'm just looking. Remembering."

He holds out his hand. "Come on, let's go and sit in the garden. I've got the kettle on, and I've bought scones and jam and cream."

"What are you? An emmet?"

"It just felt like the right thing to do!" he laughed. "Michael was up at Amethi and mentioned he had some cream, and I just had to get some. Then what's the point of clotted cream without scones and jam?"

"I'm not arguing."

I rub my back as I follow him downstairs and out into the sun-bathed garden. The air is sweet with the fragrance of flowers planted by David, and my parents, and the whitewashed walls reflect the sun so that I am almost dazzled. Sam brings a tray with tea and scones and we both tuck in, enjoying a moment of quiet contentedness. I didn't realise I was so hungry.

"Everything OK at Amethi?" I ask after a while.

"Yes!" Sam looks strict. "And now you're not allowed to ask that again for at least another two weeks."

"But it's my business…" I protest.

"Yours and Julie's. And Sue is in touch with Julie, and if there are any problems, you will know. So for now, no news is good news. OK?"

"OK," I mutter.

"Stop sulking! Enjoy it. Be in the moment. Isn't that what you tell me?"

And annoyingly, he is right. He pulls up a chair so I can rest my feet. Puts up the sun umbrella so we don't get burned. Brings the weekend paper out. He opens the main section but I don't have the inclination. If I am going to be in the moment, and if no news means good news, then I don't want to know what is happening in the outside world. Just for a few days. I'm allowed that luxury, I think.

I rest my head on Sam's shoulder, closing my eyes and listening to his breath, and the occasional turning of pages. I don't feel comfortable, but I suppose that's only to be expected.

I try to practise being in the moment. Focus on the sound of gulls crying. People walking down the steps behind the garden walls. The faint voice of the sea.

It's all going on out there, but right now I am happy to be tucked quietly and peacefully away from the rest of the world.

"Ow. Fuck." My eyes spring open and I sit up, which itself causes a sharp intake of breath.

"Alice?" Sam is immediately alert.

That was no kick, I think. No, that was something quite different. My tummy feels tight, as though it is not part of my body, but has a mind of its own.

"Ow. Yes. I think... *ohhhowww.*"

"Is this it?"

"I don't know!" I snap impatiently.

Sam gently waits and I feel my muscles relax a little. "Maybe just some indigestion from all that cream and jam."

But... no. "*Owwwwww.*" Just minutes later.

"Contractions?" asks Sam.

"I don't know! I haven't done this before!"

But I'm smiling now. I think it might be contractions. Maybe the baby is on its way.

Sam and I sit nervously, sweaty-palmed, holding hands. He slips his fingers away from mine; gets out his phone; opens the contraction timer app. I'd said it was a ridiculous thing when he told me about it, but now I am glad of it. We monitor the situation. For quite some time. It is both incredibly exciting and incredibly boring. I try to read the paper, but I keep going over the same words.

Sam attempts the crossword, but he seems to be experiencing the same problem as me. It is impossible to concentrate.

"What should we do?" I ask.

"I don't know... it's lovely out here, but I think I might be going out of my mind. It's seven minutes at the moment, between contractions, and remember, they said to call the hospital when they're five minutes apart. How about some TV?"

"OK," I agree, and he helps me to my feet, walking behind me as I make my way tentatively towards the lounge.

Sam picks up the remote control. "What do you fancy?"

"Nothing with giving birth, please."

"*Pride & Prejudice?*"

"You want to watch *Pride & Prejudice?*"

"No, but you might."

"That is lovely of you, but I think I need something new and edge-of-the-seat – to keep my mind occupied."

"OK. *Peaky Blinders?*"

"Too violent. It doesn't seem right when we're bringing a new life into the world."

"OK, well I'll put the kettle on, you decide what we're watching."

I look out of the window at the sunshine. I don't really want to be inside on such a beautiful day. A group of teenagers pass the house, laughing. I envy them. I feel like I'm missing out.

"*Ooowwwwwwww!*" That soon shakes me out of my self-pity.

"Are you OK?" Sam comes rushing in.

"Yep," I breathe out slowly. "But I think there are going to be a few more of these, so we'd better get used to them."

"Five minutes apart!" says Sam.

We've settled for reruns of *Would I Lie to You* but I've paused the TV for this latest contraction.

"What does that mean?"

"We need to call the hospital."

I am grateful for him taking control. Sam asks to be put through to the maternity ward, and explains the situation. Listens. Says, "No, her waters haven't broken." Listens.

"No, I think we need to come in now."

My ears prick up. Right now? I thought we had hours more of walking around the house, Sam rubbing my back and uttering useless words of comfort.

He listens again. "No," he says firmly, "I really think we need to come now. We're forty minutes away, anyway. We're coming in."

He hangs up. If it weren't for the intense pain of another contraction, I might be quite turned on by his authoritative manner.

On the way, the contractions seem to be coming faster – every three minutes, according to the app. Then, ten minutes away from the hospital, I realise they seem to have slowed.

"Oh, no. Branston Hicks!" I say.

"Braxton!" Sam chuckles. "We're not making a sandwich."

"Alright, smart-arse."

"Do you think they've stopped?"

"I don't know. No, not entirely. In fact…" I have to stop talking to accommodate the pain. It's amazing how quickly I've come to recognise the signs.

"Well, we're here now, or nearly. Let's just go and get checked over."

I'm put in a wheelchair, with seemingly no choice, and a porter wheels us through to the maternity unit. "Not taking any chances, mate," he says to Sam and I am momentarily irritated that I am the one left out of this conversation – it's me that's pregnant, not Sam.

At the maternity ward, Sam gives my details in at the reception desk. A midwife, Lesley, comes out and ushers us through some double doors, into a side bay. I am allowed to walk this time. Lesley helps me onto the bed. Sam is looking at me anxiously. I smile.

As Lesley begins to talk, another contraction comes on, stronger than ever. Then I am aware of a wetness, between my legs and soaking the paper that has been rolled out over the hospital bed. There is a sound like a glass of water being upended, the liquid pouring onto the floor, then quickly just a dripping.

"Ah," says Lesley.

I am shocked.

"Your waters," she says.

"Oh, yeah. So…" Another contraction comes, taking my breath away.

"Those are close together," she says. "We'd better take a look at you. Don't worry about the mess, I'll get somebody to sort that out. Sam, help your lovely lady to swivel round and get her legs up on the bed."

This is a painful manoeuvre. My back. My legs. My tummy doesn't seem to want to move this way. But somehow we manage it.

"Now, I know this isn't very dignified, but I need you to get your knickers off," Lesley says. "Are you happy for your young man to do it for you?"

"Sure." I couldn't care less.

Sam does as directed then grins and holds my hand. "Don't worry." The pain comes again. I grip his fingers. He keeps his eyes on mine, and only once the contraction has subsided do I realise how tight I've been squeezing.

"Sorry."

"Don't worry," he says again.

Lesley takes the opportunity to check how dilated I am. "Seems Sam was right to get you in so fast, Alice. You're about nine centimetres!"

"What?"

"Let me just get this on you, to check the heartbeat."

I feel like I'm holding my breath as she produces a little device and we all go quiet then breathe a collective sigh of relief as that familiar whooshing sound comes through, strong and clear.

"I'm afraid you're going to have to prepare for this baby coming sooner than we might have expected," Lesley says. "Do you think you can find a comfortable position?"

"Is there such a thing?"

"Some women find being on all fours really helps. I know it doesn't sound very dignified but you are about to give birth. Dignity doesn't come into it."

"Wait…" another pain takes hold. When it's over, I say, "I want to try that. All fours."

"You're sure?" says Sam.

"Yes, I… I think it's there. I can't move my legs," I gasp.

Sam looks panicked and even Lesley looks a bit alarmed.

"I mean, I can't put them together," I quickly correct myself. "I think there's something there."

Lesley takes a look. "Have you felt like pushing, Alice?"

"I don't know how…" I say pathetically.

"You will. And you'll want to soon, I'm sure of it. Tell me when you feel another contraction."

She waits. Watches. The room is so quiet. I want to shout, to break the silence. I've never felt such pressure.

I start to feel the tightening sensation again. Pain like I could never have imagined. "It's coming."

"Now. Push."

"*Hoooooooowww?*" I just want the pain to go away.

"Like you need a poo! I'm sorry, there's not a much better way to put it." Lesley's eyes are on mine. "Relax

287

your body and thighs and push... I know, it's easy for me to say, but you're the only person who can do this, Alice."

"*Nnnnnnnnnnn...*" I try to do as I'm told.

"That's fantastic. Wonderful, Alice. Keep going. Keep going. Keep going... now rest."

We do the same thing a few more times; I've lost count, and I'm close to saying I think we should just give up. I'm tired. But then, after the next excruciating push...

"There's its head. Do you want to look, Sam?"

He moves gingerly along the bed.

"Here, do you want to feel, Alice?" Lesley waits for my nod, then takes my hand and gently places it between my legs. The first time I touch my baby. Just the crown of its head, but it's right there. Sam looks a little green around the gills, but I am moved beyond belief.

"Now comes the really hard work, my lovely," Lesley smiles at me. "I'm going to want you to push when I say to, OK?"

I nod. It's time to push again.

"That's good. Keep going... keep going... Well done. Now, next time your tummy tightens, you push even harder, OK?"

I wait. It's happening again. I grit my teeth. Push with all my might.

"That's fantastic. Wonderful. Keep going."

Lesley sounds delighted with my progress. I wonder if I'm the best birthing mother she's encountered, she sounds so impressed.

Sam is standing by, smiling nervously when I look at him. "I feel useless," he says.

I have no answer for that. Right now, it is me, and Lesley, and this enormous baby that I somehow have to squeeze out.

"Go!" Lesley says.

I'm up for it this time. I want to please her.

"*Nnnnnnnnnnnnn*. I'm tired."

"Keep going. You can do it."

"It's not coming. It's a false alarm," I say, weakly.

"It is most definitely not that," the midwife says. "Now, come on. Sam, give Alice a cuddle. Hold her hand. Your baby's coming soon."

And she's right. The next big push. An unnerving, slithery sensation. "You did it!" Lesley exclaims, and I am awash with tears; Sam is, too. When we hear the baby cry, we are in pieces. Then Lesley is there, handing over this tiny, hot, yowling creature – red-faced and angry with the world. I don't blame him.

For it is a him. A little boy.

Sam and I have a little boy.

Lesley puts him on my chest, carefully places a sheet around us for a little warmth. I can't take my eyes off him. After a while, his crying stops, and he seems curious; big eyes looking up at me. Tears roll freely down my face and I realise I'm shivering.

Sam puts his arm around me but I barely notice.

I want to remember every moment. Every sensation. My baby's – *my baby's* – perfect, brand-new skin on mine. Have I ever felt anything anywhere near as beautiful as this?

"See if you can just move a bit like this," Lesley says, shifting me into a more upright position. "Put him near your nipple." I sense a shift in him, my son. He snuffles. His mouth finds me, the source of food, and he's there.

"Look at that!" Lesley exclaims softly. "Looks like he's done this before."

Sam and I stay silent, dumbstruck by awe at the sight. It feels alien but right. It doesn't last long.

"It's a good sign," says Lesley. "A really good sign."

She asks if we'd like her to take photos and Sam hands her my phone. She snaps away. "You'll want a load of them. But I have to tell you, Alice, it's not quite over, I'm afraid. Sam, can you hold Little One? Alice has got a bit more pushing to do."

My addled mind thinks, *Twins?* Lesley is quick to clarify: "It's the afterbirth I'm afraid, my lovely. Not as exciting as a baby, but it has to come out."

It's over quickly, and the baby – our baby – is given an injection of vitamin K. Then Lesley goes to leave the room. "You did wonderfully, Alice. I'll be back with tea and toast in a few minutes. Why don't you two get him into a nappy, and something warm?"

I look at Sam. I feel suddenly, terribly, unsure of myself. "It's easy," he says. "Don't worry."

And together, we lay out one of the tiny nappies, lie our son on it, and fasten it around his minuscule hips. Somehow manage to slide him into a vest, then a babygro. I am so grateful that Sam's done all this before. All the while, our little boy's huge eyes are fixed on us.

"You hold him," I say to Sam, handing him a blanket, and he wraps our son in it. Holds him close. Their eyes meet, lock onto each other's, and I quietly get the phone, take a photo, capture the moment. I look at Sam and see him again, that boy on the beach, who I met a lifetime ago.

I am secretly desperate to have our baby back. Sam looks at me, reading my mind.

"Here," he says quietly, and gently hands me our little boy, who is wide awake, alert, and unbelievably tiny.

I think of all the people we have to tell our news to. Mum and Dad first, of course, and Karen. I think of Julie, so many miles away from home.

I wish she could experience this. I hope she will one day.

Sam looks out of the window. "Sun's just going down," he says. "The solstice. We've got a midsummer baby."

I think back to the other solstice; the cold, dark depths of winter. Life has see-sawed, along with the seasons. In six short months, so much has happened.

My mind flits to the notes we wrote back then; the wishes which we fed to the flames. I had settled in the end on something simple. Written just one word.

Happiness.

And I'm not stupid. I know this is not going to be easy. There will be a million things to worry about, and then a million more.

Sleepless nights and extremes of tiredness, the likes of which I suspect I cannot imagine.

Tensions over whose turn it is to change a nappy.

Competition over who has had less sleep.

Fears about illness. Development. Feeding.

It's all still to come.

And that's just while he's a baby, and has no idea what it might be like to be independent; become his own person. That, no doubt, will bring other challenges. At least I've got a little idea of what to expect, courtesy of Sophie, who is now a big sister to two baby brothers.

We have it all to look forward to. I hold him close, our little boy. I never want to let him go.

Sam moves instinctively towards us, kisses my forehead and rests his head on mine.

We have already had years of being together, and years of being apart. Years of history already made.

I close my eyes for just a moment and I know that, despite all of that, this is really just the beginning.

Coming Back to Cornwall

In the Coming Back to Cornwall series, Katharine E. Smith has found a subject, and a set of characters and places, which appeal to readers of all ages. With the glorious setting of Cornwall, and unforgettable, uplifting storylines, it is very easy to fall in love with these books.

All five books are available in print and Kindle editions, with audio versions being released in 2020.

Coming Soon: Book Six!

Also by Katharine E. Smith:

Writing the Town Read - Katharine's first novel.

"I seriously couldn't put it down and would recommend it to anyone to doesn't like chick lit, but wants a great story."

Looking Past - a story of motherhood, and growing up without a mother.

"Despite the tough topic the book is full of love, friendships and humour. Katharine Smith cleverly balances emotional storylines with strong characters and witty dialogue, making this a surprisingly happy book to read."

Amongst Friends - a back-to-front tale of friendship and family, set in Bristol.

"An interesting, well written book, set in Bristol which is lovingly described, and with excellent characterisation. Very enjoyable."

Acknowledgements

I have so enjoyed writing this last book of the Coming Back to Cornwall series. I had intended this to be a trilogy originally; then it became a five-book series. I have now, thanks to the encouragement of my lovely readers, decided to extend the series again. I would never want to over-do it but whilst there are lives for these characters to live, I think I'd also like to find out what is going to happen next!

My thanks to my wonderful team of beta readers: Hilary Kerr, Katie Copnall, my 'old' friend Claudia Baker (we're not so old, really), Denise Armstrong, Louise Freeman, Julie Mitchell, Jenny Holdcroft, Wendy Pompe, Kate Webb Thomas and Claire Ingram. Not to forget (as if I could) my beta reader and adviser on all things pagan - author Nelly Harper, whose own wonderful Albion Chronicles series I highly recommend.

On top of all this, I have the support of my dad, Ted Rogers, who always reads my books in their various stages, offering excellent feedback and editorial advice (not to mention proofreading) so thank you very much, Dad.

And then, of course, I must thank Catherine Clarke, my excellent friend and wonderful cover designer. Catherine is a multi-talented artist and designer. You can follow her on Instagram to see more of her amazing work.

Finally, how can I get to this point without thanking all of you readers? I love hearing what you think of the books, and connecting with you all (if that does not sound too cheesy). I have dreamed of being a writer since I was a child, and I've been writing books for well over ten years now. This year (2019) has been a huge boost to me as an author and I really do thank you all, from the bottom of my heart.

CPSIA information can be obtained
at www.ICGtesting.com
Printed in the USA
LVHW091316220421
685238LV00018B/304